Critical Muslim 18

Cities

Critical Muslim is published quarterly by C. Hurst & Co. (Publishers) Ltd. on behalf of and in conjunction with Critical Muslim Ltd. and the Muslim Institute, London. *Critical Muslim* acknowledges the support of the Aziz Foundation, London.

All correspondence to Muslim Institute, CAN Mezzanine, 49-51 East Road, London N1 6AH, United Kingdom

e-mail for editorial: editorial@criticalmuslim.com

The editors do not necessarily agree with the opinions expressed by the contributors. We reserve the right to make such editorial changes as may be necessary to make submissions to *Critical Muslim* suitable for publication.

C. Hurst & Co (Publishers) Ltd.,41 Great Russell Street, London WC1B 3PL

ISBN: 978-1-84904-626-8 ISSN: 2048-8475

To subscribe or place an order by credit/debit card or cheque (pounds sterling only) please contact Kathleen May at the Hurst address above or e-mail kathleen@hurstpub.co.uk

Tel: 020 7255 2201

A one year subscription, inclusive of postage (four issues), costs £50 (UK), £65 (Europe) and £75 (rest of the world).

IIIT Publications

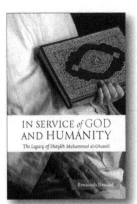

IN SERVICE OF GOD AND HUMANITY
The Legacy of Shaykh Muhammad al-Ghazali

Benaouda Bensaid

Renowned Islamic scholar al-Ghazali (d. 1996), was an outspoken critic, both of Muslim societies for their impoverished, poorly educated populations and social injustice, and of Muslims whose moral basis was fast eroding. He worked tirelessly to improve Muslim life, lay the grounds for a better elucidation of Islam, and call for a progressive, well-funded education system for all.

ISBN 978-1-56564-663-6 *pb*
ISBN 978-1-56564-664-3 *hb*
2015

THE MIRACULOUS LANGUAGE OF THE QUR'AN
Evidence of Divine Origin

Bassam Saeh

The work compares Qur'anic language to the language of pre-Islamic poetry, and the language of the Arabs past and present, to make the case that an important strand of the Qur'an's linguistic miraculousness is the fact that its Arabic was completely new.

ISBN 978-1-56564-665-0 *pb*
2015

Marketing Manager IIIT (USA) 500 Grove Street, Herndon, VA 20170-4735, USA
Tel: 703 471 1133 ext. 108 Fax: 703 471 3922 • E-mail: sales@iiit.org Website: www.iiit.org

Kube Publishing Ltd MMC, Ratby Lane, Markfield, Leicester, LE67 9SY, UK
Tel: 01530 249 230 Fax: 01530 249 656 • E-mail: info@kubepublishing.com
Website: www.kubepublishing.com

HALAL FOOD FOUNDATION

Halal Is Much More Than Food

The Halal Food Foundation (HFF) is a registered charity that aims to make the concept of halal more accessible and mainstream. We want people to know that halal does not just pertain to food – halal is a lifestyle.

The Foundation pursues its goals through downloadable resources, events, social networking, school visits, pursuing and funding scientific research on issues of food and health, and its monthly newsletter. We work for the community and aim at the gradual formation of a consumer association. We aim to educate and inform; and are fast becoming the first port of call on queries about halal issues. We do not talk at people, we listen to them.

If you have any queries, comments, ideas, or would just like to voice your opinion - please get in contact with us.

Halal Food Foundation
109 Fulham Palace Road,
Hammersmith, London, W6 8JA
Charity number: 1139457
Website: www.halalfoodfoundation.co.uk
E-mail: info@halalfoodfoundation.co.uk

@HFF_UK Halal Food Foundation

The Barbary Figs

by

Rashid Boudjedra

Translated by
André Naffis-Sahely

Buy a copy of Rashid Boudjedra's *The Barbary Figs* at
www.hauspublishing.com or by calling +44(0)20 7838 9055
and a recieve a copy of Khaled al-Berry's memoir
Life is More Beautiful than Paradise free.

RASHID AND OMAR are cousins who find themselves side by side on a flight from Algiers to Constantine. During the hour-long journey, the pair will exhume their past, their boyhood in French Algeria during the 1940s and their teenage years fighting in the bush during the revolution. Rashid, the narrator, has always resented Omar, who despite all his worldly successes, has been on the run from the ghosts of his past, ghosts that Rashid has set himself the task of exorcising. Rashid peppers his account with chilling episodes from Algerian history, from the savageries of the French invasion in the 1830s, to the repressive regime that is in place today.

RASHID BOUDJEDRA has routinely been called one of North Africa's leading writers since his debut, *La Répudiation*, was published in 1969, earning the author the first of many fatwas. While he wrote his first six novels in French, Boudjedra switched to Arabic in 1982 and wrote another six novels in the language before returning to French in 1994. *The Barbary Figs* was awarded the Prix du Roman Arabe 2010.

CM18

April–June 2016

CONTENTS

CITIES

ARTS AND LETTERS

REVIEWS

CRITICAL MUSLIM

Subscribe to Critical Muslim

Now in its fourth year, *Critical Muslim* is the only publication of its kind, giving voice to the diversity and plurality of Muslim reporting, creative writing, poetry and scholarship.

Subscribe now to receive each issue of Critical Muslim direct to your door and save money on the cover price of each issue.

Subscriptions are available at the following prices, inclusive of postage. Subscribe for two years and save 10%!

	ONE YEAR (4 Issues)	TWO YEARS (8 Issues)
UK	£50	£90
Europe	£65	£117
Rest of World	£75	£135

TO SUBSCRIBE:

CRITICALMUSLIM.HURSTPUBLISHERS.COM

HURST PUBLISHERS

41 GREAT RUSSELL ST, LONDON WC1B 3PL
WWW.HURSTPUBLISHERS.COM
WWW.FBOOK.COM/HURSTPUBLISHERS
020 7255 2201

CITIES

INTRODUCTION
DETROIT DO MIND DYING

Hassan Mahamdallie

He stumbled out from in between two corrugated-iron and wooden huts, onto the pavement and spun round to face me. I was walking towards him along one of the miles-long straight highways that bisect Detroit's suburbs. Detroit: Motor City – built by cars and built for cars. Home of Ford, GM, Chrysler, Motown records and the Nation of Islam. There was no one else on the Rustbelt stretch of road, only him and me.

He came into focus as I got nearer to him. White guy in his late sixties, swaying gently, wearing loud check golfing trousers hiked up round his belly button and a dirty-coloured T-shirt through which his scrawny arms poked. A few yards further and I could make out his creased and stubbled face, with yellow flecks of spit dried at the corners of his thin lips.

He wants some money. The story pours out – he was homeless and had been sleeping on the sofa of his nephew's shack (or 'holiday home' as the improbable sign facing the road would have passers-by believe) but his nephew was a crack-head and he had beaten him up and stole his monthly social security cheque to score some rocks and now he was properly homeless, but his sister on the other side of the city had said she would put him up and he needed five dollars for the bus. I gave him the $5. I asked him his name – it was John – and he asked me mine. 'Hassan? – are you a Muslim?' I realised he hadn't had a proper conversation for a long time. 'I was in Vietnam. I would never go to Afghanistan or Iraq – those fuckin' bastards have really messed it up for the Arabs. *I* know you are good people, I don't care what they say – Mohammed was a good man and *I* believe he ascended to heaven'.

The conversation had taken an unexpected turn. I asked him about himself and found out that he had worked for twenty-five years on the assembly line at the historic Ford River Rouge car-plant, just three miles further down from where we were standing. But he had become an alcoholic and had been sacked for coming on shift drunk one time too many, so that not even the union could save his skin. 'I've done terrible things because of drink'. His family didn't like him talking about Islam but he didn't care. He had read the Qur'an – it was a good book and he knew that it didn't have chapters like the bible, it had *soo-rahs*. 'Soo-rahs,' he repeated.

I was thinking of asking him what he thought of his city's bankruptcy and extreme decline – the factory closures, the shrinking population, the evictions, the corruption, the poverty, the dereliction and devastation – but I stopped myself. What would be the point of asking the man about the disintegration around him when he was disintegrating from within. We parted. 'Allah bless you,' he called after me.

The River Rouge plant that had taken a quarter of a century of John's life before slinging him out was the largest factory in the world when it was completed in 1928. Located on reclaimed marshland where the Rouge River runs into the Detroit River, it was a short walk from Henry Ford's childhood home in Dearborn, Michigan. Twelve miles west of downtown Detroit, the River Rouge plant was once a factory-opolis. It was a mile and a half wide and a mile long and had its own railway with sixteen locomotives and 100 miles of internal train-track, a fire department, a police force and a hospital. At its height in the 1930s it had a population of 100,000 proletarians, making sure one car rolled off the assembly line every 49 seconds. To secure the resources to shovel into its maw, the Ford Motor Company bought up coal mines, forests, iron mines, limestone quarries and a rubber plantation in Brazil. As Ford biographer Robert Lacey writes, Henry Ford 'had the vision of a total plant, the ultimate factory, where the raw materials poured in at one end and the finished cars came out at the other'.

At night the River Rouge still gives the appearance of an industrial cauldron; tall chimneys capped by gas flares, dots of glowing red lights blinking from the tops of giant sheds and the occasional rumble of freight trains leaving the plant. But it is a nocturnal illusion. Today the River Rouge plant employs just 6,000 people and is marketed as a museum destination, giving visitors 'historic' tours of the plant. This is emblematic of the decline in the city's auto-industry. In the 1950s the Motor City boasted of 300,000 auto jobs across thirty-three factories, swelling the city's population to 1.8 million. Today the city has shrunk to 700,000, with auto jobs reduced to 27,000. There are now more casinos than car factories in Detroit.

In July 2013 the city was declared bankrupt. It was the largest municipal bankruptcy ever filed in US history by debt, estimated at $18–20 billion. Was this city, once the heartland of industrial capitalism, actually dying? Would history be played backwards, and land upon which Detroit sits revert to the marshland, meadow, scrubland and forest it once was? Could such a thing be allowed to happen?

Going through passport control at Detroit Metropolitan Wayne County Airport I had been grilled by a bad-tempered immigration officer. What is my business in the city? Do I want to tell him I am writing an article for a publication called *Critical Muslim*? I tell him I'm just visiting the city as a tourist. He shakes his head. No-one comes to Detroit as a tourist. Try again. I'm an artist and I want to see the city's cultural destinations. Like where? Try again. I'm a freelance journalist researching a piece on a city in its death-throes. He grimaces 'Don't you have places like that back in the UK you can write about?' No, not really. Now he's insulted, but it's the most credible explanation thus far. He lets me through.

Detroit is an international cultural destination – of sorts. Its blighted inner-city landscape, a canvas of deserted houses, shops and buildings, is a magnet for graffiti artists everywhere. One website, detailing where to find '35 must-see pieces of Detroit's exploding street-art scene' points out that 'in case you haven't noticed, Detroit has become one of the most vibrant centres of street art in the country in recent years. Hundreds of authorised murals by some of the most famous street artists in the world now grace downtown, Eastern Market, southwest Detroit, the Grand River corridor and other hotspots'.

I follow the tour – parking my hire car on Grand River Avenue one mile before it hits the city centre. I walk the Grand River Creative Corridor (GRCC) Project – an outside gallery of graffiti pieces displayed along the roadside and on walls by local artists. I like some of it. But I am drawn to a giant mural just outside the 'corridor', painted on the side of an abandoned warehouse. It is a series of portraits of figures from Detroit's civic past. I find out later that the artist wanted to show 'everyday kind of people, people who fought on behalf of their fellow citizens'. I'm taking it in, when out of the corner of my eye I see a middle-aged African-American

Diego Rivera's Detroit Industry mural

man walking down the steps of the only property around that isn't abandoned, his hands full of stuff which he dumps in the trunk of an old car. I wonder what he thinks of the mural and does he know who any of them are. He doesn't, but he likes it. His name is Joe and the building he has just stepped out of is a hostel for the homeless. He's a nice chatty guy. I find out that he spent nearly twenty years driving an 18-wheeler monster truck, delivering auto parts to every state in the union. He tells me he loved the job – even though the pay wasn't that good because he was employed by a non-union trucking company. He becomes energised. 'You had to really concentrate you know, driving an 18-wheeler in the snow and the ice, it was hard work.' Pause. 'But sometimes I miss it,' he says softly. One day he had a terrible crash that left him disabled – he had to have a hip replaced and his shattered pelvis bolted back together. His driving days over, his only income was his state disability payments, and when the rent for his flat went so high he couldn't afford it, he had been forced into homelessness. For the past three months he had been living in 'transitional accommodation', hoping to be re-housed.

We say goodbye and I walk down Grand River Avenue towards downtown (central) Detroit – I'll be amongst the skyscrapers in maybe ten minutes. I pass by a small spotless whitewashed building. It's the Moorish Science Temple of America #25. It is locked up tight, and painted on the walls are fez-topped life-sized silhouettes, as if silently standing guard. On the back wall is a huge poster with the Moorish American Prayer: *'Allah the father of the universe, the Father of Love, Truth, Peace, Freedom and Justice. Allah is my protector, my guide and my salvation by day and by night thru his Holy Prophet Drew Ali. Amen.'* I am reminded of this particular strand of Detroit history; how the Noble Drew Ali had founded the Moorish Science Temple in Chicago in 1913, declaring that African-Americans should embrace their true nationality as Moorish-Americans and their true religion: 'Islamism'. When Drew Ali died in 1929 the leadership of the organisation broke up. One former Moorish Scientist, calling himself Wallace Fard Muhammad, then resurfaced in a poor black area of Detroit called Paradise Valley, founded what became the Nation of Islam and laid down its creed. He disappeared four years later, in trouble with the Detroit authorities, after one of his followers was detained (and later found to be insane) after committing human sacrifice to 'bring him closer to Allah'. The leadership

Joe outside his hostel

Tax Foreclosure Notice

was then taken over by Elijah Muhammad, who spent the next few decades building it into a national organisation. On the other side of Grand River Avenue still stands Nation of Islam (NOI) Muhammad Mosque No.1, as a reminder of the NOI's Detroit roots.

Just across from the Temple, set back from the road, I see a pair of boarded up derelict wooden houses. Stapled on the front of one of them is a yellow bag: Tax Foreclosure Notice. I will see many, many more of these court orders over the next few days – badges of shame pinned to broken-down homes from which the occupants have fled or been forced out. I pull the bag off and read the court papers inside. It tells me that the County Treasurer was 'seeking a judgement of foreclosure due to unpaid taxes' – in other words seizing the house because the occupants owed the county property tax arrears of, in this case, $1,095.61 (£760). The person, or persons or family who lived there had clearly moved out before suffering the indignity of being evicted, as the court hearing was not until the following month. What had been someone's home was now an abandoned lot.

The Stagecoach from Hell

Detroit Eviction Defense meet every Thursday at Old St. John's church (*'FOR WITH GOD NOTHING SHALL BE IMPOSSIBLE'*), close by the trendy Eastern Market, just north of the city centre. I push open the church door and come across a huddle being briefed on property law. Next door the group's organising committee are sat talking tactics – specifically how to avoid being arrested on a protest planned for a couple of days' time. Detroit Eviction Defense describes itself as 'a coalition of homeowners, union members, faith-based activists, community advocates, and allied groups united in the struggle against foreclosure and eviction. We believe that affordable housing is a human right, the foundation of a viable community'.

A couple of the committee acknowledge my presence with a nod and smile, and I take that as an invitation to sit down and listen in. I look round the group, trying to assess their activist 'type'. Most, but not all, are middle aged or nearing retirement. Do the maths: the '68 generation who came of age during the anti-Vietnam protests and the civil rights movement. Or even earlier. After the meeting I get into a wide-ranging

Detroit Eviction Defense mural

conversation with a very nice older woman. She explains how speculators large and small were buying up parcels of Detroit cheap, how the apartment she lives in had been bought 'by some person in Australia' who had never seen it. The reason why there was no public transport infrastructure serving the city was down to the auto-plant giants, Ford, Chrysler, GM, who had blocked it because they wanted everyone to drive their cars, and now one third of the kids in Detroit were suffering from asthma. Her name is Dianne Feeley. Later I discover that she had been politically active even before 1968, was involved in the women's liberation movement in the 1970s and was now a retired auto-worker. In 2011 she had been heavily involved in the Occupy movement in Detroit; part of the global protest against social and economic inequality. Detroit Eviction Defense was a logical spin-off from Occupy Detroit – given the crisis of hurricane-like proportions that was laying waste to the city's working class households, of which 82 per cent were African-American. Between 2002-2008 there were 19,000 tax foreclosures. Between 2008-2014 another 94,000 homes went the same way. The majority of properties were now owned by the city, it only managed to sell on a few thousand, meaning that the rest quickly fell into disrepair or were pulled down. In fact, more homes have been destroyed in Detroit than were swept away in New Orleans by Hurricane Katrina. And the process is speeding up – last year alone another 62,000 Detroit properties were in line for having the yellow plastic sleeve stapled to the door.

One Detroiter described the nightmare that stalks working class neighbourhoods as a result of the foreclosures – The Scrappers. Literally minutes after a poor family has been evicted and the bailiffs and police have driven off, bands of scavengers descend on the still-warm dwelling and dismember it. Water and heating pipes are ripped out from under floorboards and out of walls, leaving water spewing from the mains, the doors and windows and sills are prised away, the wiring pulled out like sinews from flesh, sinks, baths, toilets, taps – whatever can be carted away. One policeman told the press: 'We've seen a four-storey apartment building stripped clean in a week'.

A sunny November Sunday morning a couple of days later. I park the car up. The street is deserted. The pleasing sound of a gospel choir drifts out from a nearby Baptist Church. On the corner of 16th and McGraw in the

NW Goldberg area of the city – just a seven-minute drive from the banks and department stores of downtown Detroit – sits the ghost of someone's home. The front is hidden by a tangle of weeds and bushes. I push my way through and climb the steps onto the front porch. Laying on its side is a broken rocking chair.

Stepping through the doorway (sans door) I enter the house. It is gloomy and depressing – an old rotting mattress in a downstairs room, kept company by a cheap swivel chair. I avoid a gaping hole in the corridor floor where the strippers have burrowed for copper piping.

I climb the stairs carpeted in flakes of plaster that has peeled away from the wall. The upstairs is wrecked; there are holes punched in the ceiling, holes in the walls, and empty spaces where the upstairs windows once were; giving me a view of the equally ruined house next door, with its stapled yellow bag,

Corner of 16th and McGraw

close enough for me to read the proud slogan of the Treasurer of Wayne County, Michigan, Raymond J Wojtowicz: 'RESPECT, INTEGRITY, DIGNITY'. Standing in the wreck I try and imagine the family that once lived here and conjure up the sound of their voices, but it's impossible because the structure no longer has a scintilla of home-ness remaining.

On to Manistique – an enviably situated road in a blue collar neighbourhood on the Lower East side of the city, bordered to the south by Detroit River as it flows out into the 430 square miles of Lake St. Clair, and to the east by the exclusive Grosse Pointe waterfront area, home of the city's 'old money' families, along with their 'preppy' Ivy League offspring. Edsel Ford, the only son and heir of Henry Ford, once lived in Grosse Pointe.

839 Manistique is the childhood home of fifty-six-year-old hospital dialysis technician Lela Whitfield. She sits on a chair talking to a friend outside the well-maintained bungalow, surrounded by cheery members of Detroit Eviction Defense, who have called this Sunday afternoon gathering to protest at Lela's imminent eviction. They have pledged to organise a 24-hour watch on Lela's home and blockade it to stop the bailiffs seizing

Strippers at work

Lela Whitfield (left) and friends

the property, throwing her possessions in a dumpster and turning her out onto the streets. It is not difficult to imagine what would then happen. On one side of Lela's home is an empty overgrown lot upon which a house belonging to Lela's neighbours once stood. It was pulled apart by the scrappers. There is now not a single plank of wood to mark that a dwelling once stood there. I sense that this was once a proud African-American neighbourhood; home to generations of independent-minded home-owners who would sit on the stoop hailing the neighbours and keeping an eye on the kids riding up and down the road on their bikes. But it has taken a big hit and has been brought low in ways the residents could never have imagined, and now they struggle to keep their community together and maintain their confidence and dignity.

On the other side of Lela's is another empty plot, enclosed by a white picket fence on which a number of vivid murals have recently been painted with the slogans: 'Foreclosure Free Zone', 'Black Women's Lives Matter', 'Black Homes Matter' and 'Ain't we got a right to the Tree of Life?'

Lela's story is shocking, and tragically commonplace in today's Detroit. She grew up on Manistique, left to live her life and then moved back about fifteen years ago to tend for her ailing mother, who died in 2010. It was only then that she found that her mother had taken out a 'reverse mortgage' loan on the house she owned – a vicious financial instrument that lenders waved in front of the US's older African-American population through late night TV info-mercials and celebrity endorsements. This demographic was rendered susceptible to this hard-sell due to falling incomes and a soaring cost of living. Last year alone 12,000 Detroit retirees had their pensions reduced by upwards of 7 per cent to help pay for the city's bankruptcy.

Reverse mortgage TV hucksters included country crooner Pat Boone, actor Robert Wagner and Henry 'Happy Days' Winkler – 'Everyone trusts the Fonz'. In 2005 Lela's mum fell for their patter and took out a loan against her house. She didn't tell her daughter – I suspect she was too proud to reveal what she had done. A *Detroit Free Press* briefing explains: 'A reverse mortgage starts when a homeowner receives a loan that gives the lender an ownership stake in the property. A reverse mortgage loan requires no repayments when the borrower is alive. That's usually a senior citizen on a low income and needing cash to make repairs on the house, cover medical expenses [or] pay off accumulated taxes. The homeowner makes no payments, but interest rapidly, ominously, mounts on the loan balance. When the homeowner dies, that outstanding balance can turn out to be the value of the house'. A wicked, wicked invention of Wall Street.

When Lela found out about her mother's reverse mortgage she offered the loan company, Fannie Mae, $9,000 – the market value of the house. But they refused to sell it back to her, preferring to continually drag her to court, demanding possession of the property. The debt ballooned to $60,000. In desperation Lela turned to Detroit Eviction Defense – and they have rallied to her. She smiles as speakers at the protest excoriate Fannie Mae (the Federal National Mortgage Association) for its predatory practices and vindictiveness. Fannie Mae was an invention of the Great Depression; originally set up as part of Roosevelt's New Deal to boost home ownership by providing reasonable mortgages. It has turned into its opposite. In the 1990s President Clinton forced it into the 'sub-prime' market, a disastrous turn that detonated the huge financial crash of 2007–8, forcing the US administration to bail out Fannie Mae and its sister company Freddie Mac, to the tune of $360 billion and nationalise them.

Lela is determined and resilient – at least outwardly. 'I'm not looking for sympathy or empathy', she tells me. 'I was forced to do this. It's hanging over me and it's not a good feeling. But I have no fear.' She sighs. 'They want to evict me from my home. They should allow me to continue to be part of this community'. Lela nods to the empty plot next door. 'That was a nice home'. Her friend Shawn nods vigorously and both women reminisce about the family that 'used to live there'. I ask Shawn what happens to all the people who 'disappear'. She shrugs her shoulders. 'You see them panhandling in front of stores and getting harassed by the police. But they're not drug-addicts – they've just come on hard times.' Hard Times indeed.

Matt Clark, the lawyer attached to Detroit Eviction Defense, has a clear view of the forces at play in Detroit behind the mass evictions. 'Parts of this city look like a bomb has hit it.' But he argues that this was not the result of an off-target missile strike or a force of nature; this was done by people who knew what they were doing. He informs me that sixty-eight per cent of loans issued in Detroit were sub-prime.

Matt says that staff in one loan company, Wells Fargo Bank, privately referred to reverse mortgages as 'ghetto loans' and the recipients 'mud-people'. He is telling the truth: A lawsuit against Wells Fargo revealed that the bank pushed expensive subprime mortgages onto blacks and Latinos, even though many of them qualified for less punitive deals. So, for example, those who took out a $165,000 mortgage had to pay $100,000 more in interest then white clients in a similar financial position. Special sales teams targeted black church leaders, knowing they could be used to persuade their congregations to take out expensive loans they would inevitably default on. They did indeed use terms like 'mud people' for their victims. As one ex-seller put it, Wells Fargo 'rode the stagecoach from hell'. Matt has been fighting Fannie Mae through the court on behalf of Lela Whitfield for two years. I ask him why the government-controlled company didn't just settle with her, and take the money she is offering, rather than taking control of what is to them a worthless property. 'They don't want to keep occupants like Lela in their homes. They call it "a moral hazard".' In short, the free market, neo-liberalism, whatever you want to call it, must be seen to run its course unimpeded by any human consideration. To do anything else, to let off the hook those wriggling on it, contravenes the logic of the market, and is therefore deemed 'immoral' in this most capitalistic of countries. Matt helps Detroit Eviction Defense precisely because 'they don't back down against the most powerful organisations in the world. The banks are used to having their way, but we have found them to be very vulnerable when they have to call out the police to evict someone'. He is clear about the limits of the law: 'As an attorney I have come to understand the argument won't be won by legal virtuosity.' His view is strengthened a few days later when a court hearing, packed by Lela's supporters, sees a Detroit judge give a stay of execution, and order that both sides enter talks. Those present tell me this decision has completely wrong-footed Fannie Mae's lawyers who had expected 'victory', having confidently argued that the giant lender was 'merely living up to its legal and financial obligations' in seizing 839 Manistique.

Across the road, sitting on a porch watching the protest, are two young African-American men – Travis Thompson and Jabari Anderson. They talk to me about the 'golden years' of Detroit, how African-American families built their lives on the wages they earned at Ford, GM and Chrysler, built up neighbourhoods and communities, owned their homes, educated their kids and looked forward to their well-earned retirement. They did not foresee that the city's car industry would uproot itself and move south in search of cheap wages and higher profits, the economy fall apart, the city go bankrupt and finally the scrappers move in and literally take apart all they had achieved – leaving an urban wasteland. 'In the best times every house on this block was so nice,' says Jabari. But nowadays, adds Travis, 'you see people go – friends you have known for years, older people who led the community. It takes the spirit out of you – it brings you down.' Jabari casts his eyes around the overgrown lots: 'It looks like the countryside – you've got deer and coyote running through the middle of the city.' (Coyotes are becoming an urban problem in Detroit, with reports of them hunting in packs and eating people's house dogs, large and small.)

Travis felt like moving on, but knew that running away wouldn't solve the problem. He summoned up a feeling of self-reliance – a kind of twenty-first century version of the frontier spirit that drove the French fur trappers who founded the city back in the early eighteenth century. Abandoned by national and local politicians, abandoned by the banks, the city authority and even the retail sector who have moved their shops away, ordinary Detroiters have been forced to fall back on their own resources. 'We provide for our own people; we are not asking for help,' says Travis. 'We realise it's up to us. We can't look up to our own leaders any more.' Jabari jumps in: 'They're not helping us, they're hurting us. They're so corrupt!' He is referring to the Kwame Kilpatrick scandal. Kilpatrick became Detroit's youngest ever mayor when he was elected in 2002, at the age of thirty-one. From a family of black Democrat career politicians, the flamboyant Kilpatrick declared at his inauguration, 'I stand before you as a son of the city of Detroit and all that it represents. I was born here in the city of Detroit, I was raised here in the city of Detroit, I went to these Detroit public schools. I understand this city. ... This position is personal to me. It's much more than just politics.' What the voters of Detroit didn't realise was that the 'personal' meant embarking on a programme of enriching himself, his family and his cronies through a lavish and dissolute lifestyle paid for by the city and via bribery, kickbacks, embezzlement and the mining of city contracts totalling millions of dollars. His response to those critics who sought to reveal his corrupt dealings was to play the race card; appealing to black Detroiters as a 'nigger' being pursued by a latter-day lynch mob. Kilpatrick is presently serving twenty-eight years in prison, after being found guilty of 'pattern of extortion, bribery and fraud'. His earliest release date will be in 2037, by which time he will be sixty-three years old.

So, one day Travis decided to cultivate the empty plot next door. He showed me around his urban farm, started in 2009, which is now in its winter dormancy. In the summer he grows tomatoes, lettuce, grapevines, squash, carrots, aubergine, watermelon, strawberries and hot peppers. He sells or gives most of it away to his neighbours and the rest goes to town to be sold at the Eastern Market. School classes take trips to his farm, and visitors come from all over to admire it. There are now maybe 2,000 urban farms, large and small, across Detroit. The 'greening of Detroit' is in full swing, with the city selling off some of the 40,000 plots of deserted land they own to urban gardeners. The big auto companies, eager to generate good publicity to repair their dented image are in on the game – General Motors have converted 250 shipping crates into raised-bed planters, creating the 'Cadillac Urban Gardens'.

But for Travis, his cultivation represents something quite profound. He tells me that 'as it progressed I understood that it was a lot more than just growing food out of the ground'. Yes, it had a practical reason behind it – 'what if they close the grocery stores?' – but it was also symbolic. 'It's brought a bit of love and positive spirit to the neighbourhood, a little bit of hope amongst the heaps of rubble.' For him it is about taking back control of his life and his environment. Its sweetness counteracts the bitterness that wells up inside Travis, a symptom of the abandonment and betrayal he and his friends inevitably feel.

After the protest I swing by the Grosse Pointe neighbourhood that begins just a stone's throw away from Lela's threatened home and Travis's urban farm. I drive past mansions, manicured lawns, expensive cars and boats parked on the drives, with middle-aged white guys on their day off, out front, sweeping dead leaves into piles. I wonder whether long-term speculators have their eyes on the houses on Manistique, knowing that sometime in the future an expansion of Grosse Pointe will make the land very valuable indeed.

Dearborn

For most of the twentieth century the Detroit suburb of Dearborn was a company town, owned and run lock, stock and barrel by the Ford empire. Its height must have been in the 1920s and 1930s, for many of its prominent buildings, (like the historic buildings of downtown Detroit) are impressive examples of art-deco architecture. The houses that branch out from its main roads are very pretty dwellings indeed, and give off a tidy, contented feeling – although I notice that there are hundreds of foreclosed Dearborn houses for sale on real estate websites.

Dearborn was originally the destination for poor migrants drawn from towns and villages in south, central and eastern Europe (and Ireland). Outside Dearborn's Italian-American club stands a statue to Christopher Columbus – the 'god' who blessed them with a chance of a New World... and a job from Mr Ford. However, there were never many African-Americans allowed into Dearborn – they were segregated into other areas of Detroit like Black Bottom, Inkster and Paradise Park. In the 1940s Dearborn voters elected the notorious Mayor Orville Hubbard 'who built a political career lasting more than a third of a century on the well-understood and thoroughly redeemed pledge to "Keep Dearborn Clean"', according to Robert Lacey. Hubbard was not afraid to say publicly 'If whites don't want to live with niggers, they sure as hell don't have to. Dammit, this is a free county.' (In a subtler, but equally racist manner, real estate agents in Grosse Pointe operated a secret points system by which they debarred blacks, Jews, Greeks and Italians from buying property.)

We don't know (although we might guess) what Hubbard would have made of the fact that today his fiefdom has become the celebrated home to the largest-Arabic speaking population in North America. Dearborn's Arab-Americans – Lebanese, Yemenis, Iraqis, Syrians and Palestinians – today constitute some 40 per cent plus of its 98,000 population. As writer Mark Binelli puts it in his book *The Last Days of Detroit*, 'The best restaurants in metropolitan Detroit, for my money, are here, along stretches of Warren and Vernor that feel like neighbourhoods in Damascus or Beirut, if either of these cities have mini-malls. As the state of Michigan continued haemorrhaging residents, one demographic experienced a minor growth

The Arab American National Museum in Dearborn

surge, about five thousand new arrivals in the Detroit metro area in 2010 alone: Iraqi immigrants.' Binelli, tongue-in-cheek, concludes: 'So that was something. Dire though things had become, Detroit, apparently, remained a more desirable place to live than postwar Baghdad.'

In the library of the Arab American National Museum in Dearborn, I spot a recent issue of the DC Comics graphic novel series 'Green Lantern' on the shelves, nestled amongst religious, historical and philosophical tomes. In this superhero tale that began fictional life in 1940, a succession of humans become imbued with powers given by a ring forged by aliens. The latest recipient of the ring is Simon Baz, a Lebanese American Muslim from Dearborn. In his backstory, which begins on 11 September 2001, Baz and his sister Sira are persecuted – Sira has her hijab torn off by 9/11 vigilantes. Against the backdrop of Detroit's financial crisis, Baz is fired from his auto plant job, discovers a talent for car-jacking, and one night steals a van, which to his horror he discovers is carrying a bomb in the back. He drives the van onto the site of the now closed-down car plant, where it detonates without loss of life. However, Baz, being Arab, is suspected of being a terrorist, arrested and is brutally interrogated. The Green Lantern Power Ring finds him, allowing him to bust out of captivity. And so it goes on! The storyline is written by Geoff Johns, who is a half-Lebanese Detroiter. It's an inspired example of the huge, energising impact of Arab-Americans on Dearborn, Detroit and wider American society. Of course there are plenty of real life examples of famous Arab Americans celebrated at the museum – from scientists to writers and trade union leaders to politicians. But Baz should have his place as well alongside the others. Like other immigrant communities, they have had to fight their way into the American mainstream. But by the 1990s Arab-American Dearborn could boast that it had produced the CEO of Ford, a US senator and the head of the United Auto Workers union. However, due to the times we are living through, they can still find themselves under scrutiny as a 'suspect' community. While I was in Detroit the November 2015 massacre in Paris was carried out. The Dearborn community automatically steeled itself, and lo and behold, a few hours later came the death-threats and then calls from US politicians to bar the entry of anymore refugees from the Middle East 'until we can find out what the hell is going on!'.

The Arab American National Museum does its bit in educating the visitor, with displays on Islam and Muslim heritage, the history of its community, as well as giving space for exhibitions with a bit more of a contemporary edge – such as the striking photo-portraits of young Somali men that I viewed in the museum's art gallery. After I have gone round I chat with Katherine, the cheery young woman on reception. Her family come from a small village in Lebanon – 'back home' as she calls it. She had spent two years in Lebanon attending the American International School, but was now back in Dearborn studying medical case management. As well as putting in time at the museum, which she sees as an enjoyable duty, she volunteers for ACCESS (Arab Community Center for Economic and Social Services), a grass roots organisation that was 'founded by a group of dedicated volunteers in 1971 out of a storefront in Dearborn's impoverished south end'. Katherine had been out the previous week with an ACCESS team, boarding up abandoned houses and cleaning up garbage in the south end. She tells me she was named after a much revered older member of her family and the community – Katherine Younis-Amen, who was one of the original founders of ACCESS and of the museum.

In reality, the Dearborn community does not fit the one-dimensional stereotype thrust upon it by the bigots. It is very diverse – a mix of American-born and newly arrived immigrants, Arab and Chaldean, Palestinian, Iraqi, Lebanese, Syrian, Shia, Sunni, Catholic, Orthodox and Protestant, wealthy and working class, business men and business women, public-sector workers, civil rights activists and law enforcement county deputies. Out of this diversity has emerged a particular fusion of grass-roots social activism and entrepreneurial flair. Wider Detroit also exhibits aspects of this – created by the huge vacuum left both by the retreat of the state from the lives of the city's inhabitants and the ravages of the free market.

Small business start-ups are popping up across the city; encouraged by a combination of favourable tax breaks, access to funding, cheap rental property, and the stark truth that Detroit clearly needs help from someone. I arrange a meeting with a couple of representatives of this new business culture: Amany Killawi and Chris Abdur-Rahman Blauvelt are happy to show me around Green Garage, the eco-friendly building in mid-town Detroit that houses a number of 'third sector' organisations, including LaunchGood – their Muslim orientated crowdfunding business. These two young Muslims aim to enter the space that the city's disintegration has opened up: 'It's like a laboratory – a Silicon Valley for social entrepreneurialism'.

Chris and Amany take their religion to heart. For them, Islamic values are intrinsically ethical and progressive, and therefore Muslims have a particular role and responsibility in reviving the city's social and financial fabric. LaunchGood is built on that which they hold dear. Their website states: 'Too often we are constantly telling others who Muslims are not, that we rarely can tell them who we are. We are proud of our heritage as pioneers, inventors, entrepreneurs and bearers of all things good. We believe in Muslims doing great work that benefits everyone, not just Muslims.'

They advise organisations and individuals on how to crowdfund for good causes; such as raising money for a new roof for the home of a poor family, donations for medical aid to Syria, funding the rebuilding of black churches recently burnt down in racist arson attacks in the southern states, and a fitness DVD for Muslim women. Chris and Amany take me to the local halal café for lunch where they tell me what they are trying to do. Amany's parents left Syria in the 1980s, and after a spell in Louisiana, migrated to

Amany and Chris of LaunchGood

Detroit where they raised their family. She is clearly a product of Detroit's activist and social justice tradition. Chris was born in Kuala Lumpur where his father was working at the time, educated in the US, and at fifteen converted to Islam, partly inspired by the biography of Malcolm X. Both cite 9/11 as a watershed moment in their lives, convincing them that their mission as Muslims was to 'do good'. In its first year their organisation helped raise over $1 million for more than 100 projects across thirteen countries. They are now up to the $5.5 million figure. They eschew the corporate approach that has done so much damage to their city. Amany tells me, 'Purely maximising profit is not sustainable; we believe sustainability lies in creating value in the community.' Chris adds 'Detroit has a do-it-yourself culture. That's what we love about this city.'

They also see the value in alliances across the different embattled communities – for example, that Muslims must unite with the black community: 'African-Americans have the cultural power here in America and the immigrant communities have the wealth. If you can come together, you can do more than government or private investors can.' They connect with a bigger entrepreneurial hub – 'Dream of Detroit' – another Muslim-led initiative that is attempting to reverse the tide of foreclosures by buying up land and renovating houses. Its declared goal is to 'build a dense, thriving community on the west side of Detroit based on prophetic values of compassionate living and concern for one's neighbours'. Perhaps Dream of Detroit and LaunchGood represent the green shoots of a new Detroit? Or is the task too great and the city just too far down the line?

No place like Utopia

This issue of *Critical Muslim* examines The City from all angles – as historical memory, as an existing entity, as a concept, a metaphor, a dream and a living nightmare. Yet despite this panoramic range, it is hard to ignore a plain truth – something has gone horribly wrong. The dissonance between humanity's needs and the twenty-first century city clangs in the ear. As David Harvey says in his book *Rebel Cities* 'the traditional city has been killed by rampant capitalist development...driving towards endless and sprawling urban growth no matter what the social, environmental, or political consequences'.

Javaad Alipoor, in his imaginative contribution for this issue, 'Utopia in Tehran', argues that the classical utopian concept of the city in harmony with the needs of its inhabitants has, like Tehran, 'become sprawling, contradictory and covered in the muck of history's most violent century'. As Alipoor highlights, more than in any other period in history, cities today are the site of the struggle for and against 'democracy' and 'rights'. Dictators fear the insurgent forces that cities contain, and yearn to control common spaces where people may gather, dominating them symbolically through statues and monuments. Peter Clark, writing lovingly of Istanbul, which for him is still 'the capital of the world', tells how Ataturk had a statue of himself raised on the headland Sarayburna in 1926, 'but he only came to the city for the first time, full of apprehension, the following year'. In 'Tashkent Odyssey' Eric Walberg writes that in the post-Soviet period the president/dictator of Uzbekistan Islam Karimov opened a museum commemorating national hero Amir Timur on the site where a statue to Karl Marx once stood – and for good measure replacing 'a quiet tree-lined park which was a beloved meeting place for ordinary Tashkenters'. Walberg paints a fascinating picture of his time in Tashkent, from where he began his personal journey to Islam, pushed down the road by the dictator's brutality, and beckoned 'by waking to the gentle *adhan* and the sweet Uzbek women offering a share in their *iftar*'.

David Harvey argues that the only way to seize control of cities from dictators and rampant capitalism and to 'build and sustain urban life' is to assert our 'unalienated right to make a city more after our heart's desire'. This heartfelt leap of the imagination is at the centre of Syima Aslam and Irna Qureshi's contribution: 'Festive Bradford'. They describe how they launched the Bradford Literature Festival as a way of wresting the identity of the city back from a powerful media, who, ever since the Rushdie affair, have framed the northern city as a hotbed of backward, violent, book-burning religious fanatics. On the other side of the world, but in a similar vein, Irfan Yusef in 'Muslim Life in Sydney' good-naturedly debunks the lazy Islamophobic stereotypes that abound, to reveal that Sydney's Muslim population have the same diversity and drive exhibited by Dearborn's Arab-Americans.

Nimra Khan's vivid account of the heroic resilience of Lahore's Third Sex community in the face of bigotry and hypocrisy, reminds one that although cities are harsh unforgiving places, common humanity will be found amongst the marginalised. We inevitably yearn for a simpler, less complex social organism. Robert Irwin, in his hugely evocative and entertaining essay on medieval Basra tempts us at every turn. Although ninth-century Basra was most likely a rough old place, who wouldn't want to be transported back for a day, to walk through the *Mirbad*, where the Bedouin parked their camels and the lizard vendors displayed fat skinks (a local delicacy) for sale, before bumping into the famed goggle-eyed scholar and bibliophile al-Jahiz, on his way to be locked up in a bookshop for the night.

Detroiters are rightly proud that their city remains famed worldwide for its cultural innovation that has always been driven by the beat hammered out in the city's car plants. In 1932 Mexican artist and revolutionary Diego Rivera, accompanied by his wife Frida Kahlo, was invited by art enthusiast Edsel Ford to Detroit. After spending time sketching in River Rouge and other factories Rivera produced *Detroit Industry* – the truly magnificent panoramic twenty-seven panel mural decorating all four walls of the courtyard of the Detroit Institute of Arts. You can only stand in awe, your vision sweeping across a combination of scenes of heroic workers toiling on production lines, depictions of the power of twentieth-century industrial invention, entwined with symbols and vistas from Mexican land-mythology.

Berry Gordy worked on the Ford assembly line (including a spell at the foundry at River Rouge) before going on to found Motown records (Motor-City Records). He modelled his hit-factory on Henry Ford's original idea – artists in one end and perfectly crafted three-minute pop songs out the other: 'Every day I watched how a bare metal frame, rolling down the line would come off the other end, a spanking brand new car. What a great idea! Maybe, I could do the same thing with my music. Create a place where a kid off the street could walk in one door, an unknown, go through a process, and come out another door, a star.' He even set up a system at Motown called 'quality control' and famously filmed Martha Reeves and the Vandellas' 1965 hit 'Nowhere to Run' on the Ford Mustang assembly line. Later on the 1970s thrash guitar band MC5 (the Motor City 5) served as a seminal influence on the punk rock explosion. MC5 fan, the idiosyncratic rock star Iggy Pop, who hails from the nearby Michigan city of Ann Arbor, claimed that he was inspired by 'the industrialism in

John Collins of Underground Resistance

Detroit…what I heard walking around…boom boom bah – ten cars… boom boom bah – twenty cars.'

Today the city's mantle of industrial musical innovation rests with Detroit Techno. John Collins, a central figure in the movement, shows me around the headquarters of Underground Resistance – round the corner from the Motown Museum. A former auto-workers' union hall, the building is part museum, part studio, part record distribution centre and global destination for techno aficionados. John has a real sense of history, he is endowed with a broad vision, and is a man very much worth listening to. He gives me a quick history of the musical form. It was founded by 'the Bellville Three' – three black high-school friends from a Detroit suburb, who, in the early 1980s, absorbed the diverse influences of the industrial/ cultural life of Motor City in decline, the legacy of Motown and funk, sci-fi such as Star Trek, and electronic music coming from bands in Europe – most notably Kraftwerk whose most famous tune is, fittingly, called *Autobahn*. The result was a futuristic, soulful, electronic musical sound that also served (and serves) as a musical commentary on post-Fordist decline and social distress.

Collins is busy, but takes time out to educate me on the pioneers of Black Detroit, such as the city's first African-American mayor Coleman A. Young, elected in 1974, much to the horror of the city's white racist power structure. I'm certain that many people feel that the majority black population is today being punished by the powers-that-be for having the temerity to take political control of Detroit. Underground Resistance also has echoes of the legendary Underground Railroad – the hidden chain of sympathisers along which escaped slaves from the southern plantations made their way north to Detroit, and the final leg of their perilous journey, across the Detroit River to Windsor, Ontario, and freedom. John refuses to allow the present state of Detroit to obscure its history, its unique spirit and achievements. 'A lot of good things have always gone on in this city.' It will rise again. 'Detroit is like an alcoholic. It has hit rock bottom many times. But it always picks itself off the floor'.

Later that evening, walking through the Eastern Market district, I pass by a bar. I stop to glance through the window. Inside mixed couples, black and white, are drinking and enjoying themselves after a hard day's work. Some are squeezed onto the tiny dance-floor, dancing and singing along joyously. I can't hear the music, but I fancy it is the urban blues number Joe L. Carter wrote while working the line at River Rouge in 1965:

Please, Mr. Foreman, slow down your assembly line.
I said, Lord, why don't you slow down that assembly line?
No, I don't mind workin', but I do mind dyin'.

At this moment they look like they don't have a care in the world.

ISTANBUL:
CAPITAL OF THE WORLD

Peter Clark

Istanbul, Constantinople, al-Āsitāna, Qustantiniya, Tsarigrad, Mucklegarth – Bolis – the city on the Bosphorus, the largest city in Turkey, means many things to many people. For most of its life its geographical position, as a port bestriding two continents, has made it an international and cosmopolitan city. For a thousand years it was the principal city of Christendom. For nearly five hundred years it was the capital of the most successful Islamic state in history. It has always attracted people from the rest of the world, traders, scholars, writers, adventurers, men of religion. In the sixth century it imported wine from Gaza and in later Byzantine times herrings were brought from England. In the twenty-first century a community of Turkic speaking Uighurs provides the government with Chinese interpreters.

In the last twenty years or so the city has attracted people from the former Soviet Union. Poorer people flock to the cheaper hotels of Aksaray, and services are advertised in Russian; the wealthier migrate to the Taksim area and luxury clothes shops in Nişantaş advertise their wares in Russian. More recently Aksaray has housed thousands of refugees from civil war-torn Syria; here services are advertised in Arabic.

Its most famous monument, the Church of the Holy Wisdom, Haghia Sophia, Ayasofya, built by the Byzantine Emperor Justinian in the sixth century, was converted into a mosque by Sultan Mehmet after the Turkish conquest of the city in 1453. It became a 'museum' in 1935. Islamists want to turn it back into a mosque as they have done with the Ayasofya in Trabzon, Trebizond. It is the prototype for almost all subsequent mosques in the Ottoman Empire and beyond, to such an extent that a dome is still commonly regarded as an integral feature of a mosque.

Everybody has his or her own Istanbul, and anyone can feel at home there. The quarters, the cemeteries, the alleyways, the docks are all like a palimpsest of universal history. Napoleon is said to have claimed that if the world had to have a capital it should be Istanbul.

The twentieth century saw great changes to the city. The century started with bursts of architectural activity. The many different communities were being challenged by a new nationalism that transformed the city during the First World War. The implosion of the Ottoman Empire led to a Turkification of Istanbul, and other communities were expelled, decimated or chose to leave. A monoculture was imposed. But the dawn of the twenty-first century has seen a revival of the city's globalism. It has become a regional financial capital, a cultural metropolis, with some exciting new architecture. Constantly expanding, its transport systems have remarkably kept up with a tenfold increase in population in the last fifty years. This means that nine out of ten of the inhabitants of the city are not from Istanbul. Mostly the newcomers are from Anatolian villages.

From 1453 to 1923 it was the capital of the Ottoman Empire. When Mehmet Fatih, the Conqueror, took over a ravaged and shrunken city, he encouraged whole populations to come to his new capital. His immediate successors welcomed the Muslim Arabs and the Jews expelled from Spain after the Christian Reconquest; their skills were valued and needed. The Ottoman Empire was dominated by Sunni Muslims but was a diverse, multicultural, multilingual, multi-ethnic society. There was certainly a hierarchy of communities, but the empire had a far greater tolerance of diversity than was the case in contemporary Renaissance Europe. It is misleading to call the Armenians, Greeks, Jews and other communities 'minorities'; that effectively delegitimises them. Insofar as there was a political philosophy the varying communities were seen as elements – *anāsīr* – of the body politic. Each community had a contribution to make to the whole, comparable to different parts of the body. An arm was as integral as an eye. Of course things went wrong; there were breakdowns of community relations, persecutions and even massacres. But usually the empire was sufficiently resilient for a balance to be restored that allowed the empire to survive. It was only at the end of the nineteenth century that ideas of exclusive nationalism undermined the Ottoman system. And the geography and demography of the capital reflected that inclusiveness.

Istanbul was not rigorously cantonised. Districts were not exclusively Muslim or Christian or Jewish. Social divisions were as much horizontal as vertical. The poor shared the same space, had the same dilemmas, constraints and opportunities; as did the rich.

The nineteenth century saw outside powers anticipating the collapse of the Ottoman Empire and coveting juicy provinces. The observation attributed to a Russian tsar, that Turkey was the 'sick man of Europe', was often repeated, anticipating this collapse. Yet we must remember that the Russian Empire actually predeceased the Ottoman, albeit by six years. The Ottoman Empire also outlived the Habsburg and Hohenzollern empires. For most of Europe the First World War lasted from 1914 to 1918. But the Ottoman Empire was continually at war from 1911 to 1923. Insofar as strength is seen in military terms the Ottoman forces did not do too badly during that war. They had to fight on four fronts. They repelled an international invasion – from Britain, France, Australia and New Zealand – of the Gallipoli Peninsular; they captured an Anglo-Indian Army (including its British General) in Mesopotamia; they extended territory in southern Arabia; they did not surrender Medina until the end of the war; and, in spite of early reverses, they regained territory in eastern Anatolia lost in the war with Russia in 1878. From the 1920s there were over twenty succession states to the empire. The national narrative of each was based on rejection of or revolt against the Ottomans. These states included not only the non-Turkish states of the Balkans, Middle East and North Africa but also the Turkish heartlands themselves. The Republican Turkey that emerged from the ashes of the empire was based on a repudiation of the multinational Ottoman state. In the generation after the First World War, loss of empire made Istanbul a sad place: like Vienna, it was built to be the centre of a great empire. Modern Turkey stressed its Turkishness; in spite of its secularism, the identity of a Turk overlapped with being a Muslim. In the early 1920s, with the exchange of populations between Turkey and Greece, the country was purged of its Greek Christians, most of whom had Turkish as their first language. They left to become second class citizens in the Kingdom of Greece. A few thousand Greeks stayed behind in Istanbul, some of whom insisted that they were Turks, not Greek. These Turkish Orthodox Christians kept their church at Panaghia in Tophane.

The historical narrative of all the succession states painted the Ottoman Empire in the most unfavourable light – coinciding with the Turkophobia of elements of Western war propaganda. It has only been from the end of the twentieth century that a revised version of the past has had some support. Ethnic conflicts in the former Yugoslavia and then the troubled chain of events in the Middle East have led people to think that the empire must have had a more successful formula. Liberals have reinterpreted the Ottoman Empire as a valid experiment in multiculturalism. Islamists have looked back on the empire as a successful Islamic political institution. The boundaries of the Ottoman Empire were very similar to those of the empire it succeeded – the Byzantine Empire, which always saw itself as the continuation of the Roman Empire. (It was only in the sixteenth century that western historians started using the term Byzantine.) Administering an empire from the same city meant that, in spite of religious differences, the Byzantine and Ottoman empires – *sub specie aeternitatis* – had much in common. For most of the people in the Eastern Mediterranean world in the fifteenth century the Fall of Constantinople / Conquest of Istanbul was a regime change. Inevitably, the managers of each successive empire were constrained, to some extent, by geographical determinism and by the same opportunities and constraints. There was never any question, in each case, that the city was the focus and capital of the empire. One successor considered shifting the capital to Mecca to emphasise the Islamic nature of the empire, but that would not have made any strategic, political or economic sense. Both empires saw themselves as universal entities with a unique divinely ordained mission. In practical terms, there was a similar degree of delegation to the provinces, with gradations of autonomy defined by pragmatism. There was even the implicit idea that Istanbul's sovereignty over its co-religionists extended beyond the bounds of the empire.

Mehmet Fatih (1432–1481) saw himself as the successor of the Roman Empire and indeed, with his patronage of the arts, could be seen as a Renaissance Prince. But there were other Byzantine legacies. Architecture for both was a symbol of power. Until the 1960s most people coming to Istanbul approached the city by the sea and Ayasofya, first as church and then as mosque, dominated the landscape as the outsider approached. In the early nineteenth century the Selimiye barracks on the Asian side of the Bosphorus, when it was built, was the largest garrison in the world, and was another display of military power, designed to overawe the visitor. Although the first sultans left most churches in the hands of Christians, successive sultans built enormous mosques that dominated different quarters of the city. Byzantine emperors and Ottoman sultans both ensured that the city had adequate fresh water supplies with aqueducts and fountains. Ottoman taxation was based on Byzantine precedents. The Byzantines had built up a customs mechanism based on duties on incoming ships that were moored on the Golden Horn. *Kommerkion* was the word used for a customs payment due, from which, through Latin we get the word commerce. The word was also borrowed by the Ottomans and evolved into the word *gumruk*, a word familiar to every visitor to Turkey and the Arab world. The common Turkish word *efendi* is also derived from the Byzantine Greek word for 'gentleman'. One faith gave each sovereign its legitimacy but other religions were permitted. The quarter of Eyub, with the tomb of one of the Companions of the Prophet was always a site of pilgrimage. In the Byzantine city there were other destinations of pilgrims. Holy wells abounded and the city became famous for its unrivalled collection of holy relics. With the Fourth Crusade in 1204, when the city was plundered by western Christians under the leadership of Venice, these relics were looted and dispersed all over Europe. But the Ottomans continued with the policy of collecting holy relics. This was particularly the case after Sultan Selim attached Egypt to the empire in 1517. From Cairo he brought relics to the imperial palace, Topkapı, most notably a mantle believed to have belonged to the Prophet Muhammad.

Out of the chaos of the collapse of the empire and the twelve years of warfare which had brought dislocation and loss to almost every family in Anatolia and Istanbul, Mustafa Kemal (Ataturk, after the introduction of surnames in 1934) brought the country together on his own terms. Imperial nostalgia was banished, a new regime and a fresh new politics, albeit rooted in the later Ottoman reforms, was launched. The windy Anatolian hill town of Ankara became the new republic's capital and seat of government. It was cold in the winter, hot and dry in the summer, a contrast to the moderate Mediterranean climate of Istanbul. Few of the new elite actually came from Ankara or central Anatolia. Public servants and those who sought to be close to men of power reluctantly shifted their bases to Ankara, but hastened back to the Bosphorus for the summer months.

Mustafa Kemal's own feelings about the city were ambivalent. He came from Salonica and was one of a succession of men from the Balkans who have had a profound impact on the city. (The Byzantine Emperor Justinian and the sixteenth century all-powerful statesman Sokullu Mehmet are two others who spring to mind.) Mustafa Kemal first came to the city as a seventeen-year-old cadet at the War College (now the military museum in Harbiye). He enjoyed the glamour and pleasures the city provided, and in some ways he became the quintessential late Ottoman Pasha, speaking French, moving in the best circles, familiar with the imperial palaces, staying at the Pera Palas, taking rooms in Beşiktaş, self-consciously concerned about his dapper appearance. He was not alone in absorbing ideas and political programmes from France or Britain. But he grew to abhor the cosmopolitanism of the city, its Levantinism. He looked for an authentic Turkishness and, although his personal relations with the non-Turkish Muslim elements were often excellent, Istanbul represented for him all that was distasteful and an obstacle to the new Turkey of which he dreamed.

After he had raised the standard of revolt against the Sultan's authority in 1919, he avoided the city for eight years. In 1926 he authorised a statue of himself to be raised on the headland, Sarayburnu; the promontory that separates the Sea of Marmara from the entry to the Golden Horn. This was a defiant statement against an Islamic objection to statuary, but he only came to the city for the first time, full of apprehension, the following year. He had already travelled all over Anatolia where he was greeted with adulation. In the summer of 1927 he arrived by yacht. City and President greeted each other graciously. The President stayed at the Dolmabahçe Palace, architectural symbol of sultanic authority. He received delegations of support and the streets were crowded with well-wishers. Security was tight, for several leaders from the war years had been assassinated. But the ice was broken, and Mustafa Kemal came thereafter every year to Istanbul. He established his own villa at Florya to the west of the city. He had strong ideas on architecture, as on most things, and hated domes, eaves, pitched roofs and everything that made up quaint orientalism. He insisted that his villa, now a museum, be made up of straight lines. It is a straightforward structure of brutalist simplicity, an eloquent testimony of the man's own simplicity and single-mindedness.

Ataturk became a regular visitor to Istanbul and enjoyed the dancing and parties at the Park Hotel near Taksim. He fell ill in 1938, and after a visit to Ankara in May stayed in Istanbul for the remaining six months of his life. Too ill to move back to Ankara, he spent a lot of time on a yacht, bought for his personal use by the government. There he received visitors but from July he was terminally ill. He stayed at his modest Florya villa but in the summer he moved to the less modest Dolmabahçe Palace. He went into a coma on 16 October, came to from time to time but sunk into final unconsciousness two days before he died on 10 November. His body lay in state for seven days in the lavishly ornamental Throne Room at Dolmabahçe Palace – a room that he must have loathed – and people thronged to pay their respects. Two days after he died the crowds were so out of control that several people were trampled to death.

In the last half century the city has emerged again from the eclipse into which it had been plunged by Republican policies. The city represents the history of the land that is Turkey and has bounced back to vigorous life. Ankara may be the political capital but in every other respect Istanbul is dominant. As well as being the largest city in population, it has become the financial and artistic capital. Most of the newer inhabitants from Anatolian towns and villages have brought their own perspectives, way of life and culture. Older Istanbullus are anxious that their city has been taken over by the peasants of the interior. The newcomers have provided the main support for the AKP and the Islamist policies of President Recep Tayib Erdoğan, to the dismay of the liberal internationally-minded elites who easily relate to the outlooks of their counterparts in Paris, Milan, London and New York. There is a social gulf between the sophisticated quarters of Istiklal Caddesi in Beyoğlu or Bağdat Caddesi on the Asian side on the one hand and the suburb of Sultanbeyli and the area around the Fatih Mosque on the other.

The different classes come together in their enthusiasm for different football teams. The three main Istanbul teams – Beşiktaş, Galatasaray and Fenerbahçe – have their supporters all over the country. The fourth team of the country is not based in Ankara but is from Trabzon (which has also seen a remarkable transformation in recent years). However, the traditional base of support for each of the Istanbul teams reflects the social history of the city. Beşiktaş is the oldest team with a stadium that occupies the site of the imperial stables attached to the Dolmabahçe Palace. It is seen as the team of the working class. Galatsaray is named after the old elite school in the centre of Beyoğlu and represents the older elite of the city. The Kurdish leader, Abdulla Ocalan, in an interview once expressed his support for Galatasaray and many Kurds now support the team as a result. And Fenerbahçe with its stadium on the Asian side of the Bosphorus – a location that does not prevent the team from participating in the European World Cup – is the team of the new meritocracy. The Nobel Laureate, Orhan Pamuk, typically, is a supporter. Football is followed intensely and bitter are the rivalries. As they enter the stadiums supporters are frisked for weapons and opposing fans directed to terraces behind high wire netting. The whole country follows key matches, especially between two of the three teams, and crowds pour onto the streets to celebrate or bemoan the result. I could write a book about the different quarters of Istanbul (indeed I have). Nearly every part has its stories; a modern mosque, a monument, a cemetery, a piece of Byzantine wall, an Art Nouveau shop front. Let us pause in Balat, an old Jewish quarter; Istiklal Caddesi, the spine of Belle Epoque Istanbul and Yildiz Palace, home of the last powerful Sultan, Abdülhamid II.

Balat is a suburb on the west side of the Golden Horn about four kilometres from the Bosphorus. It lies below the old Byzantine Palace of Blachernae. The word Balat is derived from the Greek *Palation*, meaning simply Palace. Originally Balat was a suburb allocated to Christians. There had been a small Jewish community in Byzantine Istanbul but it was augmented in the sixteenth century when the Sultan encouraged migration to the new Ottoman capital. Initially the Jews came from the Balkans but after the final fall of Andalusia, Jews (and Arabs) were specifically invited to Ottoman lands. They came in large numbers and settled in Balat.

From the early seventeenth century until the middle of the twentieth century Balat was the predominant Jewish quarter of Istanbul. The Andalusian Jews brought their own Spanish dialect, *Ladino*, with them and a distinctive Judaeo-Spanish culture prevailed. There were already synagogues in the area, named after Balkan locations – Plovdiv and Ohrid for example. It was predominantly, though not exclusively, Jewish, as Turkish Muslims, Armenians and Greeks lived there alongside them, generally in harmony.

Large changes affected the area from the nineteenth century. The Jewish community was conservative and observant. The main divisions in the nineteenth century came from a secular education which challenged the authority of the religious leaders. Istanbul also admitted Jews from Italy and Ashkenazi Jews from Eastern Europe. Prosperity also led to migration from Balat outwards to the other side of the Golden Horn around Galata. The 1940s and onwards further diminished Jewish Balat. Imposition of a property tax in the Second World War targeted non-Muslims and many chose to emigrate, the wealthier to France and Canada, the poorer to the new State of Israel. Istanbul was noted for its urban conflagrations. One happier, though unexpected, outcome of these fires was that from the 1860s there was a coherence in the urban planning and architecture of the area known before the republican period as Pera, and since as Beyoğlu. It was the home of the wealthy, the elite (of all religions) and the foreigner.

In the nineteenth century, Istiklal Caddesi was the spine of non-Muslim Istanbul. Even in Byzantine times this suburb, situated across the Golden Horn from the main city with its great mosques and the Sultan's palace of Topkapı, was separate. It was *pera*, beyond the city, and was the base for the Genoese, who were uncertain allies of the Byzantines. From the Galata Tower two town walls descended to the Golden Horn. Some parts of these Genoese walls can still be seen, including a gate with the Genoese symbol above the doorway. A walk along Istiklal Caddesi, previously known as Grande Rue de Pera – happily, largely pedestrianised – is an encounter with the social, cultural and architectural history of the last century and a half. In the last twenty years there has been a tension between commercial interests in smashing and rebuilding on the one hand, and preserving and celebrating this heritage on the other. There have been victories on both sides. Some buildings have a distinctively Istanbul architecture. Many of the architects were French and Italian, though the owners of the land were often Ottoman Muslims. The Balians, the Armenian family who designed palaces, mosques and barracks are represented by the entrance to Galatasaray school. Several shopping malls, *pasaj*, on the pattern of those in Naples and Brussels, have been restored in recent years. It is worth looking at all the buildings, for some gems may be overlooked. For example, the small Asnavur Pasajı has a narrow entrance, but above it and on the upper balconies are fine examples of Art Nouveau ironwork, as well as mosaics on the floor. On the eastern side is another gem, at number 201. It houses an old fashioned shop selling clocks and antiques. On the iron grille doorway is an Art Nouveau giant beetle. The walls and windows could have been designed by Charles Rennie Mackintosh. Like many smaller buildings, the name of the architects is on the wall. In this case the architects were called Yenidunia and Kyriakides, a Turkish-Greek partnership.

On the other side of the road is a larger building, the Elhamra Pasajı, built in 1920. The architect was Turkish — Ekrem Hakki Ayverdi, and it is in an extraordinarily bold eclectic style. Gothic arches frame the windows. Slender classical columns between the windows rise to a neo-Islamic *muqarnas* blind archway. It is worth pausing to contemplate this example of multiculturalism frozen in stone. Purists would condemn the mixture of styles, but it is in many ways a reflection of the universal quality of the city, which was, even as it was being built, vanishing. The building occupied the site of a French theatre to which, in 1861, a ballroom called the Crystal Palace was added. A feature of the street was its commitment to pleasure. Cinema in Turkey began here. Betwen Yeşilcam Sokak and Sakizağaçı Cadesi was one of the great Istanbul cinemas and theatres, originally called the Gaumont (or Gomon) and then the Glorya. Louis Armstrong once played there. It was lost in the first decade of the twenty-first century, although today several cinemas still remain along the road.

Music was a feature of Ottoman Istanbul. Along the street at the corner of Nuru Ziya Sokak the Commendiger family used to have a shop selling classical musical instruments. The Ottoman ruling family were among their most loyal customers. In 1847 the Commendigers hosted the Hungarian composer and virtuoso pianist Franz Liszt. He played to the imperial family and gave lessons to some of its members. Sultan Abdülaziz was no great reformer but he did love music. He, and other members of the family, composed music. His son, Abdülmecid, was a lover of music and also a painter.

The cousin of Abdülmecid, the Sultan Abdülhamid II, has had a bad press. He is generally portrayed as paranoic, suspicious and reactionary. He had built for himself his palace at Yıldız, then on the edge of the city, a couple of miles up the Bosphorus. He was, like the rest of his family a lover of western classical music, in his case opera. He had a small theatre built at Yıldız where an Italian company would put on operas by Offenbach and

Verdi. But he did not like unhappy endings and in *La Traviata* he directed that Violetta should not die a consumptive death but be restored to vigour in the final act. The theatre survives. Abdülhamid was also a patron of architecture. Unlike members of the family of the previous generation he did not go for the outrageous extravagance and splendours of the palaces of Dolmabahçe or Beylerbey, but a relatively modest extended villa at Yıldız. This palace had extensive grounds that stretched down to the Bosphorus, with one or two independent buildings as guest houses. The whole enclosure was surrounded by walls about five metres high. He was suspicious and had every reason to be. His uncle, Sultan Abdülaziz, had been either driven to suicide or murdered; his immediate predecessor and brother, Murad, was deposed; he himself survived an assassination attempt. He concentrated power in the hands of himself and a few trusted servants, but he also had a reforming vision that owed more to Metternich than to John Stuart Mill. During his reign there was a huge expansion in education. His palace, now a museum, reveals his personality. As well as his theatre, he also had a carpenter's workshop where he liked to make furniture, some examples of which are in the museum. He was also a builder. His favourite architect was an Italian, Raimondo D'Aronco, who built much of the palace. Abdülhamid also commissioned the Yıldız mosque just below the palace. This was designed by the last of the Armenian Balian family of architects. It has Gothic windows and to this mosque the Sultan would drive the hundred yards from the Palace each Friday.

Sultan Abdülhamid also built up his own personality cult, strange for a reclusive. He saw the importance of visible symbols of monarchy. In his youth he had accompanied his uncle, Sultan Abdülaziz to London; he even went to Balmoral as the guest of Queen Victoria. He read of the Queen's Golden and Diamond Jubilees, and celebrated the twenty-fifth anniversary of his accession with much ceremony. His personal arms and portrait appeared on school textbooks.

His reign, 1876-1909, saw a weakening of the empire and the loss of Christian provinces in Europe. At the same time Muslim refugees arrived from Central Asia and the Caucasus, fleeing from advancing Russian imperialism. The ideology of the empire became more explicitly Muslim. The idea of the caliphate, *khilafa*, took on fresh life under Abdülhamid. He reached out to Muslims beyond the empire, especially in India. He was particularly committed to retaining the allegiance of the Syrian provinces. Some of his closest advisers were Syrians. There still survive throughout the empire – in Jaffa and Aleppo for example – clock-towers he had built. These were symbols to bind the empire. Of course in the end he failed.

In his person the Sultanate and the Caliphate were united, an identity both secular and religious, a revival of the Caesaropapism of the Byzantine Emperors. In 1923 Mustafa Kemal abolished the Sultanate, but for a year retained the Caliphate in the person of the music-loving painter Abdülmecid, nephew of Abdülhamid. But he was sent packing in 1924, in spite of protests from India. During the 1920s and 1930s there were several possible contenders for the role of Caliph, including King Farouk of Egypt. The notion of caliphate went into eclipse until it was revived this century.

Istanbul carries its inheritance lightly. It is a modern city but a palimpsest of two millennia of artistic and cultural endeavour. Fifty years ago there was a touch of provincialism about the city. The main political and economic decisions were made in Ankara. But today it is the dominant city of the country – New York to Ankara's Washington or Sydney to Canberra.

Not only has it asserted itself as Turkey's major city once again, it has also resumed an international role. The internationalism is less visible than in the late nineteenth century, but it is possible to see public signs in Istanbul today in more than half a dozen languages. Visitors, residents and tourists arrive from all over the world.

The political and social changes since 1960 – three military coups, democratic elections, mass immigration into the city from rural areas, extensive developments in architecture and transport – have not undermined the essential personality of Istanbul. You are never far from the waters of the Golden Horn, the Bosphorus and the Sea of Marmara. If there are unsightly tower blocks in one direction, there are the age-old monuments of faith and power in another – Süleimaniye mosque, Ayasofia, the Selimye barracks.

Istanbul is eternal. It still has something for everyone. It is the most exciting city in the world.

MEDIEVAL BASRA:
CITY OF THE MIND

Robert Irwin

'I made up my mind to go to sea and so I went off to buy a variety of trade goods, as well as other things that I would need for the journey. I boarded a ship and sailed down river from Basra with a number of other merchants. We then put out to sea and sailed for a number of days and nights, passing island after island and going from sea to sea and from one land to another. Whenever we passed land, we bought, sold and bartered, and we sailed on like this until we reached an island which looked like the meadows of Paradise ...' So begins Sinbad the merchant's narrative of his travels. Basra was the port of the Abbasid Caliphate. Baghdad became the political capital of that caliphate, but Basra remained its literary capital as well as a port.

Anyone who thinks about the history of Arabic literature in the Umayyad and Abbasid periods, from the seventh until, say, the eleventh century, must be struck by the enormous number of first-rank writers and thinkers who were either born in Basra or who lived and studied there. They include Sibawayh and Khalil ibn Ahmad, the founders of Arabic grammar, lexicography and prosody, Hasan al-Basri the first great Sufi mystic, Rabia al-Adwiyya, the most famous of all women Sufis, Bashshar ibn Burd and Abu Nuwas, the most famous poets at the Abbasid court (or, in the case of Abu Nuwas, perhaps the most notorious), Ibn al-Muqaffa', al-Jahiz and al-Hariri, the acknowledged masters of literary prose and the scientific encyclopedists known as the Ikhwan al-Safa, or the Brethren of Purity. As the great, if somewhat crazy, Orientalist, Louis Massignon put it: 'Basra, in fact, is the veritable crucible in which Islamic culture assumed its form, crystalised in its final shape in the classical mould ... in the seventh to tenth centuries. It was the site on which the main components of Arabic literature were manufactured. It was the forcing ground for Islamic philosophy, theology, oratory and science.'

The strange thing is that in its origins the place was mostly inhabited by illiterate Bedouin soldiers fighting in the service of Islam and the jihad. Basra was and is situated almost 300 miles south of the capital Baghdad (though old Basra and modern Basra do not occupy identical sites). Basra (the name means 'black pebbles') is in the Shatt al-Arab region where the rivers Tigris and Euphrates come together. Though the city was very close to the Tigris, it was not actually on its bank, but rather situated on a canal drawn from the Tigris. Basra was threaded with canals and bridges like Venice – and, as in Venice, people and merchandise used to be carried through the city on gondolas (or bélems) poled by keffiyed Bedouin gondoliers.

Founded in 635, in its earliest years the place was an army camp strategically situated close to the war front with the disintegrating Persian Sassanid Empire. As Arab troops pushed on further, they went on from Persia into Central Asia and for several decades the Islamic territories conquered in Central Asia, including Khurasan and Merv, were administered by Arab army officers resident in Basra. Five great tribes from the Arabian Peninsula settled in Basra. The camp soon became a city. At first the troops and their families lived in huts made from reeds and the first great mosque was similarly an enclosure roofed over with reeds. Later mud brick replaced reeds and later yet baked bricks were used in the houses of the comfortably off, but there were always many poor people living in slums of reed huts during Basra's first centuries. The early military population enjoyed tax breaks and received pensions from the caliphs and these privileges they passed on to their non-military progeny. Basra's privileged fiscal status and its population of pensionaries is one reason for the place's early prosperity.

The Great Mosque was eventually rebuilt in mud brick and stone. The prison was next door to the Mosque and so was the residence of the commander-in-chief of the Arab army. The Mosque was the centre for prayer, especially the Friday lunchtime prayer. But its importance went wider than that. It was the favoured haunt of the *masjiddyun*, the 'mosquey' people, these people came not so much for prayer, though they prayed occasionally, as to pass the time in literary debate and other matters. These were afternoon men, often recipients of military pensions, men with time on their hands and a disposition to take an interest in culture. So the Mosque was a kind of club or salon. Poetry was recited in the Mosque and *rawi*s, professional commentators, explained that poetry. It was common to 'publish' one's work in poetry or prose by reciting it in the Mosque. As the Arab army was decommissioned and progressively replaced by foreign levies, mercenaries and slave soldiers, Basra acquired a fairly idle population of retired military men and the children and grandchildren of soldiers. Over the centuries, the military genealogies of Basra were diluted by the influx of Persians, Indians, Malays, Greeks, Javans, Zanzibaris, East Africans and others. Deserters from the Sassanian army made their way to Basra. Two Jewish ghettoes, Talmudic and Karaite, were established in the city. The place's proximity to the sea, two days upstream from deep waters, made it a cosmopolitan city. Despite the place's horrible climate, the medieval city acquired a population of some hundreds of thousands. One mosque no longer sufficed and the geographer al-Yaqubi claimed that there were 7,000 mosques in Basra. (He had not counted them of course. He just meant that there were a lot of mosques.) The main mosques were the centres of the great Arab tribes.

Downstream from the city there were mudflats where poor people made mats of reeds and where pious people went out to meditate and do penance on isolated muddy little islands. There was also a small garrison fort to protect against pirates and a lighthouse to warn of the mudflats. Big ships could not reach Basra, but docked at the nearby port of al-Ubullah. The river-going ships of Basra, with their lighter drafts, were built of teak and were whitened with quicklime and grease. The ocean going dhows had to discover the world for the Arabs – first the real one – India, China and Sumatra – and then, beyond that, the fictional one found in the adventures of Sinbad or those of Captain Burzugmihr – the City of Brass, the Valley of Diamonds, the Island of Waq Waq where human-headed trees grew, and the Tree at the End of the World.

Basra came into existence in the region where the sand of the desert gave way to rich black earth. The immediate rural hinterland of Basra consisted mostly of fertile palm groves and villas hidden in the palm groves. Fifty different kinds of date were grown in the environs of Basra. The famous translator and political theorist Ibn al-Muqaffa' lived as a gentleman farmer on one of those palm grove estates. The indigenous non-Arab rural population of Iraq were known as Nabataeans and they spoke Aramaic. The Arabs tended to treat the Nabataeans with scorn. As we shall see, Nabataean writers tried to get their own back. But the Bataih, the area to the north east of Basra, was mostly inhabited by Indians, gypsies, and blacks. The blacks, mostly East Africans, were engaged in plantation slavery and working on land reclamation. The gypsies herded water buffaloes. Michael Asher's life of the explorer Wilfred Thesiger, describes the Iraqi marshes as they were before Saddam Hussein drained them:

> The canoe cut through jungles of reeds, into glades and lagoons of smooth water, along waterways and across permanent lakes, passing villages of reed houses each on its own floating island – a flotilla of galleons riding at anchor, each with its squad of water-buffaloes mooning around a smoky fire in its open bows. Giant wild pigs haunted the reed-beds and swam in the water; four different kinds of otter trawled around the floating islands; flights of ducks and geese exploded at the canoe's approach in a shimmer of light; coot and heron skimmed away from them in a snap of wings. In the evenings, when the light from the slit doorways of reed houses fell like pillars of fire across the water, the world was filled with the croaking of a billion frogs.

But let us turn back from the marshy hinterland to the city itself. The Great Mosque was an important literary centre. But the Mirbad was an even more important one. *Mirbad* means literally a place for tethering animals and that was indeed one function of the great open space, as the Bedouin parked their camels there. The word Mirbad derives from r-b-d, to lie, to rest of animals, thus *mirbad*, a place where animals lie down to rest and then in modern Arabic, by extension, *rabid*, a suburb. Situated to the west of the city, on the edge of the desert, the Mirbad was topographically on the edge, but in most other senses, it was the centre of Basra. The Mirbad was a halting place for caravans. It was also the place where Bedouins brought their livestock to sell and it was precisely because of this that the place became the centre for literary research and debate. Arabic was the language of God, the language of the Qur'anic revelation. Not only that, but all of a sudden Arabic had become the language of a great empire. But the language was a difficult one and there were many contentious points regarding the vocabulary and grammar of the Qur'an and early Islamic poetry. And the desert-dwelling Arabs were known to be the guardians of the purest form of Arabic and their memories were the best guide to how things had been said and done in the lifetime of the

Prophet. So it was that theologians, grammarians and poets went out regularly to the Mirbad to talk with the men from the desert. Philologists and grammarians spent more time in the marketplace than they did in libraries. So did Persians, Nabataeans and others who wanted to learn good Arabic and in that way advance their careers. And there is another consideration. The Arabs had just conquered two great empires, the Byzantine and the Sasanian, which had both possessed rich cultural traditions. The new Arab ruling class had no culture of painting, architecture, literary prose or music. But they did have one cultural achievement of which they could be justly proud and that was the fabulously rich and sophisticated pre-Islamic poetry composed by Imr'ul-Qays, Shanfara, Ta'batta Sharran and others. This poetry was not at first written down in books (and papyrus was in the early years very expensive). The poetry was preserved in the memories of Bedouin and transmitted by them to the city-dwelling Arab litterateurs who wanted to study and emulate the great pre-Islamic poets. Urban poets learned to sing about deserted campsites and the rigours of desert life. To risk an oxymoron, much of Basra's literary culture was oral and, as in Ray Bradbury's novel *Farenheit 451*, men turned themselves into walking, talking books.

The half-Persian ninth-century poet Abu Nuwas used to go out to the Mirbad very early in the morning with a tablet on which he jotted down Bedouin vocabulary and verses. That was the foundation of his future greatness. The people who frequented the Mirbad in order to acquire learning were known as the *Mirbadiyyun*. Poets used to declaim their poems in this great open space and we know that literary debates took place there. Poetry often took the form of flyting – that is to say that it was competitive and abusive. There were several reasons for this. First the poets were often the spokesmen of the five great tribes and it was seen as their job to magnify the achievements of their own tribe and diminish those of the rival tribes. (Incidentally, it also seems to have been the case that some of the poets forged pre-Islamic poetry in order to heighten the literary prestige of their tribe.) Additionally non-Arabs who had mastered Arabic and Arabic prosody used poetry in order to belittle and satirise the Arabs. Poets also needed patronage. One obvious way was to compose *qasida*s, or odes, of panegyric addressed to a particular patron, but the other hardly less obvious way was for the poet to make himself a master of *hijja*, or satire, so that he had to be paid for his silence or, alternatively used as a kind of hired pen against designated enemies. In the Umayyad period the flying contests of the Arab poets Akhtal, Farazdaq and Jarir were particularly famous and much discussed and compared in the literature of later centuries. Jarir and Farazdaq belonged to the Tamim tribe that dwelt in the south-east part of the city. They had their fixed pitches where their fans assembled. Literature apart, the Mirbad was also the haunt of snake charmers, mountebanks and storytellers. It must have resembled the great open space in front of the Jami al-Fana in today's Marrakesh. The Mirbad was also often the place where rumbles took place between rival Arab tribes.

The lizard market was situated on the south-east corner of the Mirbad. Lizards were sold to be eaten. Though the Bedouin regarded lizards as a delicacy and lizard-eating was in early years a mark of authentic Arabdom, it was common for the Persians, Indians, Nabataeans and others to sneer at the Arabs as eaters of lizards and locusts. Bashshar ibn Burd, an eighth-century Persian who composed poetry in Arabic, boasted in verse that 'Never did we roast a skink with its quivering tail/ nor did I dig for and eat the lizard of the stony ground'. Apart from the nutritional value of lizards, I have read in Norman Douglas's treatise on aphrodisiacs, *Paneros*, that the skink was held by the Bedouin to have aphrodisiac properties. (As for locusts, 'The locusts eat us and we eat the locusts' was a famous Bedouin saying.) From the 780s onwards the governor of the city's house was located on the edge of the Lizard Market. The famous essayist al-Jahiz quoted Ja'far ibn Suleiman, governor of the city in 790, saying 'Iraq is the eye of the world, Basra is the eye of Iraq, Mirbad the eye of Basra and my house the eye of Mirbad ... '

Undoubtedly Basra's most famous citizen and the star of Arabic literature was al-Jahiz (or Goggle-Eyed, for that is what the Arabic means). Jahiz was born in Basra in the 770s, made a career of sorts for himself in Baghdad, but returned eventually to Basra to live and die there. He was the grandson of a Black African porter. As a child, he studied the Qur'an at a *Kuttab*, or Qur'an school, in the Banu Kinana quarter. Basra was divided into five big quarters (and never mind the mathematics of that) named after the five Arab tribes that had settled in the original encampment. Jahiz moved to Baghdad at the invitation of one of the caliphs. This was a common feature

of life in the Abbasid period – intellectuals from Basra were imported by
the caliphs and viziers in Baghdad. In Baghdad, Basra's literati sang for their
supper, composing songs and jokes and turning themselves into *nudama*,
that is professional conversationalists or cup companions. The Basrans in
Baghdad tended to stick together hanging around in the district of the Ibn
Raghban Mosque. They might spend years at the court surviving on literary
patronage, but they usually returned to Basra – as Jahiz did. He was famous
for his spiky satirical wit, his passion for books and his ugliness. Once he
applied to be the tutor of one of the caliph's sons, but when the caliph
interviewed him, he decided that Jahiz was much too ugly to be employed
at court and gave him a large sum of money and sent him away.

Jahiz's various and numerous works were in large part a compendia of
the wit and wisdom of Basra. He has been described as the incarnation of
the city's collective genius. He took care always to entertain as he
instructed and he had a terror of being boring. He had a digressive comic
style that anticipated *Tristram Shandy*. His favoured form was the *risala*, a
letter that was really an essay. Whoever the letter was formally addressed
to, it was really addressed to the Arabic reading public at large. He wrote
about the round and the square, animals, misers, lepers, the respective
merits of the back and the belly, singing girls, Mutazilite philosophy, the
cultivation of palm trees, the Qu'ran, the respective merits of boys and
girls, stranglers, Christianity, thieves, rhetoric, Turks, the respective merits
of summer and winter, lame people, kings, judicial verdicts, the envious
and the envied, Jews, nostalgia, slave mothers, the afterlife, Persians,
saddle-makers, emaciated people, presents, orators, plagiarism, apostates,
getting hot or cold, a perfume shop, fornication, prophecy, Zoroastrians,
ugliness, keeping secrets, in praise of wine, the land tax, gatecrashers,
booksellers, people who pester their friends, the disputation between the
cross-eyed man and the man blind in one eye, horses and atoms among
much, much else. And much of what he wrote has alas been lost. The
diligent Abbasid book cataloguer, Ibn Nadim went on for pages listing
Jahiz's writings. The Abbasid historian al-Mas'udi wrote that Jahiz's books
'polished the rust of the mind ... Those writings are very well organised
and set down with consummate art. When the author fears that he is
boring or is tiring his audience he skilfully passes from the serious to the

entertaining, and leaves the grave tomes of science for the lively ones of amusing stories'.

One other thing he wrote about was the respective merits of Basra and Kufa and the fierce rivalry of the two cities:

> The traveller making for Qasr Anas espies an expanse of moist earth, with soil like camphor; he finds people hunting lizards, pursuing gazelles and fishing with both line and net, and hears the song of the boatman at his tiller as well as the chant of the camel-driver in the saddle. Above the cemetery at Basra is a place called al-Kharir, where people say the air is cooler, the breeze gentler and the evenings pleasanter than anywhere. The people of Kufa say that Basra will be the first town in the world to be ruined, that it has the worst soil, is furthest from heaven, and will be the first to be engulfed by the waves; the water will come up out of the sea, submerge it and return to the ocean. But what do they know about it, seeing that they only manage to bring floodwater to their reservoirs after raising it thirty cubits in the air?

Jahiz continues in praise of Basra's water, which, among other things, accounts for the intellectual well-being of the inhabitants of the city. The city is also estimable for the whiteness of its crockery, the colour of its brickwork, its palm trees, its plentiful supply of money, moderate prices, cheaply built houses, its useful reed beds and its access to the Indian Ocean. Kufa, by contrast, is a vile ruined little hole that is haunted by jackals and foxes and the Kufans make their houses out of bricks of dung. Moreover 'the people of Kufa dislike the people of Basra more than the latter dislike them. The people of Basra are friendlier, less conceited'. (One thing you will take away from reading Jahiz is a realisation of what a terrible place Kufa is. Not that I have ever been there. I am just relying on what Jahiz said.)

By the way, the respective merits and demerits of Basra and Kufa was a stock theme in Arabic literature. The tenth-century historian al-Mas'udi (who was unusual in being a writer who did not come from Basra) reported one such debate. One of Mas'udi's friends declared that 'Truly I can think of no more apt a comparison for Kufa than a beautiful girl of noble birth but no fortune, so that when her poverty is mentioned, her suitors withdraw. Basra I can only liken to a wealthy old lady who boasts in vain of her property and riches – still no one comes forward to claim her.' To which Ahnaf ibn Qays, a man, like Jahiz, famous for his ugliness and wit, replied that 'Basra has reed below, woods in the middle and meadows above. We have more teak than you, more ivory and silk brocade, and likewise more sugar and more coin. Truly it is a city I always enter with joy and leave with regret', (which to me sounds like the boasting of the old lady).

To return to Jahiz, he loved books. According to an acquaintance 'whatever book came into the hands of al-Jahiz, he read it from start to finish'. He used to pay to be locked up in bookshops so that he could read there all night. It is related that he died when a pile of books collapsed on top of him (but God knows best). Before that, he wrote in praise of his library: 'If these books are noble, beautiful and excellent, and surpass all others, it is because their contents are designed to meet the expectations of eminent men. They contain, first, elegant and unusual anecdotes, subtle and beautiful sayings transmitted by Companions of the Prophet, and hadiths calculated to encourage the acquisition of praiseworthy qualities and the performance of noble deeds worthy to go down to posterity; but they also contain information about the conduct of kings and caliphs and their ministers and courtiers, and the salient features of their life-stories.' Jahiz was a one-man intellectual ferment. Between them Jahiz and Ibn al-Muqaffa' (on whom more shortly) hammered out Arabic prose.

One factor behind Jahiz's productivity and the explosion of literature in Basra more generally was the spread of the new paper technology. Paper allowed Arabic literature and it also underpinned an Arab bureaucracy. The parchment that was used earlier was seriously expensive. The first paper mill was established in Baghdad towards the end of the eighth century and paper was in common use in the eastern Islamic lands. Baghdad remained the centre of papermaking in the medieval Islamic lands. Prior to the ninth century, Arab culture was mostly oral, consisting as it did of orally transmitted *hadiths* and orally transmitted poems. (Even the Qur'an at first only existed in the memories of men and in scraps carved in bits of bone, wood and leather.) But in the Abbasid period, the advent of paper licenced new genres, such as cookery books. There was no copyright. There were no print runs. Jahiz kept himself going mostly by dedicating books to wealthy men. The alternative strategy of making name for oneself as a master of invective has already been mentioned. Some people were prepared to pay good money to keep their names out of poetry. The novel was unknown in medieval Arabic literature and short stories were often, even usually, presented as if they were non-fiction.

Poetry was the literary art form. The Arabs first golden age of literature was that of the Jahili or pre-Islamic poets. This body of poetry was really the only culture that the early Arab soldiers and settlers possessed. It was not much in bulk to set against the great bulk of Persian literature. The Basran scholar and mnemotechnician, al-Asma'i (d.828?) was the first to systematically collect and study Jahili poetry. A particular specialist in language, al-Asma'i produced classified lists of Bedouin vocabulary. Some of that vocabulary was rather specialised. In the early nineteenth century the German Orientalist Freiherr von Hammer Purgstall made a special study of one aspect of this sort of material and found that there were 5,774 words for camels and camel-related things.

Arabic poetry was difficult. *Ruwat*, reciters who also provided glosses on what they recited, were often necessary. *Tarab*, or robe tearing, was a traditional mark of emotion at hearing a poem or on seeing human beauty.

Basra produced or at least nourished hundreds, or more likely thousands of poets. The flyters Jarir and Farazdaq have been mentioned. I will mention only two more of the most famous poets here. Bashshar ibn Burd (c.718–784) was a Persian born in Basra. He was blind from birth, so he was never able to see how spectacularly ugly he was. He knew Jarir and al-Asma'i. He was the sworn enemy of the great local Sufi, Hasan al-Basri. Bashshar was rude and arrogant and his rudeness and arrogance fuelled his invectives and satires. Women found him sexy. He moved to Baghdad soon after it was founded in 762. He was a pioneer of *badi'*, the ornate, metaphor-heavy, modern style of poetry that came fully into fashion a little later in the ninth century. The licentiousness of his verse attracted a lot of criticism from the pious, but it was a political satire that led to Bashshar's being tortured and then sewn into a sack that was dumped in the Tigris.

As for Abu Nuwas, the book-cataloguer, Ibn al-Nadim wrote that Abu Nuwas was so celebrated that there was no need to go into the details of his biography, but perhaps his fame has faded a little in modern Britain. Abu Nuwas, born in Ahwaz around 755, was half Persian (on his mother's side) and spent his youth in Basra. It has already been noted how he went out early in the mornings to the Mirbad to talk to the Bedouin. It was in Basra that he fell in love with Janan, a slave-singing girl. (The singing girl was a feature of Iraqi society. The best of them were educated somewhat like geishas and sang from a repertoire of Arabic poetry that was commonly accompanied on the lute. Jahiz wrote a treatise entitled *In Praise of Singing Girls* that was actually an attack on them.) Abu Nuwas went to Baghdad in search of patronage and eventually became the cup companion of the Caliph al-'Amin. Later, he served as the cup companion of Harun al-Rashid (and as such features in several of the tales of *The Thousand and One Nights*). Abu Nuwas composed wine poems, hunting poetry, satire, homosexual love poetry, heterosexual love poetry, satires and ascetic poetry. He is best known for the wine poetry that shaded into erotic poetry as the carousing poet often found himself fancying the bearer of the wine, or the singer in the background or one or other of his cup companions. Or he would fall into drunken regrets for his lost youth. Lost youth was a great theme in pre-Islamic poetry. But wine poetry (*khamriyyat*), oddly, seems to start in the Islamic period. The sale of wine was particularly associated with Zoroastrian Persians, who feature frequently in poems as dealers in liquid ecstasy. It is surprisingly difficult in the Abbasid period to sort out the homosexual poetry from the heterosexual, because of the conventions regarding pronouns in medieval poetry and sometimes poets used male pronouns to refer to women, perhaps in order to protect their honour. Besides writing homosexual poetry, Abu Nuwas wrote in praise of *ghulumiyyat*, young women who had disguised themselves as men. By the time Abu Nuwas set up his stall, the *ghazal* or love poem had acquired its fixed cast of characters – the blamer, the jealous watcher, the go-between, and a few others.

He was also the leading poet of hunting and he celebrated hunting oryxes and wrote in praise of falcons:

'Oft I go forth in the early morning, while the night is still black, a dark-bay colour, sending the birds flying as it breaks up. It is the morn of one desiring the hunt. With a hawk ruddy in colour or light-bay with a blaze on her cheek. The Maker has fashioned her with finest body; she is the same before and after the hunt ...'

In the hunting poetry he worked perforce with highly specialised Bedouin vocabulary. The words were *gharib*, strange. He liked to shock and featured in *The Thousand and One Nights* as a trickster, a rogue and a kind of court jester. Probably his most famous poem is a parody of the traditional *qasida*, which traditionally opened with a dismal lament over the abandoned campsite. Besides composing a great deal of hedonistic poetry, Abu Nuwas also wrote ascetic poetry (*zuhdiyyat*). Perhaps these poems should be seen as the product of old age and repentance, but then again perhaps the old rogue was simply trying his hand at another literary genre. He died in 810.

Turning now to some other prose writers, the Basran Khalil ibn Ahmad (718–791) was the pioneer of Arabic lexicography. It was more or less inevitable that Basra with its Mirbad should be the birthplace of the Arabic dictionary. Khalil, the earliest of the dictionary makers, had to establish an alphabetical order. He thought that the alphabet should be ordered according to where the noises were made in the throat or the mouth. Since *ayn* was made at the far back of the throat, he began his *Kitab al-Ayn* with that letter, hence the title of his dictionary. As an additional refinement he included all words that had *ayn* as one of their radicals in the first section of his dictionary, only subsequently moving on to *ha*, the next most guttural letter. (The dictionary ends with *ya*.) This complex system of permutations is difficult to manage and eventually had to be abandoned. However, even today Arabic dictionaries are not organised according to straightforward alphabetical order, but rather according to the roots. Most words being formed on the basis of a trilateral root. *Maktab* means office, but you don't look that up under m, instead you go to K and k.t.b. – *kataba*, he wrote, from which also provides the trilateral root of the word 'office', as well as words for scribe, library, book and so on.

Khalil's dictionary set a tradition in Arabic lexicography of quoting heavily from poetry. A dictionary's purpose was in large part to elucidate the obscurities of pre-Islamic and Bedouin poetry. Usage was illustrated by such heavy quotations that dictionaries were in large part literary treasuries and collections of anecdotes. It was not just the lexicon of the camel that featured specialised vocabulary. As M.G. Carter put it in his summing up of Arabic lexicography: 'we turn with gratitude to the dictionary to find, for example, that *bahlasa* means "he arrived suddenly from another country without any luggage". Ignorance of the verb *bahlasa* is probably harmless, but it was always an article of faith that the well-being of Islam at large depended on a thorough knowledge of Bedouin linguistic conventions. The dictionaries are thus more than mere repositories of information in a certain order: rather they are alphabetical lists of the ingredients of an entire civilisation.' Khalil also worked out the pattern and rules of Arabic metre. It is said that he was inspired to do so while in the Azd quarter of Basra, listening to the rhythms of a blacksmith's hammer. Khalil was famous for his scholarly asceticism and he lived in a house of reeds. He was an archetypically absent-minded intellectual. It was while he was working out how to teach his slave girl how to do sums when paying for food that Khalil collided with a pillar in a mosque and died of the impact.

Khalil taught the Persian Sibawayhi (d.793), the first and leading grammarian of Arabic. His name derives from the Persian '*sibuya*' which means 'the scent of an apple'. He was later to acquire an even more strangely named pupil, Qutrub. *Qutrub* means 'werewolf'. The young student was called werewolf because he used to turn up so early for Sibawayhi's classes that people joked that he must have spent the night scavenging for corpses in graveyards. But back to Sibawayhi himself.

Sibawayhi had come to Basra intending to study religious traditions and law, but having proved himself to be stupid in law classes and made lots of mistakes, out of sheer shame he turned to the study of language instead. The grammar he produced was entitled *Kitab Sibawayhi*. There was no precedent in Arabic culture or for that matter in the earlier Graeco-Roman culture for the compilation of a systematic grammar. Sibawayhi divided the Arabic lexicon into nouns, verbs and marginal items. He conceived of speech as a social act, so that the listener as well as the speaker had a role in determining the form of speech.

As has been mentioned, it was quite common for people to fake pre-Islamic poetry. One of the important functions of early Arab grammatical study and lexicography was the detection of fakes. These disciplines were born of debates with Bedouin in the Mirbad and a reapplication to the Arabic language of the ideas underpinning Islamic law. Besides testing ancient poetry, grammar was needed to set Islam's non-Arabic citizens right. And even Arabs needed grammar in order to elucidate the text of the Qur'an – a text that with every generation came to seem increasingly obscure and threw up points that needed glossing. Basran grammarians were conscious of competing with the grammarians of Kufa, for Kufa was also a centre for study of grammar and lexicography. But Kufans tended to study the exceptions and anomalies, (*shawadhdh*), whereas Basrans concentrated on the general rules. Basran grammar after Sibawayhi became prescriptive, setting out those rules, whereas Kufan grammar tended to be descriptive. Basrans and Kufans competed in lobbying for Baghdad's approval and they of course composed poetry abusing one another.

We do not have precise dates for the birth or death of Ibn al-Muqaffa', this despite the fact that he is one of the grandest figures in classical Arabic literature. He was a Persian, born in Firuzabad in the early eighth century. He learnt Arabic in Basra and made a career as a scribe, translator and author. He was at least nominally a Muslim though some of his rivals accused him of being a crypto-Manichean. He was generous and ambitious – the two qualities went together, as generosity tended to be used to build up a clientele. He was arrogant about his command of the Arabic language, which was better than that of the Arabs around him. I believe that he put together his famous fable collection *Kalila wa-Dimna* in order to teach foreigners and children good Arabic. *Kalila wa-Dimna* is a collection of stories first put together in India and called in Sanskrit the *Panchatantra*. It was then translated into Pahlavi Persian and somewhat expanded. Ibn al-Muqaffa''s Arabic elaboration on the Persian version has further additions to what was originally a base structure of five frame stories: 'The Lion and the Ox, The Ring Dove and Her Companions, The Owls and the Crows, The Ape and the Tortoise and The Ascetic and the Weasel'. Morals, maxims and fables, stories boxed within stories, purporting to give guidance to rulers and their counsellors were inserted into this framework. But did rulers actually read this sort of thing and learn from it? Clearly *Kalila wa-Dimna* had a much wider readership and, as so often in early Arabic literature, it was a work of entertainment posing as a work of edification. Much of the book deals with the murderous but eloquent jackal Dimna who pleads for his life at the court of King Lion. The book serves as a kind of shop window for oratory. Insofar as the book taught anything, it was not so much statecraft as good Arabic style and rhetoric. Ibn al-Muqaffa' wrote a wonderfully limpid prose, and unlike Jahiz, Ibn al-Muqaffa''s syntax and vocabulary were easily accessible.

More generally Ibn al-Muqaffa' specialised in translating and adapting old Persian texts and he wrote on political theory. He was prolific, but like most authors of the time, most of his work has been lost and we have to guess what has been lost from references in Ibn al-Nadim and elsewhere.

As the fate of Bashshar ibn Burd suggests, writing was one of the dangerous professions. Ibn al-Muqaffa' became the victim of a political murder sometime in the 750s and he died under torture.

The other great writer of prose fiction, Al-Hariri (1054–1122) spent most of his life on a palm tree plantation outside Basra though he also lived in Basra and in Baghdad for a while. Together with Ibn al-Muqaffa''s *Kalila wa-Dimna*, al-Hariri's *Maqamat* is the most famous work of classical Arabic prose. The *Maqamat*, often translated as 'Sessions' but literally 'Standings', is a collection of fifty short rhymed prose picaresque sketches, all featuring in various disguises the eloquent and wily rogue Abu Zayd. Unlike *Kalila wa Dimna*, the Arabic of the *Maqamat* is ferociously difficult – allusive, punning games-playing. It has to be studied with a commentary. It represents a newish and distinctive kind of fiction. In his last speech in the book, Abu Zayd addresses the citizens of Basra 'O ye people of Basra! May God keep and guard you and strengthen your piety; how far-spread is the fragrance of your fame and how surpassing are the virtues that distinguish you ...' and he carries on praising the place for its fertile pasture grounds, the accuracy of their mosques' orientation towards Mecca, the rivers and date palms, its position as gateway to Mecca, its exclusively Muslim foundation, never soiled by heathen practices. And there is more. Basra has lots of shrines and holy tombs, 'In [Basra] meet the ships and saddle beasts, the fish and lizards, the camel-driver and the sailor, the hunter and the tiller, the harpooner and the land-serf ...' Abu Zayd points out that Basra has been home to Islam's greatest ascetic, Hasan al-Basri and to the creator of poetics, Khalil ibn Ahmad. The place also has the best muezzins. As a final indication of the blessedness of this city, the Prophet had predicted the rise of Basra even before it was founded.

Turning now to science, or at least what purported to be science, al-Kindi, was the son of the governor of Kufa, but he was educated in Basra. The man who wrote the short chapter on him in *The Cambridge History of Arabic Literature* (Fritz Zimmerman) found the man's work difficult to summarise. As he says, 'Al-Kindi wrote on questions of mathematics, logic, physics, psychology, metaphysics, and ethics, but also on perfumes, drugs, foods precious stones, musical instruments, swords, bees and pigeons. He wrote against the false claims of the alchemists, the atomism of the *mutakallimun* [theologians], the dualism of the Manichaeans, and the Trinitarian doctrine of the Christians. He supported astrology, calculated the duration of the Arab empire, and speculated on the causes of natural phenomena such as comets, earthquakes, tides or the colour of the sky. He took an interest in distant countries and ancient nations ... ' and so, on and on. He was less stylish and witty than Jahiz and he was simultaneously both more of a scientist and an occultist than was Jahiz. Jahiz was the son of a porter, but al-Kindi, as his name, which refers back to the ancient tribe of Kinda, may suggest, was an aristocratic Arab. He died some time after 865. At first sight, what he studied and how he studied might be seen as representative of a lessening of interest in Persian culture and a growing interest in that of the Greeks, but as Dmitri Gutas has shown, Persian patrons in Abbasid Baghdad and elsewhere were inclined to regard all serious wisdom as originating in the *Avesta* (the Zoroastrian holy scriptures). Since they believed that the Greeks had taken over Persian scholarship at the time of Alexander's invasion of Persia, it followed, they thought, that Greek science was really Persian science in origin and it therefore followed that to translate works by Aristotle, Euclid, Ptolemy, Hippocrates and others was to reclaim elements of ancient Persian culture.

Al-Kindi did a lot to recycle Greek philosophy and science and to dress that philosophy up in Islamic terms. In recent years I have had the misfortune to read rather a lot of potted accounts of the Arab transmission of Greek science and philosophy to the West — the Arabs as postmen of Greek letters. Such accounts generally fail to assess the value of what was being translated. Perhaps the authors of those accounts have not actually read the texts in question. In the case of al-Kindi, for example, his treatise on optics survives in a Latin manuscript, *De Radiis*. *De Radiis* is occult bunk, full of astrological and other misconceptions. The chief misconception was that al-Kindi believed that sight depends on rays projected from the eyes. One might also question the scientific value of the *Qanun*, the medical encyclopedia of Ibn Sina (Avicenna), with its purported cures for such maladies as werewolfism and love sickness.

Jabir ibn Hayyan, the famous eighth to ninth century alchemist (known to medieval European alchemists as Geber), can hardly be claimed as a citizen of Basra, as it is probable that he never existed. He was supposed to have lived in the eighth century and studied with the Shi'i Imam and master of the occult sciences, Ja'far al-Sadiq. But the excessively copious literature attributed to him shows signs of being influenced by Shi'i ideas prevalent a century later, as well as translations later made from the Greek. Jabir's or rather pseudo-Jabir's treatises ran into their hundreds. In the middle ages it was common for authors to ascribe their books to other more famous personages in order that their books might survive. Works by the school of thinkers and writers calling themselves Jabir covered philosophy, medicine, astrology, talismanic magic and mathematics from an alchemical point of view. There were also treatises on ingenious mechanical devices, toxicology, music, grammar prosody, physics, military stratagems, botany, the properties of stones, numerology and human biology. In much of what they wrote they relied on the lore of craftsmen such as the glassblower, the smith, the dyer and perfumer. They ranged widely, so that amidst all the speculations about the true nature of metals and transmutation of base metals into gold and silver, one may also find advice on how to raise pigeons, a description of a pharaonic perpetual motion machine, a talismanic idol that will keep flies away from the table, the technique for constructing speaking statues, a Chinese technique for waterproofing silk, a discussion of frightening voices, a discussion of why the human skull is the shape that it is, a talismanic spell for keeping awake at night in which an effigy of a Chinaman is placed is placed in one's bed (I can well conceive that this might actually work), a discussion of the origins of language, a description of *al-bahit* the laughing stone, recipes for invisible inks, and an exposure of the fraudulent miracle of the Fire at the Holy Sepulchre in Jerusalem, the sea doctor that was a fish with a stone fixed in its head and which went swimming around curing sick fishes, and so and so on. (It is all a bit like Borges's famous Chinese encyclopaedia.) The treatises all refer one to other treatises in a kind of maze of mutual referentiality. Medieval Arab alchemy was very much a reading activity. Most Jabirians do not seem to have thought that a furnace or an alembic was necessary.

Jabirians divided substances into three kinds: spirits, metals and bodies. Spirits were volatile substances, such as mercury, sulphur and sal-ammoniac. Then there were seven metals including silver and gold, but also the mysterious Chinese iron that was available only from a remote Asian valley. Bodies were earths. The substances were all combinations of hotness, coldness, dryness and wetness. Gold was the only perfect metal, the only healthy one. All the other metals were in a sense sick and the alchemist strove to be their doctor. The medicine he sought to administer was *al-iksir* (al + Greek *xerion*, a dessicative powder for wounds). Though the word derives in part from Greek, the actual idea of an elixir seems to come from China. The elixir would be a substance made pure by sublimation so that it had a single nature. The alchemist for example tried to separate out the wetness from the coldness in water.

Jabirians were fascinated by the possibility of animating talismans and in using organic putrefaction to create homunculi and other monsters. Like Paracelsus centuries later, they were obsessed with the filthy dispensary of corpses, turds, urine, semen and menstrual blood. Jabirians wrote of building Frankenstein-like creatures. By combining the various parts of a man and a woman it might be possible to construct an artificial hermaphrodite. Or by using bird's semen and other materials it might be possible to make a flying man. More ambitious yet was the Jabirian project to build *al-Insan al-Kamil* the Perfect Man, a millennial figure in Shi'ite thinking who would lead the Shi'ites to victory in the Last Days.

There was a political aspect to alchemy. The Jabirians, who seem to have been ninth- and tenth-century Ismaili Shi'ites, tended to use coded allegories to conceal their chemical recipes. But it seems that these codes were also used to conceal politico-religious messages urging revolt against the caliphate. So that some treatises that seemed to deal with chemistry were actually talking about revolution. Others again were discussing sexual matters in a disguised fashion. To finish with Jabir, it only remains to add that popular accounts of the transmission of Greek wisdom and Arab science to the west like to refer to Jabir as the father of modern chemistry.

Ibn Wahshiyya was an Iraqi intellectual, was reputed to have flourished in the tenth century, but, like Jabir, he may never have existed. Ibn Wahshiyya, whoever he was, made himself spokesman of the despised Nabataeans of Mesopotamia. The work attributed to him, *Filaha al-Nabatiyya*, 'On Nabataean Agriculture' sounds innocuous, but it is in fact a treatise on witchcraft. The occult agriculture book, probably written around 900, pretended to be a translation of a pre-Islamic text produced by an ancient people called the Kasdanians and it drew on hidden books of forbidden knowledge (a bit like the *Necromicon*, which the horror writer H.P. Lovecraft attributed to the mad Arab, al-Hazred the Damned).

The *Kitab al-Sumum*, Ibn Wahshiyya's treatise on poisons, features many curiosities including the poison maiden (reared on years of low doses of arsenic so that intercourse with her is lethal), the recipe for producing a human-headed cow, killer castanets, and the stone which, when it is seen, makes the one who has observed it literally die of laughter. Like pseudo-Jabir, Ibn Wahshiyya (if that really was his name) was most interested in the creation of an artificial man and he tells how a magician called Ankabutha created a man, though without speech or intelligence and the magician kept this avatar of Frankenstein alive for a year. Ankabutha's success was only partial, for it is difficult to construct a complete man.

The same magician created a white goat which could not bleat but could open and shut its eyes. Ibn Wahshiyya, who wrote in bad Arabic, intended to celebrate the glories of the ancient Chaldaeans and at the same time denigrate the vaunted wisdom of the Arabs: 'It splits your belly because of the envious ones, the ignorant who blame the Nabataeans and who are ashamed of their nationality, language and all the rest of it.'

The *Ikhwan al-Safa*, or 'Brethren of Purity', was a learned secret society which flourished in Basra, probably in the tenth or the eleventh century. These scholars, who may or may not have been Isma'ili Shi'is, produced an encyclopedia entitled *Al-Risala al-jami'a*, (The Collected Letters). This was an encyclopedia of all the sciences and it placed great stress on mathematics: 'the science of numbers is the root of other sciences, the fount of wisdom, the starting point of all knowledge, and the origin of all concepts'. The authors were also keen on craft techniques, but mystical and occult preoccupations furnished the foundation of this compendium of knowledge. The universe is the macrocosm, while man is the microcosm of the universe, so that unseen harmonies connect the two. Through study of mathematics and the dependent sciences the human soul might return to its origins in the godhead. The world is a prison from which man may escape and then hear the unearthly beauty of the music of the spheres. The *Ikhwan* flourished in the cosmopolitan port of Basra and their theorising drew upon Hindu, Buddhist and Zoroastrian thought, as well as on Arab fiction.

Al-Hasan al-Basri (642–728) was of Persian ancestry and has been described by some as the first Sufi. He has also been described (by

Massignon) as the true founder of Sunni politico-religious thought. He was famous for his austere piety and for his eloquent sermons against moral laxity. He exhorted his audiences to penitence and he made full use of the rhetorical battery of the medieval Arabs: rhymed prose, antitheses, parallelisms and balanced periods. Rabi'a al-Adawiyya, who died in 801, is a semi-legendary figure. Some of the earliest Sufi verses are attributed to her. It is said that she was orphaned at an early age, kidnapped and then enslaved. But eventually her master, observing her fervent piety, thought that he had better free her, as he would probably go to hell if he did not. It is said that she was once seen with a bucket of water and a flaming torch marching down one of the streets of Basra. When someone reasonably asked why, she replied that she was on her way to burn down the gardens of paradise and douse the flames of Hell, so that she could serve her God without desire for the one or fear of the other. It is also said that she was making a stew one day when an onion dropped from heaven, but she ignored it, saying 'My lord is not an onion merchant'. The earliest manifestations of Sufism were rather ascetic and devotional in character, and they lacked the theoretical and mystical elaborations which came a little later.

The famous or notorious Sufi al-Hallaj 857–922 was born in Fars but he studied in Basra. Louis Massignon in a massive three-volume study of the man, presented Hallaj as a Christlike Sufi saint and martyr. People living closer top al-Hallaj's time tended to have a more hostile view. According to the assiduous cataloguer of books, Ibn al-Nadim, 'al-Hallaj was a crafty man and a conjuror who ventured into Sufi schools of thought, affecting their ways of speech. He laid claim to every science, but nevertheless his claims were futile. He even knew something about the science of alchemy. He was ignorant. Bold, obsequious ...' According to another story, Hallaj took to the wandering life of a Sufi after hearing apocalyptic prophecies about the destruction of Basra by fire and water (and Basra was indeed the subject of many apocalyptic stories about its imminent destruction by fire or water). He was alleged to have spent time in India where he learnt various conjuring tricks which he used to seduce the credulous into believing in his sanctity. He taught that it was possible through supreme love to attain total self-identification with God. Eventually he came to Baghdad where he attracted the enmity of many, but also the patronage of others and for a while he exercised a Rasputin-like influence at court. He was arrested and charged with heresy, and eventually in 922 condemned to be flogged and to have his hands and feet cut off before being crucified. His last words were (or may have been for there are many variant accounts) 'Here I am in the dwelling place of my desires', before being beheaded.

Basra's collective nose was put out of joint by the foundation of Baghdad in 762 and Basra's political and military importance declined from then on. However, economically the place became more important than ever, as so much commercial traffic en route for Baghdad passed through Basra and, as we have seen, its literary culture certainly continued to thrive for another two centuries or so. But Basra suffered badly from successive revolts first by the Zott gypsies and later by the Zanj black plantation slaves in the late ninth century. Then in 923 the city was plundered by Carmathians, members of the revolutionary wing of Isma'ili Shi'ism. In the course of the Sunni revival, from say the eleventh century onwards, the *madrasa*, or religious teaching college, became the chief vehicle of further education that was more narrowly focused than before on the religious sciences. The old wild ways of acquiring learning by shooting the breeze in the main mosque or going out to the Mirbad to talk to the men of the desert were over.

THE NEW CITADELS OF CULTURE

Boyd Tonkin

Say what you like about the luxury hotels of the Gulf: they do know how to lay on a proper breakfast buffet. One morning, in Abu Dhabi, I was gathering my usual hybrid artery-clogging spread – scrambled eggs, turkey "bacon" and grilled mushrooms on one side; labneh, zatar and flatbreads on the other – when a curious sight hovered into view. This particular hotel occupies the upper storeys of a high-rise block – one of dozens now – that shoots up near the immense halls of the National Exhibition Centre. It has a Guinness World record-verified idiosyncrasy: an 18-degree tilt from the vertical that begins half-way up. No hotel in the world leans further. Why? Search me.

This morning, a stiff breeze was blowing from the Persian Gulf. It often does, with a welcome cooling effect. Outside the restaurant windows, though, half a dozen human figures swung perilously in the gale as they inched down the building. External window-cleaning at 150 metres can never count as a relaxing job. Factor in the fitful wind, and the world-beating angle, and the breakfast browsers witnessed a heart-stopping spectacle. The suspended toilers tried to combat both gravity and gusts. They had to clutch onto the steel exo-skeleton of the tower in order to polish each massive pane. Every now and then, one of the workers would fall back to the perpendicular, swinging in the wind mid-air, before a colleague hauled him back to find a grip on the glass-and-steel wall.

Everyone wore a hard hat and sturdy protective clothing; their safety harnesses and support platforms looked robust enough. All the same, even the greediest of breakfast guzzlers must have shared a little of their terror. Turning in the breeze without any hand-holds, dangled twenty storeys above a car-park, thousands of miles from home, did these (most probably) Indian, Nepalese, Bangladeshi, Pakistani and Sri Lankan window-cleaners decide then or later that the higher pay on offer in the Gulf amounted to sufficient compensation for the risks, shocks, insults and humiliations that every day blew in?

I saw no sign that those cleaners suffered treatment any worse than hundreds of thousands of fellow-expat toilers across the region. In fact, upmarket hotels filled with international visitors who may well talk to staff, and report on what they see, tend to offer comparatively attractive wages and welfare conditions. Their workers form a fraction of the 88 per cent or so of Abu Dhabi residents and employees who do not and never will acquire UAE citizenship. Mostly bound by the *kafala* system of restrictive sponsorship by employers, routinely forced to pay recruitment fees that even UAE law deems illegal, this disenfranchised proletariat builds the palaces of fun, rest and business that sprout over the Gulf. They seldom enter the luxury abodes they create and maintain. And they stand at constant risk of expulsion if a job ends, or if they argue with a sponsoring boss. Still, as our hair-raising breakfast show revealed, no binding contract or police supervision will ever keep these dispossessed toilers entirely out of sight, or mind.

The mid-air ordeal compelled by a Western architect's no-expense-spared gimmick offered a salutary image. As the Gulf monarchies learn to depend less and less on hydrocarbon extraction as the pipeline to wealth and influence, so global services and trades of every kind – from diamond-dealing and financial brokerage to tourism and culture – must make up for the growing shortfall. Showpiece architectural schemes, tilting hotels and all, both symbolise this push towards a 'post-oil' future and act as drivers for fresh investment.

These 'diversification' strategies have been in place for a decade across the nations of the Gulf Co-operation Council (GCC). However, the plummeting oil prices of 2015 – caused in part by a strategic decision by Saudi Arabia to sustain its production levels – will intensify the trend. The UAE as a whole planned to run a 2.1 per cent budget deficit in 2015. As the senior emirate, home of the ruling al-Nahyan family and traditional leader of the federation, Abu Dhabi finds itself especially vulnerable to the price plunge. Oil still supplies Abu Dhabi with around 80 per cent of export revenues. Yet the cost of a barrel has fallen off a cliff: from $110 in early 2014 to a 2015 average of around $50. As I write, in early December 2015, it has temporarily dropped even below $40.

Given the secrecy of the al-Nahyan dynasty, picking the chief power-brokers among the many offspring of the UAE's founding father, Sheikh Zayed, can be a tricky task. By common consent, though, Crown Prince Mohammed – half-brother of the Emir of Abu Dhabi and UAE President, Sheikh Khalifa – runs several key branches of the state. Earlier this year, he welcomed the eventual expiry of the hydrocarbon economy, saying that 'If today we are investing in the right sectors, we will celebrate that moment.' Those sectors stretch from the Formula One race track and 'Ferrari World' theme park on Yas Island to the 'green city' of Masdar, which pioneers sustainable technologies.

Prestige cultural ventures, each with their own obligatory royal sponsor, have since the early 2000s also helped to spearhead Abu Dhabi's diversifying mission. Conceived as a magnet for high-end global tourism, and a shop-window of globalised modernity, these schemes can also serve the internecine rivalries of the UAE. They help to solidify the image of Abu Dhabi as a stylish and sophisticated destination, in comparison with the supposedly downmarket, shopping-fixated glitz of upstart Dubai just down the (accident-prone) road.

In 2007, I first sampled the status-enhancing culture of the Gulf when I reported on the unveiling of the Kalima translation project. This ambitious programme aimed to produce and distribute high-quality, copyright-controlled Arabic editions of classic literature and other key texts from around the world. From Adam Smith to Isaac Newton, Haruki Murakami to George Eliot, Albert Camus to Umberto Eco, the opening catalogue boded well for genuine pluralism. Never before has the director of an arts venture told me that 'Money is the least of our worries'. It also set out to correct some deep-seated weaknesses in the publishing culture of the region, with routine state censorship, a near-total lack of serious retail outlets and rampant piracy all commonplace. As can happen in the UAE, internal politics later shrunk the scope of Kalima, although it continues with a narrower focus on educational works. Nonetheless, its unstable compound of high ideals, elite surveillance and patchy execution introduced me to the shifting, even baffling, landscape of 'soft power' in the region.

On Saadiyat Island, a wedge-shaped sand plateau of around 10 square kilometres a few hundred metres over the road bridge from the Abu Dhabi port district, those contradictions have reached their apogee. First announced in 2008, the 'cultural quarter' of Saadiyat (the 'island of happiness') carried an initial budget of $27 billion. It occupies just under three square kilometres of the island, with the remainder given over to upscale hotels, residential estates, a marina, beaches, golf courses and nature reserves. Although much of Saadiyat remains a gigantic building site, some venues are up and running, as the most glittering cultural showcase of a 'post-oil' society rises from the sands.

At the visitor centre, the cool and elegant Manarat ('beacon') of Saadiyat, elaborate models of the quarter whet the appetite. Meanwhile, taster exhibitions deliver selections from the collections that will, in due course, fill the island's new museums. Amid these dunes and plains, the world's most illustrious 'starchitects' have lined up to set in stone and metal their homage to the post-fossil fuel economy and culture envisaged by the al-Nahyans.

Jean Nouvel has designed the Louvre Abu Dhabi: a separate institution to the Paris mothership, but still the same brand of 'universal museum', and still tied to France both by the hire of curatorial expertise and by the payment of more than £500 million in licence fees. Frank Gehry has conceived the Guggenheim Abu Dhabi, second in line to launch, with a focus on post-1960 visual arts. Norman Foster is creating the Sheikh Zayed National Museum, to be built in the shape of the falcon as a tribute to the late ruler's preferred pastime, and with the British Museum as its international partner and adviser. Further down the road, both in terms of space and time, a new performing arts centre will come from the avant-garde studio of Zaha Hadid. Japanese architect Tadao Ando has also been contracted to build the Maritime Museum.

Over the past three years at the Manarat, the Louvre has offered a sample of its treasures (Asian, African and Arab as much as European), the National Museum has hosted a UAE-customised version of the British Museum's popular blockbuster 'A History of the World in 100 Objects', and the Guggenheim has put some highlights of its own on show. All of these displays have celebrated Saadiyat, and by implication the UAE, as a crossroads and a meeting-point: a nexus of both trade and ideas where cultures can come together in a spirit of openness, curiosity and exchange. The Saadiyat project describes itself as 'a centre for global culture, drawing local regional and international visitors... housed in buildings constituting a statement of the finest architecture at the beginning of the twenty-first century'. It will, according to the masterplanners of the Abu Dhabi Tourism Development and Investment Company (TDIC), 'fuel the imagination, foster interaction and encourage people of all backgrounds to embrace a common bond of creativity'.

Other Gulf states have chosen the big-ticket arts blueprint as a focus of diversified development in a globally connected economy. Abu Dhabi's closest rival in high-status cultural enterprise is Qatar. There, the maverick, Wahhabi-influenced Al-Thani family – often at odds with the UAE – has overseen the creation of a world-leading Museum of Islamic Art and a still-unfinished National Museum, also designed by Jean Nouvel. So far, however, no *grand* project in the Gulf can equal Saadiyat as a high-stakes bid to re-position an extractive neo-feudal monarchy as an inter-cultural hub.

On these wind-scoured sands, as grit from the building sites blows between the estate agents' show-homes, the finely-combed hotel beaches and even the transplanted English public school (an overseas branch of Cranleigh), every thoughtful visitor can sniff the paradoxes on the air. Most obviously, these flagship monuments aim to show the way beyond oil dependence. Yet their very completion will turn, in part, on the fluctuating price of crude.

The Louvre Abu Dhabi was supposed to launch in December 2015. Behind schedule, the final piece of cladding for Nouvel's iconic dome, with its 7,850 star-shaped pieces of aluminium and steel, slotted into place in late September 2015. At the earliest, the museum will open its modernist-Islamic doors at the close of 2016. The timetable for the Guggenheim (due to be ready for 2017) and the Zayed Museum (2018) may also slip off target. Backlogs in the sourcing of labour and materials account for some delays. The shrinkage of state revenues has also played its part. Just now, the original estimated date for completion of the entire complex – 2020 – looks not so much hopeful as fanciful.

Even deeper conundrums blow around these sites in the form of their ethics and ideology. The new museums proclaim their commitment to the values of free and open exchange between peoples. But they will owe their material existence to an employment system that many critics treat as not far off slave labour.

After a period of silence and indifference, protests and boycotts began to swirl like a sandstorm around TDIC. The Gulf Labor group has spent five years documenting the plight of Saadiyat workers and seeking improved conditions for them. Since 2011, more than 2,000 international artists and writers have vowed in petitions to refuse all collaboration, with the Guggenheim in particular, unless the workers get a better deal. Gulf Labor has recorded over-crowding, under-payment and various degrees of bonded labour. The most alarming evidence comes not from the island itself – where the Saadiyat Accommodation Village offers a clean and spruce public face to investigators, right down to the cricket pitch for South Asians starved of their favourite sport – but from the more distant camps where nosy campaigners seldom go.

Beyond the illegal recruitment fees, the twelve-hour shifts and the thuggery that greets periodic strikes, a Gulf Labor report in 2014 found it 'crucially necessary' to address 'the removal from view and understanding of the men who are building the UAE from its citizenry and its visitors'. A venue devoted to making ideas and cultures visible depends on the occlusion of its makers.

In July 2015, Gulf Labor issued an updated report. It revealed, for example, that a Pakistani worker had died during the installation of the final 'stars' on the Louvre dome. 'He was not the first, and will likely not be the last, fatality on Saadiyat Island.' As before, the researchers by and large worked with the co-operation of the UAE authorities. For the state, an evident desire to attest to openness and humanity competes with older, and cruder, repressive instincts.

Andrew Ross, a Saadiyat campaigner and professor at New York University (which has just opened a campus on the island), was denied entry to the UAE in 2015. So were several fellow-activists. All the same, Gulf Labor and its allied artists have sought to keep dialogue with officialdom and with the overseas institutions alive. In comparison with the despotisms in Central Asia, say, the UAE has opened its doors to a degree of scrutiny. It also has laws that, if implemented, would protect migrant workers more securely than they do.

In the course of a commission for *Vice* magazine to interview and draw workers on Saadiyat, American artist Molly Crabapple wrote that 'Defenders of Western institutions in Abu Dhabi are right about one thing. They are not unique. The labour abuses at the Louvre or NYU are the same labour abuses that are happening throughout the UAE. The UAE is not the worst country for workers in the Gulf, and the Gulf is not the worst region for workers in the world. Most countries sustain themselves on the labour of transient, disposable people.'

In the UAE, the kind of reform that even the authorities might approve has arrived slowly, if at all. After five years of activism, Gulf Labor reports that 'despite repeated assurances that the Guggenheim Foundation and TDIC shared our goals, they have yet to deliver any tangible results on behalf of workers.' The researchers also travelled to India to interview workers who had returned from the Gulf. They found that 'routine wage theft and under-payment, coupled with, in many cases, informal high-interest loans, left them with little extra to show for their time and labour in the UAE.'

So the pharaonic temples of Saadiyat are still rising from a barren ground of repression and exploitation. A hard-headed historian might counter that every august monument to culture – from Gothic cathedrals to Europe's own 'universal museums' – has grown in the same harsh soil. 'Who built the seven gates of Thebes?' Bertolt Brecht asked in his poem, 'A Worker Reads History'. 'The books are filled with names of kings. / Was it the kings who hauled the craggy blocks of stone?' Planners, builders, even artists, have often shared Zaha Hadid's chilling sentiments when, in 2014, she parried questions about the deaths of labourers on construction projects in Qatar. 'I have nothing to do with the workers,' she replied. 'I'm not taking it lightly but I think it's for the government to look to take care of. It's not my duty as an architect to look at it.'

Tales of injustice and oppression among the toiling expatriates have now become near-obligatory in media despatches from Saadiyat, as from Qatar. If TDIC and the ruling family wished to bury the evidence, they have failed. In part, this failure even gives grounds for hope. Might the liberal façade of UAE's cultural grand designs deepen into something more solid than a desert mirage?

Recent signs do not look promising. Like their cousins around the Gulf, the al-Nahyans reacted with alarm and even panic to the Arab Spring in 2011. They had good reason. That year, I attended the award of the International Prize for Arabic Fiction – the 'Arabic Booker' – at another swanky hotel in Abu Dhabi. The Iraqi poet and novelist Fadhil Al-Azzawi, chair of the jury and a veteran secular leftist, saluted the 'storm' that had lately burst across the region. Even this select audience broke into a thunderclap of spontaneous applause.

Not long before, 133 prominent Emiratis had signed an online petition asking for full direct elections to the Federal National Council: the representative body which can advise the government but cannot itself pass legislation. The signatories included senior professionals such as lawyers, academics and doctors. Elsewhere, Facebook, Twitter and YouTube hosted a flowering of demands for democratic change. In his book *After the Sheikhs*, optimistically subtitled 'the coming collapse of the Gulf monarchies', Gulf specialist Christopher Davidson quotes a typical blog by UAE economist Nasser bin Ghayth. 'No amount of security – or rather intimidation by security forces – or wealth, hand-outs, or foreign support, is capable of ensuring the stability of an unjust ruler.' Although such manifestos hardly amounted to a call to overthrow the state, the authorities moved swiftly to stifle dissent. Over the next two years, the UAE security services unleashed a reign of terror on internal opponents.

In 2011, the 'UAE Five' – including Dr bin Ghayth himself – went on trial. He received a two-year sentence, was later pardoned, but now (December 2015) has disappeared again into the limbo of indefinite detention. In July 2013, the wave of repression broke with the trial of the so-called 'UAE 94'. As always, the state threw at defendants accusations of involvement with Islamist organisations such as the Muslim Brotherhood or its local offshoot al-Islah, the 'Reform and Social Guidance Association'. Radical Islamists have certainly operated within the UAE. But the net of arrests, detentions and (in well-documented cases) ill-treatment was cast much further than those circles.

In November 2014, an Amnesty International report concluded that 'at one stroke, the authorities removed their most prominent critics and the country's leading advocates of reform from the public arena, while signalling to other potential dissenters that they will not tolerate open political debate in the UAE'. Around sixty of the UAE 94 remain in jail, serving sentences of up to ten years. Some allege both torture and the harassment of spouses and children. They have no right of appeal. Meanwhile, a 2012 law against 'cybercrimes' has widened the remit of the already-repressive Press Law of 1980 into digital media – a popular, and officially feared, vehicle for dissent. It resulted in prosecutions such as that of Waleed Al Shehhi, for tweets about the UAE 94. He was fined 500,000 dirhams and sentenced to two years in prison. As in many authoritarian regimes, the UAE constitution in fact contains some fairly robust guarantees of freedom of expression. They remain pretty much dead letters.

Yet, on the world stage, the UAE cannot afford to look too much like North Korea. Official ripostes to evidence of human-rights violations stress the common struggle of the country, along with Western nations, against Islamist extremism and terrorism. Amna Al Muhairy, director of the Human Rights Department at the foreign ministry, regretted that Amnesty had issued 'a one-sided and inaccurate report' that 'repeats familiar politically motivated accusations from groups seeking to undermine and overthrow the UAE's successful model of a stable, peaceful, tolerant and diverse society'. Above all – the clincher – Al Muhairy voices disappointment that the Amnesty analysis 'completely borrows the narrative of the Muslim Brotherhood and its affiliates'. In other words: back us, or give comfort to the jihadis and their sidekicks. No third way exists.

This strategic appeal to the shared values of pluralism and tolerance could nonetheless backfire. Some Emirati citizens will start to take it seriously. All the Saadiyat Island mood music about cross-cultural exchange and frank dialogue might, in due course, plant a seed. It could well grow, even on this infertile terrain. At events during the annual Abu Dhabi book fair, I have heard young Emirati authors, and audience members, speak up for freedom of expression in the tone of genuine seekers rather than regime mouthpieces.

The more the 'cultural quarter' flourishes as a hub both for local artists and global visitors, the louder those voices might become. Moreover, any reformist pressure could strike a chord within sectors of the governing elite itself. According to the Gulf Labor investigators, 'We hear anecdotal evidence of power struggles within the ruling families over the exact course of UAE's development and can only assume that there is a tug-of-war between factions who favour liberalisation, and the hardliners'. It would be hard to dispute that assessment. So far, outside analysts of the Gulf states have yet to perfect the sophisticated art of 'Kremlinology' that, during the Cold War, allowed Western observers to spot trends, pick winners and calculate the balance of power within the closed Soviet system. After all, these family oligarchies rank as allies – and increasingly close ones – rather than enemies. So the drive to dig beneath the ceremonial surface of power comes more from stray investigative journalists and under-resourced pro-democracy pressure-groups, such as the Gulf Centre for Human Rights, than from established universities and think-tanks.

Besides, many Western universities now enjoy new centres for the study of Middle Eastern or Islamic affairs, courtesy of lavish funding from the Gulf monarchies themselves. One conspicuous example, among many in the UK: the LSE's principal lecture theatre is named, in honour of a generous donation from the Emirates Foundation for Philanthropy, after the UAE's patriarch Sheikh Zayed. As Christopher Davidson puts it in *After the Sheikhs*, 'Most of these gifts have no strings attached per se, and there is generally no follow-up control after the gift is made. However, donors have usually been able to rely on a culture of self-censorship taking root in the recipient institutions.'

So Emiratis who hanker for greater freedom, or even just the constitutional monarchy that the protesters of 2011 sought, will have to build it for themselves. They cannot depend on outside support from any group that carries clout with their rulers. Yet, according to the iron law of unintended consequences, a prestige-seeking performance such as the Saadiyat cultural quarter might still open a chink in the armour of social management.

Curators, managers and executives, both local and expat, already do their jobs according to the 'universal' and inter-cultural ideals that the museums proclaim. They are not hypocrites, although they may work under severe constraint. No one should mistake a pivotal figure such as Zaki Nusseibeh, the Jerusalem-born ex-journalist who advises the UAE President on cultural affairs, for a stooge. As he has said about the masterplan for museums and universities, in an interview for *Bidoun* magazine: 'Of course, in the back of your mind – of the leadership's mind – is the thought that this is necessary for our own survival, but also it is necessary for the stability of the region and for our relationships with the rest of the world. The communities have become so interrelated now: Europe and the Arab world and the Gulf… And so we have a role to play. What is this role? It is to provide this kind of liberal, open education, but at the same time, to strengthen our roots even as we open to the rest of the world.'

True, imported or transplanted narratives that buttress this 'liberal' vision of the future are still subject to a process of desert acclimatisation. Look, for instance, at the British Museum's 'History of the World in 100 Objects' as it travelled to the Manarat al-Saadiyat. The BM did not simply authorise an identical touring version of the show. If anything, it looked even more splendid on Saadiyat than in Bloomsbury. The design curved across millennia and continents to highlight the artworks and artefacts that tell the human story. In their new surroundings, some of the treasures had a special resonance: the Iraqi writing-tablet that records the beer ration due to workers (3000BCE), the cute clay camels from the Silk Road, the wall paintings from an Iraqi harem, or the Yemeni bronze hand (100–300CE) that commemorates the worship of a pre-Islamic deity. Such artefacts did help to ratify the UAE's self-image as hub, harbour and crossroads.

However, a visitor would have searched in vain for (say) the Warren Cup, the BM's Roman silver chalice with its depiction of male lovers having strenuous sex. '100 Objects' was not only resprayed, but re-engineered. The displays now served to wave a discreetly patriotic flag, and to affirm that 'the UAE's identity has been formed on the exchange between the regional and the international'. At the exit, the organisers even installed a new exhibit: a foot-controlled car designed for disabled drivers by a (female) student in Abu Dhabi, Reem Al-Marzouqi. So the global grand tour received its Emirati certificate of approval.

For all its nationalistic colours, Reem Al-Marzouki's car at least supplements the BM's narrative with an example of women's agency and autonomy. As the Saadiyat museums refine their mission, so their professions of faith in cross-cultural humanism and unfettered creativity will leave an identifiable trail of thought through the public spaces of the UAE. The Guggenheim Abu Dhabi, for example, promises to 'contribute to a more inclusive and expansive view of art history that emphasises the convergence of local, regional, and international sources of creative inspiration rather than geography or nationality'. Sceptics might suspect that such a façade of liberal cosmopolitanism will only attract a tiny Emirati fringe, and thus pose no threat to entrenched hierarchies of power. After all, for a decade the grandiose Emirates Palace hotel on the Abu Dhabi waterfront has hosted 'free' art exhibitions, in theory open to all. But invisible barriers will keep most citizens, let alone migrant labourers, from ever walking through the hotel's fortress-like neo-Mughal gatehouse.

However, it is the precisely the professional elite most likely to appreciate Saadiyat that stands most at risk of contamination by the values that they might find voiced within its galleries and halls. An institutional rhetoric fashioned for one purpose – which in today's UAE means the delegitimation and destruction of radical Islamism – may perform other tasks. In July 2015, the UAE even passed an anti-discrimination law that outlaws hate-speech on the basis of race or creed. The immediate target was fundamentalist propaganda: derogatory terms for non-Muslims such as 'kafir' are thus now illegal in the UAE. Still, that kind of self-serving legislation might conceivably, in the hands of independent-minded lawyers, boomerang back to strike the framers of the law.

Into this whirlpool, or rather quicksand, of contradictory development step the Western art mandarins who have chosen to accept the generous partnership deals on offer in the UAE. In a new collection of Gulf Labor documents, *The Gulf: High Culture/Hard Labor*, Andrew Ross of NYU argues that 'Over the course of the last decade, Western high-culture institutions have been following in the path of corporations that went offshore twenty years ago. The underlying motive – to beef up their balance sheet – is more or less the same, but the rationale for operating overseas has to be presented as more than a monetary undertaking. More often than not, these initiatives are couched in rhetoric about spreading the virtues of Western-style liberal arts, which at times can sound little different from the nineteenth-century credo of the "mission civilisatrice".'

That Victorian civilising mission often ended up by giving the 'natives' subversive ideas. How might they hold the imperial governors to their own lofty principles? The skewed societies of the Gulf, where 80 per cent and more of all residents work as dispensable hired hands, will block the creation of any mass movement in the anti-colonial mould. All the same, the fast-extinguished fires of protest in 2011 showed that dissent can, and will, extend beyond the Islamist foes whose threat licenses almost any repression in the eyes of Western allies. Saadiyat, and other cultural spectacles, may eventually help to ignite that spark again. Indeed, we may not have to wait too long to witness one flashpoint.

If, as now scheduled, the Louvre Abu Dhabi opens towards the end of 2016, then the UAE's rulers will wish to cut the ribbons with a fanfare that echoes around the world. The continuing incarceration of peaceful, non-jihadi dissidents, and the conspicuous abuse of migrant labour, would surely spoil the fun of a top-level diplomatic circus. So the Saadiyat project may spin off some measure of at-least cosmetic reform sooner rather than later. I only hope that those hapless window-cleaners will not forever dangle in the wind.

TASHKENT ODYSSEY

Eric Walberg

It was 1989, and I was in Moscow. I had come at the invitation of *Moscow News*. From my editor's office on Pushkin Square, I watched on television the last Soviet troops leave Afghanistan and arrive in Uzbekistan, retreating across the Amudarya River on the Friendship Bridge (built in 1982 to ferry Soviet troops into Afghanistan). Even as the troops retreated, *mujahideen* snipers continued to target them, with US arms still being poured into what was already a powder keg. I was intrigued by this little-known part of the world, and remembered a dream-like trip as a Russian language student in 1980 to Tashkent, with its elegant opera house and its bountiful fruits, soaring mountains and hospitable people.

After five years in Moscow, I had had enough of the city in upheaval, where food was scarce and expensive, and people were losing their laid-back Soviet ways and embracing the worst features of the West. I was robbed a number of times (once by the train police waiting in a suburban station on the way to Uzbekistan), and remember gunshots in my Vikhino apartment building entrance one night, then being told the next day someone had been found murdered just a few feet away from me. Moscow had lost its charm. I yearned to live in a Muslim society. Uzbekistan seemed to be the most developed, cultured of the Soviet 'stans' and a short hop away from Mazari-i-Sharif. My 1980 memories made me decide to take the leap. I looked on the budding internet (still in its infancy 20 years ago) and signed on to a 'friends of Uzbekistan' notice board, where I found a call for English speakers to teach at the new English-language university in Tashkent. Despite protests from my Moscow friends ('You will be mugged or killed by the Muslim insurgents. Russians are all escaping, and you are going there willingly?'), I made the wild leap to Tashkent to teach at the University of World Economy and Diplomacy (UWED), and bought a $15 *platzkart* (third class) one-way ticket, bracing myself for the long journey in mid-August heat. As the train pulled out, as if on cue, a band of robbers climbed through our open window (they were later kicked off trying to rob someone further down the car).

I am not the first western adventurer to find romance in Tashkent. Tashkent has benefited, as do the more attractive colonial possessions, from pampered rakes from the imperial centre. The most famous, or rather infamous, was Grand Duke Nicholas Constantinovich of Russia (1850–1918), first-born son of Grand Duke Konstantin Nikolayevich of Russia, grandson of Tsar Nicholas I. Born in St Petersburg, he was a gifted military officer and an incorrigible womaniser. His scandalous affair with the American Adventuress Fanny Lear had led him into a plot to steel three diamonds from his mother's icon. He was declared insane and banished to the far reaches of the Russian empire in 1874, eventually settling in Tashkent in 1881. Despite his notoriety as a diamond thief, he still had his family fortune, and he used it to build a modest palace in 1890 and sponsor a number of philanthropic and entrepreneurial projects. He was renowned as an engineer and irrigator, constructing two large canals, the (now silted up) Bukhar-Aryk and the much more successful Khiva-Aryk, later extended to form the Emperor Nicholas I Canal (atoning for the betrayal of his royal family?), irrigating 12,000 *desyatinas* (33,000 acres) of land in the Hungry Steppe between Djizak and Tashkent. Most of this was then settled with Slavic peasant colonisers. He used his palace to show his large, priceless collection of works of art. The palace became the Lenin Young Pioneers Palace in 1935 and reopened in the 1980s as the State museum of arts of Uzbekistan. Since 'independence', it has been closed to the public and used for foreign ministry receptions, a few of which I attended. It is itself a priceless gem, one of Tashkent's few.

The rebel gene was passed on to the Grand Duke's youngest granddaughter, Princess Natalia Alexandrovna Romanovskaya-Iskander, born in fateful 1917, the last Romanov and the only Russian among the Romanovs to remain in Russia following the Revolution. Her father Alexander died in 1918 and her mother kept the family in Tashkent out of the upheaval of the Civil War. They eventually moved to Moscow under a new name and miraculously survived, despite their Romanov blood and the fact that her uncle Artemi died fighting for the Whites. The princess becoming a professional vertical motorcyclist, an army driver during

WWII, and secret agent of Lubyanka. She would visit the Pioneer Palace in Tashkent, fondly remembering that it was their family home. Natalia died in 1999, having witnessed the Revolution from start to finish.

One day, I stumbled upon a tiny museum opened in 1981, dedicated to another Russian adventurer, one of modern Russia's great poets, Sergey Esenin (1895–1925). The museum is, appropriately, on Tolstoy Lane on Pushkin Street, near Pushkin metro station (now Independence St and Salar metro), commemorating his visit to Tashkent in 1921. Esenin had a lifelong fascination with Central Asia; his lyrical poems include a series 'Persian Motives'. In what was now Soviet Tashkent, he met local poets and read his poem 'Pugchev' which he had just finished. Esenin was originally enthusiastic about the revolution but became disillusioned, writing such poems as 'The Stern October Has Deceived Me'.

When I arrived by train from Moscow in the summer of 1994, following the same journey of the more illustrious Esenin and Grand Duke, life was peaceful, but Uzbeks were looking on with unease at the anti-communist whirlwind a mere 300 miles to the south. Afghan President Muhammad Najibullah was still alive though without a government, living in the UN offices in Kabul. The Taliban only got to Kabul in 1996, when they seized and castrated him before hanging his body from a lamp post.

The four-day trip across steppe and desert in an open sleeping car of eighty people is a blurry but pleasant memory now. The Soviet tradition of comradery on crowded, spartan trains was still alive, in this instance surrounded by genial Asian faces, all of whom spoke Russian, encouraging me with stories of life in Uzbekistan. I was covered in soot upon arrival in Tashkent, but was relieved to find a dapper fellow named Alisher from the University of World Economy and Diplomacy (UWED) on the platform. We took a 'taxi' (most taxis are just private cars which you hail on the street) to the elegant university, formerly the Communist Party school, renamed in 1992. I joined the staff along with a British Council language teacher Martin, a tall, gangly fellow from Leeds, who was a like-minded adventurer. He became a good friend, and a passport into the diplomatic world of expat parties that were a lifeline to the distant West.

City of Stone (and Trees)

Public life in Tashkent unavoidably centres on the figure of Amir Timur (1337-1405), the legendary Turco-Mongol conqueror and the founder of the Timurid Empire in Persia and Central Asia. Timur is considered the last of the great nomadic conquerors of the Eurasian Steppe, and his empire set the stage for the rise of the more durable 'Gunpowder Empires' in the 1500s and 1600s, which once blazed and now limp along, their baneful effects enduring. Timur envisioned the restoration of the Mongol Empire of Genghis Khan, claiming descent (probably falsely) from the even more legendary and ruthless twelfth-to-thirteenth century Mongol conqueror. He even justified his Iranian, Mamluk and Ottoman campaigns as a re-imposition of legitimate Mongol control over lands taken by usurpers, referring to himself as the 'Sword of Islam' and patronising educational and religious institutions. Scholars estimate that his military campaigns caused the deaths of 17 million people, amounting to about five percent of the then world population. He was not as bad as Genghis, who is considered responsible for closer to 40 million deaths. (The Brits are somewhere in between, overseeing 27 million deaths in British India, mostly due to famine.) Timur paid no attention to Tashkent. He made Samarkand his capital in 1370, where he brought the world's best artisans and had constructed fabulous Islamic mosques and madrassahs. He was the grandfather of the renowned Timurid sultan, astronomer and mathematician Ulugh Beg, who ruled Central Asia from 1411 to 1449, and great-great-great-grandfather of Babur, founder of the Mughal Empire which ruled parts of South Asia for over three centuries, from 1526 until 1857.

Just as Mongolia fetes Genghis Khan as their patron saint, Timur is now officially recognised as Uzbekistan's national hero. His museum is in Tashkent, opened by Uzbekistan's President Islam Karimov, occupying the place where Karl Marx's statue once stood. Appropriately, it is near Amir Timur Square, where the world's largest statue of Lenin formerly stood, replaced by a globe featuring a geographic map of Uzbekistan at its centre. And in the Karimov tradition, the museum replaced a quiet tree-lined park which was a beloved meeting place for ordinary Tashkenters. 1996 was declared to be the 'Year of Amir Timur', and the 660th anniversary was widely celebrated, reaching a peak with the inauguration of the museum by Karimov who declared, 'Every man visiting this museum can make sure to my words, that this museum is like a great mirror, reflecting both our past and present and our great future.'

There is no question that Timur was a genius, if a cruel one. He took counsel with Muslim intellectuals such as Ibn Khaldun (1332–1406) and Hafiz-i Abru (b.1380). But whitewashing his genocidal acts and seeing him as the inspiration of 'our great future' raised eyebrows at the time. It is no coincidence that Karimov is also a Samarkander, and as Karimov spoke of 'our future', he was no doubt using the royal 'our', having turned Tashkent into his personal fiefdom.

Tashkent, literally 'Stone City', is the capital of Uzbekistan and largest city in the 'stans', with a population of two and a half million – big but not too big. Due to its position in Central Asia, Tashkent came under Sogdian and Turkic influence early in its history, before that of Islam in the 8th century AD. After its destruction by Genghis Khan in 1219, the city was rebuilt and became an important way station on the Silk Road. In 1865 it was conquered by the Russian Empire.

With the collapse of the Russian monarchy, changes in Tashkent mirrored those elsewhere in the former empire. In March 1917, Tashkent celebrated the first revolution in Petrograd with a parade by Russian workers marching with red flags, Russian soldiers singing *La Marsellaise*, and thousands of curious onlookers. Governor-General Aleksey Kuropatkin closed the events with words 'Long Live a great free Russia'. The First Turkestan Muslim Conference was held in Tashkent in April 1917, dominated by the *Jadid*, Muslim reformers (think Young Turks). A more conservative faction emerged in Tashkent centred around the *Ulema*. This faction proved more successful during the local elections of July 1917, forming an alliance with Russian conservatives, while the Soviet became more radical. The Soviet attempt to seize power in September 1917 proved unsuccessful, as it was mostly Russian-based, Russians being twenty percent of the population, but soon prevailed after bringing in *Jadid* types.

The historic Congress of the Peoples of the East was a multinational conference held by the Communist International in Baku, Azerbaijan (then part of Soviet Russia) in September 1920, attended by nearly 1,900 delegates from across Asia and Europe and marking a commitment by the

Comintern to support revolutionary nationalist movements in the colonial East. The gathering adopted a formal 'Manifesto of the Peoples of the East' as well as an 'Appeal to the Workers of Europe, America, and Japan'. Muslim religious leaders attended, but the congress was solidly secular and anti-imperialist.

In April 1918, Tashkent became the capital of the Turkestan Autonomous Soviet Socialist Republic (Turkestan ASSR). The new regime was threatened by White forces and *basmachi* (read: *mujahideen*) revolts from within, and purges ordered from Moscow. The anti-religious campaign of the time was not as severe here as in Russia, but signs of independent movements were repressed. In 1930 Tashkent fell within the borders of the Uzbek SSR, and became the capital, displacing Samarkand.

When Nazi Germany invaded the Soviet Union in June 1941, whole factories were dismantled and 'shipped' to Tashkent. This led to great increase in industry, and the Russian population increased dramatically; evacuees from the war zones increased the total population of Tashkent to well over a million. In addition to groups forcibly deported (mostly Koreans in 1938 and Crimean Tatars in 1944), Russians and Ukrainians eventually comprised more than half of the total residents of Tashkent. Many of the former refugees stayed in Tashkent to live after the war rather than return to former homes, but many left after 1991, and Russians now comprise less than ten per cent of the population.

During the postwar period, the Soviet Union established numerous scientific and engineering facilities in Tashkent. After the war, Japanese prisoners of war built the stunning opera house. Soviet archeologists did important work documenting the past. Being sent to Tashkent was deemed a plum location for winter-plagued Russians. In 1966, much of the old city was destroyed by a huge earthquake (7.5 on the Richter scale), leaving 300,000 residents homeless. In a spirit of socialist comradery, the Soviet republics, and some other countries such as Finland, sent 'battalions of fraternal peoples' and urban planners to help rebuild devastated Tashkent. They created a model Soviet city of wide streets with parks, immense plazas for parades, fountains, monuments, and acres of apartment blocks. A beautiful metro was built, with fine mosaics of Uzbek poets (Alisher Navoi) and scientists (Ulugbek).

The 'new' city was noted for its tree-lined streets, numerous fountains, and pleasant parks, at least until the tree-cutting campaigns initiated in 2009 by President Karimov. He mortified Tashkenters by cutting down the towering century-old chenars (plantanes), planted lovingly by the Russians at the turn of the last century in the central square, now Amir Timur. Probably they were seen to overshadow the sparkling new museum. The park was lovingly called Broadway by locals (too lovingly for Karimov), a lively meeting spot where people could get relief from the summer sun under the legendary chenars.

Teaching Uzbeks

My excuse for being in Tashkent was to teach sons and daughters of the new elite. I was given a room in the dormitory, ate in the cafeteria during the day and used the communal kitchen to make simple meals (there being no fridge). It was spartan and when I was offered possession of my own apartment by a local performing legend in exchange for an occasional English lesson, I jumped at the chance. Alisher was the drummer in Yalla, one of the most popular Soviet folk rock bands in the 1970s and 980s - but by 1994, long past its due-date. His English was already fluent and he said he would be on tour most of the time. I thought I had luckily discovered an inside track to the Uzbek cultural world. But once he had me trapped, his apparatchik haughtiness was revealed with a vengeance, and he started to demand daily (free) lessons, making life unbearable. A good lesson for me about the worst type of 'Soviet man', used to ordering people around, lying, with no religion and no social graces.

The students had to go to the fields to pick cotton in November and I pestered the administration to be allowed to go with them. They promised yes, but then one day the students were gone – without me. Hardly surprising, as this is called forced labour by the Anti-Slavery International, and Ikea, Adidas, Marks & Spencer and others boycott Uzbek cotton. The authorities were unlikely to let the curious Westerner nose around their dirty laundry. My students later told me they mostly did nothing in the fields as they could pay a bribe to have someone else gather their quota. They treated it as time off to party. But that only works for the rich students.

By the end of the school term, I'd had my fill of spoiled students eager to move up the ladder in the brave new capitalist world, and had enough contacts to find a normal rental apartment. I landed work on contract with a UNIDO privatisation project. My landlady was an Evangelical Christian who after a few months politely asked me to leave to accommodate a church member. I politely declined her offer to share her flat ('You can stay with me'). So the second of six moves, but a Godsend, so to speak.

I finally found what was to be my main home, settling into a rather pricey apartment with a phone and a delightful Tatar landlady right next door; cultured, Muslim and with stories to tell about Soviet life. It was on what is now called Bogishamol Kychasi (Botanical Breezes Street) near the Botanical Gardens, across from the new Intercontinental Hotel and new western-modelled Tashkentland children's park. The pricey theme park is enclosed by high chain link fence, and consists of treeless expanses (what *does* Karimov have against trees?), a water slide and rollercoaster. It had just opened, replacing the modest, wooded Soviet children's park, which had been gratis and fenceless, but lacked the water slide and roller coaster.

What had drawn me to Tashkent was both the fact that it was largely Muslim and precisely the fact that it was still very much a Soviet remnant, not yet invaded by the West, though the Intercontinental Hotel and Tashkentland were forebodings of things to come. I had always been impressed that the Soviet experiment, despite its flaws, was a viable alternative to capitalism as a way of organising society, stressing social equality and mobility, de-emphasising materialism — all borrowings from the Qur'an. Its major flaw was its long tradition of discouraging religion as the alternative to material pursuits, and this was already changing when I got there. The street name changing and Tashkentland-type buildings were already taking place when I arrived. For instance, Gorky metro station was changed to the unpronounceable Buyuk Ipak Yolli (Great Silk Road) and Pushkin was changed to Salar (Persian meaning leader). The tree cutting would move into full gear later. They both are examples of Karimov's obsession with blotting out all evidence of Russian and Soviet heritage.

The president, Islam Karimov, had a promising name, but this turned out to be a misnomer, as he was the most ruthless of the pre-independence Soviet apparatchiks, quickly dispensing with any likely rivals, muzzling all media. Being in the right place at the right time, during the chaos of Gorbachev's perestroika (1985–1991), he became head of the new version of the old Communist Party, the People's Democratic Party of Uzbekistan, now the Uzbekistan Liberal Democratic Party, and wasted no time taking control of the reins of power after declaring 'independence' on September 1, 1991. He has been the dictator presiding over fake elections ever since, and has killed, tortured and imprisoned thousands of mostly Uzbek Muslims. When the killing gets too scandalous the West cools its relations, but the exigencies of geopolitics and Uzbekistan's strategic importance has brought him forgiveness more than once. Relations with the West now are cool but correct.

I had survived the grind of teaching Economics and English but wanted to explore life here. I eventually stumbled onto the beautiful old Chorsu Turkish banya, with a flavour of both Turkish and Soviet tradition of steam and sauna to make the summer heat bearable (soon privatised, now an upscale club). As a result of my earlier trip to Astrakhan, I had written articles for the *Moscow Tribune* (Russian sails around the world from Caspian Sea, animal rights, cold bathes, the banking pyramid scandals in Moscow). I reinvented myself as a journalist, wrote the *Privatisation Newsletter* for UNIDO and prepared an English language paper *Good Morning* for the main daily, *People's Word*, and the Canadian *Peace Magazine,* carefully steering clear of Uzbek politics.

I took time out for trips to the magnificent Chimgan mountain, only an hour and a half by bus, Uzbekistan's highest peak, part of the Tien Shan range which merges with the Himalayas. There, I met Nuf, a wiry old Kazakh tour guide, now retired after years in service in Chimgan, Uzbekistan's only ski resort. We became friends and I visited Nuf often, and did some paragliding, skiing, and trekking with a Russian New Ager Vadim who lived there.

To keep my visa, after the UNIDO contract ended, I hustled to get work at – of all places – the President's Office, translating presidential decrees and pro-Uzbekistan 'news', continuing my own writing but, with the new opportunity the internet offered, under a pseudonym. After 9/11, internet news sites proliferated and there was interest in the West for this new ally of the US. *Canadian Press* and the *Economist* business reports actually provided some cash.

I made good friends, Mubin an editor and Yuri a designer at the *Tashkent Business Weekly (TBW)*; where, as an employee at the dread President's Office, I had use of a desk and computer to translate the *TBW* English page. We enjoyed carousing and hiking. They were not 'new Uzbeks' though both would like to have had a better life. They, like most Uzbeks and most Soviets, bemoaned the collapse of the Soviet Union. 'We were once living in a borderless world covering a sixth of the globe. We were a respected world power,' sighed my hiking friend Rashid, a Tatar whose family was from Kazan.

My friend Vladlen (Vladimir-Lenin acronym) and his friend Anafi are Tatars whose families were deported from Crimea in 1944 as punishment for Tatars cooperating with Nazi invaders. Vladlen's grandfather had been an imam, suffering Mubin's grandfather's fate. Vladlen (he was born in 1967 on the fiftieth anniversary of the Russian revolution) was from a broken family and grew up off-and-on in orphanages. Though life was grim growing up, he was well-educated and enjoyed reading psychology. His favourite painter is Dali.

There was no sign of anti-Russian sentiment (apart from a brief period during the collapse of the Soviet Union and the early excitement at independence). Everyone spoke Russian and the Uzbeks would slip into Uzbek among themselves. I diligently studied Uzbek, but when I tried to speak it, my interlocutor would laugh and reply in Russian. I played piano with an Uzbek musicologist, Olim, and his Jewish violinist friend Sasha. It was a pleasant life, not rushed. My friends were a mix of Uzbeks, Russians, Tatars, Koreans and Ashkenazy Jews from European Russia. The legendary Bukharan Jews had by now got their US green cards or Israeli passports, but many Russian Jews had no interest in emigrating, enjoying their lives as part of the intellectual and artistic elite.

Horse-riding in Iranov Nature Reserve (don't tell anyone)

On a three-day mountain hike in the Tien Shan, my Russia friend decided to take a shortcut back, which meant going through the nature reserve, which is off limits. Of course we were found out. The patrol leader, Zhora, as he introduced himself with a Russian diminutive, put his hand on his heart to show respect (though our party was clearly not Muslim), and proceeded to explain that this was a sanctuary, and hunting and hiking were forbidden. He was short and athletic, missing a few teeth with a few others capped in gold, but with the traditional Tajik flashing eyes and a well-shaped, handsome face. They made a half-hearted attempt to fine us, but Sasha said no one would ever keep track of the paperwork. Zhora was intrigued to meet a Canadian. I was equally intrigued by this fresh young Tajik mountain dweller, and said how great it must be to do his work on horseback. 'Come and I'll take you on an expedition,' he offered.

I accepted and a few weeks later, showed up in his village, Nevichu, unannounced, phones being a luxury back then. Zhora has six brothers and four sisters, and the family is mostly able to live off nature (gardening, fishing and poaching, for as the ranger he earned a measly $8/month). I found Zhora at a 'toi' for the neighbourhood, hosted by a friend from schooldays named Bakhodir, who was celebrating the birthday of his new-born daughter.

'Why such a big deal?' I asked Zhora after enduring long speeches of gratitude and many vodka toasts. 'Bakhodir is a very generous guy. He was a teacher, but took advantage of commercial possibilities after independence in 1991 and became rich. He's always helping people out with their weddings and funerals, circumcision ceremonies and whatever. But for seven years, he and his wife had no children. That is a terrible thing for young people, and when his wife finally gave birth, he decided to show his thanks to Allah, and celebrate by inviting all his neighbours and friends.'

It was in fact quite a do, with endless food and drink. I didn't point out that strictly speaking the vodka was taboo. This after all was the Soviet Union for seventy years. Old habits die hard. I ended up at the table with bachelors and heavy drinkers, who tried to get me tipsy, but after a hard four hour bike ride in 30 degrees-plus heat, I craved only tea and the succulent watermelon and early grapes which I gathered from abandoned tables nearby. The drinkers lost interest in me. In fact, one was soon hanging his head in an unsightly stupor, and one of his cohorts quickly ushered him out, a great example of the evils of liquor. Knowing your limit is very important in a Tajik village, where everyone knows everyone and there is little news other than neighbourhood scandals.

It struck me that this village dynamic harks back to ancient traditions which are an integral part of Islamic culture. It certainly was not something that was introduced when Uzbekistan embraced capitalism at its independence in 1991. It seemed like a combination of the North American native tradition, where it was the duty of their well-off tribal members to blow their surplus on big *potlach* parties, plus a dose of Muslim paternalism: 'Praise Allah for your blessings.'

In any case, though many in Nevichu may be jealous of Bakhodir for his successes, he seems to be unanimously admired and respected, and is playing a vital role in distributing some of the wealth among direly poor neighbours. For example, Zhora has a respectable job as reserve inspector, but takes home about $8 a month, with which he must feed his wife and four young children, not to mention build a house and save for the inevitable 'toi's. In addition, there is the day-to-day danger which he must now face. Last year several inspectors were killed by bandits (shade of the old basmachi and the nearby mujahideen) and there are militia currently patrolling the area.

With her eleven children, Zhora's mother was a Hero of the Soviet Union, though that doesn't hold much water these days. His father was inspector at the nature reserve for forty years, so Zhora came by his job almost by inheritance; certainly love of nature is in his blood. His grandfather lived in the territory of the reserve until the 1930s and part of the reserve is actually named after him - the Iranov valley and river.

After the 'toi', I said in a respectful jest to Zhora's father: 'You are probably the richest person in Nevichu. After all, children are wealth, and you have eleven healthy children and countless grandchildren.' He laughed and said: 'Not true. I'm still trying to marry off my three youngest sons. Have you any idea how much work they have been?' But I think he was rather more proud than frustrated, and if I could judge from Zhora and his equally handsome younger brother, who brought us my horse for our trip, there would be little problem in finding eager partners for the remaining unmarried sons.

The expedition was a challenge, the horse fully aware that I was a greenhorn. The serious danger of a tree branch stump ripping open my designer jeans didn't enter my mind till after the fact, giving me a nasty scrape and sprinkling the path with the pocket contents, including my keys, and ripping the arm off my glasses. Fortunately I found them, but we had no needle and thread (along with bandages, an absolute essential on such hikes), so Zhora later used his hunter-gatherer wiles, found a bit of electrical wire in his bag, stripped out some filaments, and showed me how to use a match stick as a needle and the metal filaments as thread until we got home. For dinner, he caught six trout (a 1,000 soum fine for each one!) while I prepared the fire and some tea. We spent a lazy day, gorging on fish and tippling on vodka (I know, shame on us), swimming in a pool in the river and lounging on hot rocks, specially worn down for us by Mother Nature.

This adventure confirmed my love of the Uzbeks/Tajiks, who have kept their culture and traditions through thick and thin, love their big families and find true wealth in them. Even the new Uzbeks that I knew were not cold and calculating. Bakhodir, who I worked with on another UNIDO privatisation project and befriended, was very much the new Uzbek (actually half Tajik). He started up his own consulting business, was generous with neighbours (and me) and not obsessed with money.

Brave New Uzbekistan

Ploff dinners at Mubin's home are a fond memory. He lived with his mother as the youngest son, in a traditional Uzbek *mahalla* (neighbourhood) of one/two storey adobe homes with a courtyard, all surrounded by a high adobe fence. His mother had been a translator of Russian novels, his sister Sayora a professional singer, his older brother is a noted artist. His good friend Hasim became a slot machine owner, raking in cash and saving to go to the US. He came over after dinner and we all stood around in the courtyard shooting the breeze. As virtually all young people here believe, America is the magical heaven on earth where they can earn lots of money and come back home to live like kings. That prompted me to ask:

'What do you think about Bush's plans to attack Iraq?'

'That's just to gain control of the oil there,' he said in a matter-of-fact way. His friend Salim piped in: 'Afghanistan, Iraq ... the US has lots of weapons. It has got to use them up. War's good for the economy.'

I thought that wasn't far off the mark, considering their only sources of news are word of mouth and official Uzbek news – which is slavishly pro-American.

Somehow the conversation came around to what it was like 'before' – before the Soviet Union collapsed.

'Life was secure then. We had communism and didn't realise it,' said Hasim sheepishly. 'You didn't think much about money. Studying was free. Now our kids have to hustle to pay for everything. They don't have time to study properly. Or play.'

'And the US thought twice before bombing another country into oblivion,' I couldn't help adding.

'We were part of a powerful country that the world respected,' said Salim. 'Where are we now? A backwater, cut off from the world behind tightly controlled borders.'

It was getting nippy, so Mubin and I bade farewell and joined his family. As the youngest son, he had settled into the family home when he married, and he looks after his energetic, no-nonsense mother, this being the Uzbek and Muslim tradition. In fact, she needs little looking after, though she is pushing 80. The garden is a riot of color in the summer, full of flowers, persimmons, figs, pomegranates, apples, berries ... She had just finished a biography of her father, who studied in Turkey until 1925, and, as with so many of the intellectuals of the Soviet Union, disappeared during the 1930s one day, never being heard from again.

Despite this, Barno *opa* (*opa* means elder sister, a term of respect) never suffered being a child of an 'enemy of the people'. The family, though devastated when he disappeared, fantasised that he had gone back to Turkey somehow. She became a noted journalist, joined the Communist Party, and lived a full and interesting life; a strong, independent woman who had no need for 'women's lib'. She had read Khrushchev's speech denouncing Stalin, but only learned the fate of her father after the floodgates opened under Gorbachev in 1989, over fifty years later. He had been arrested along with eighty other leading Uzbeks, and was one of fifteen who were spirited off to Moscow and shot without trial for advocating a pan-Turkestan independent republic.

'But didn't you know about the gulag?' I asked her. 'Didn't you suspect that he had been 'repressed'?'

'No. We knew that there were many unjust arrests and murders under Stalin, but I never thought this had happened to my father,' she said.

As a result of this shattering revelation, Barno *opa* welcomed Uzbekistan's independence, and supported Karimov, refusing to bemoan the collapse of the Soviet Union that had done so much, both good and bad, for her. She accepts the entrenching of a petty dictator (who incidentally was a destitute orphan and yet was able to rise to be president), the extreme censorship of media, the jails full of ordinary believers. In her twilight years, she doesn't worry about the radical economic changes and the brave new world growing up around her. What's important to her is that her father's picture is in the Museum of the Victims of Colonialism, which lumps Russian and Soviet periods under one imperialist yoke. It's hard to blame her.

Nonetheless, I suggested that perhaps it was a tragedy that the Soviet Union collapsed. As if to end any further criticism, Barno *opa* said firmly, 'I'm proud of our new independent Uzbekistan.' But Mubin's beautiful, smartly dressed sister, Sayora, surprised me by readily agreeing with me. 'I'm a professional singer and lived comfortably in Soviet times, with no worries about hustling to find engagements.' Her charming personality and talent convinced me of that. Their mother remained silent, but Sayora's husband, Temir, an erstwhile Communist Party member, launched into a critique of the Soviet Union as being state capitalist. He is a budding businessman and during perestroika was active in organising a 'trade union of entrepreneurs'. As we were both economists, I started to protest his obvious misuse of terms. 'Of course, it wasn't a trade union in the real sense of the word, but at that time, we had to use acceptable terms to organise,' Temir explained smoothly. You know the type: he would have fit well into the ideology section of some Soviet ministry, and now, if his English were better, he would be snapped up by Saatchi & Saatchi to dream up ads in Uzbek for Dentamint. He struck me as having less of a grip on reality than the street-smart Hasim, and with a lot more pretensions.

'Yes, poor Gorby,' I said rather undiplomatically and proceeded to poke holes in Temir's trade union for entrepreneurs and his theory about the Soviet Union. 'Gorbachev had these naive ideas that if things were loosened up a bit, people would honestly work together, form real cooperatives, and the reforms would succeed,' I continued. 'Instead, everyone grabbed what they could and Yeltsin tore the whole system down.' Maybe they were just being polite, but no one dissented. Even Barno *opa* didn't have a good word for Yeltsin, except that by scuttling Gorbachev's attempt to salvage the Union, he had paved the way for Uzbekistan to become independent.

Such a stew of contradictions – the worship of the American dream, but also the cynical awareness that the US is selfish and violent on a world scale. People lived well under a harsh but egalitarian system, but either their personal tragedy or just their gullibility undermined their faith in it. They have to come to terms with their brave new world, and it's not easy.

In Soviet times, it was the US that was the cause of the problems. Now President Islam Karimov told parliament in August that 'the shadow of the USSR' was a major reason for its present problems. He hailed the new generation growing up free of 'the totalitarian heritage' of the Soviet Union. As Karimov told parliament in 2002, 'Having visited one of the schools, I asked the children, "Do you know who Brezhnev was?" They answered, "No, we don't." Then I asked them, "Who is Gorbachev?" They again said that they didn't know. Then I told them that they are doing great.'

Whew. The saving grace in all this stew was the fragrance and (muted) voice of Islam, which had proved impossible to eradicate. Given what Karimov was up to, it was now the only remaining path not sullied by the clodhopping Soviet past and Karimov present.

Journey within

For the first few years, I hadn't seen or heard much evidence of Islam, other than the *adhan* from the Mirzo-Yusuf mosque near my home in 1996, which was soon banned, and an invitation at the UNIDO office by some shy Uzbek women to join in their *iftar* in February 1997. True, Uzbeks said a blessing for meals and ran their hands down their face then and every time they passed a cemetery. Russians kidded them about this, but Uzbeks paid no attention. There was talk of the Islamic Movement of Uzbekistan (IMU), but no violence occurred until 1999, when six car bombs exploded in Tashkent, killing sixteen and injuring more than 100, in an attempt to assassinate Karimov.

The collapse of the Soviet Union is what led me to search for some answers in Islam, which I knew was also a bedrock of anti-imperialism, notably in Palestine, and which, as a socialist, I saw, approvingly, as a bedrock of a just society. With the collapse of the communist dream, I finally found my 'Damascus moment' in events which unfolded in 2005 in Andijan, one of the oldest cities in the Fergana Valley.

Many Uzbeks had kept their faith through all the Soviet repression, which had subsided. There were only 500 functioning mosques in the Soviet Union in the 1970s, and public religious observance was not allowed, but religious practice was not outlawed. It was not expected that the new post-independence order would repress religious observance, let alone return to the practices of Stalin. But when peaceful Muslims tried to make a public protest, asking only for the municipality to issue licenses to form businesses based on Islam principles, 1,000 were gunned down while sitting in the city square in Andijan.

When the news of the massacre spread, I was shaken. 'It is necessary to honour them. Teach me the Muslim prayers and let's pray for them,' I told Mubin. Though a believer, he was embarrassed, as he didn't know them. After all, his grandfather had been killed in a purge in the 1930s, and his mother, though a believer, was a communist. But he was also shaken and began to learn the prayers. He is no revolutionary: 'There's no point losing your life trying to overthrow a dictator as ruthless as ours. I will keep on educating my children in the straight path. One day we will win.' Karimov's viciousness was galvanising many into affirming their faith.

That began my journey to Islam (thank you Mr Karimov). But wait. It was not just the horrible massacre in 2005. It was much earlier, in 1996, waking to the gentle *adhan*. And the next year, when sweet Uzbek women offering a share in their *iftar* at work. I only signed on the dotted line later in Cairo, where I moved in 2006, once the precious visa was denied me in Tashkent.

Following the massacre, Mubin and I went every Juma to the modest Kukeldash Madrasah, which serves as one of the few functioning mosques. It was built in 1570 and went through many different transformations, as a caravanserai in the eighteenth century, and later a fortress. In the twentieth century it was a museum, first of atheism, and later of folk music (I remember going to a disco there in 1980 as a Russian language student in Moscow), before returning to its roots in the 1990s as a centre of Muslim education. The modest open-air courtyard serves as the most central mosque in Tashkent. The Khast Imam Mosque, like Kukeldash, is also in the old city, but is less accessible, more a museum, containing the Uthman Qur'an, considered to be the oldest, dating to 655 and stained with the blood of murdered caliph, Uthman. It was brought by Timur to Samarkand, seized by the Russians as a war trophy and returned in 1924. Far more gawking western tourists see it than Uzbek and non-Uzbek believers. Karimov has purposefully avoided building a large public mosque in the capital. Mubin and I were taking our chances worshipping at Kukeldash Madrasah as it was watched like hawks by Karimov's police.

A lovely memory of that time is walking in the Botanical Gardens. The gardens were unkempt, very Soviet, spacious; a blessed riot of restful green. I discovered a meandering, overgrown brambleberry thicket, and often went there to struggle to reach the berries through the thorns. For some reason the activity gave me satisfaction. I suppose I sensed how it expressed metaphorically my own struggle to find the precious reward in the thorny, hostile surroundings, all the tastier for the struggle.

Tashkent brings back haunting memories with their fleeting beauty. I kept on looking for such treasures through the new pathways I trod. There was no happy ending to my thirteen years in my special city, but there were many happy moments, and the greatest treasure I found there was Islam, which found Turkestan in the eight century, where *Sahih Bukhari*, the most authentic of all hadith compilations, was complied in the ninth century, and where Ibn Sina wrote the definitive medical encyclopaedia of the time – *The Canon of Medicine,* in the eleventh century. Both are ageless works.

My journey to the Other could have been to Kuala Lumpur, Konya or Karachi. What's important is being the Other. Tashkent is almost exactly half way around the world from my birthplace, Toronto, and at the same latitude. I like to imagine: what if my soul had been plopped down on the other side of the earth, growing up in this exquisite mountain river valley, with small farmer traditions enduring, living a tough but peaceful life, rich in culture, Muslim. But Tashkent became my Other, one that will last my whole lifetime. I had not put this piece into the puzzle of my life until I relived it here in the telling. Recalling this vital Other has been like combining different themes/melodies in my private symphony, which I compose anew each time I move through the experiences. The different 'flats' (sic), some dark, some light, some major, some minor. The different acquaintances – the growling drummer Alisher, the prying Garifovna, the flashing smiles of the dark, handsome Mahsud and his radiant wife Nargiza, the men in their *duppis* (square embroidered skullcaps), the women in brightly coloured dresses and scarves. Tashkent allowed me to find the spiritual path that Marx ignored.

Karimov is an especially appallingly dictator, but one whose power is skin deep (an unfortunate metaphor). Uzbeks remain a charming, handsome people. Despite the torture and killing of innocent Muslims, the accumulating scars in Tashkent, the treeless and *faux* Disney amusement parks, the burgeoning *mahallas* for the super-rich, the inherent beauty of the Uzbek people and their magical Tashkent prevail. Dictatorships eventually crumble, and good Muslims like my friend Mubin are preparing a new generation to pick up the pieces, just as his mother and Vladlen's mother survived Stalin's dictatorship and brought fine sons into the world.

But I do owe a vote of thanks to Karimov, the ogre of Uzbekistan. Thank you for not boiling me in oil upon discovering a naughty gadfly on your staff. Yes, I betrayed your confidence, but in my defence it was mostly just to prevent myself from going mad, and my scurrilous internet screeds did not seem to harm you in the least. What's more, they turned me into the writer I am today, fighting injustice but with a sense of humour, and a foundation in what you hate most – Islam.

UTOPIA IN TEHRAN

Javaad Alipoor

That is from the news of the cities, which we relate to you; of them, some are (still) standing and some are (as) a harvest (mowed down).

The Qur'an 11:100

This meant nothing to me. 'In which country is that?' I asked. 'In the country to which your index finger cannot point,' he said, and I realised that this old sage was very wise.

Suhravardi al-Muqtal, *The Song of the Tip of Gabriel's Wings*

From Plato's *Republic* onwards, the idea of a politics built on an imagined city has allowed generations of thinkers to engage with the vision of a radical rupture, a break from how the world is now, and how they think we may get to that other place. In the nineteenth and twentieth century, the Islamicate world produced a number of thinkers that sketched, and in some cases, built their cities. We have the desire of the celebrated poet and philosopher, Mohammad Iqbal, to fuse the spirit of the eastern poet with the western engineer, Ayatollah Khomeini's vision of the *Vilayat e Faqih* (Guardianship of the Jurisprudent) where religious scholars oversee a utopian society, and the black banners of Daesh (ISIS) that want to expunge colonial borders as part of their dystopian programme. But unlike the Islamic utopians of previous centuries, from al-Farabi's *The Ideal City* to Sohravardi's *Nakuja-abad* the utopians of the twentieth and twenty-first century have not yet explicitly designed a city. Instead, ideas have piled up and the city, rather than taking the form of Isfahan, commanded consciously by a newly world conquering Shahenshah, has, like Tehran, become sprawling, contradictory and covered in the muck of history's most violent century.

A truly authentic vision would have to show the contradictions and mutual exclusiveness of what Marxist philosopher Henri Lefebvre calls 'the possible impossible' register of modern utopia. It would have to be a text that synthesised fiction, history and theory. It would have to sketch a city that could simultaneously hold the resolutely opposed aspirations of a revolutionary like Ali Shariati and a theologian such as Ayatollah Khomeini, of someone like Fazlallah Nouri, who fought against democracy and Ayatollah Taleqani who died mysteriously for democracy. It would have to be a text to be discovered, guided and pieced together by someone who knows the city. It would be found in the ruins of the slums that used to hang from the southern tip of Tehran, edging out into the desert. It would tell the story of a journey through the city. Like the eleventh-century philosopher and traveller Naser Khusraw's description of Fatimid Egypt, the accounts of the places visited don't always seem to map onto real places, but rather the unveiling of a city as a code of politics, religion and power. It would have to show the mediation and fissure intrinsic to the comparative image of utopia, corresponding to the respective vicissitudes of the concepts and ideas of 'Utopia' and 'Nakuja-abad'. As such, it would require two voices. The first would be the fractured and broken voice of Tehran, straining towards the divine. The second would be framed by a voice representing the European tradition, by turns uncovering and obfuscating it.

It would be an act of the imagination. This is how it might read.

In 2008, I was invited to the Goethe Institute Tehran, to review a collection of papers that had been bought by an American scholar of Iranian religion who had bought them in a bookshop, near Tehran Sharif University. Some of them were burned and charred. They all seem to be written in the kind of dirty ink that implies a speedy composition, under pressure. Given the times described, and the politics described by the author, not to mention the clear parallels with the prison memoir style that developed in twentieth century Iran, it seems reasonable to place these writings in that tradition. I have examined the fragments that were not too fire damaged, and tried to piece them together.

From the Slums of the South to the Imperial Museum

I write this so there will be a record and so people will know the journey that brought me here. When, God willing, this Pharaonic regime falls, the people will remember martyrs, in the way I remember martyrs now. We who die to build the government of love, trade individuality for eternal life. Hussein is remembered, but who can name all the seventy-two? My life as a Muslim, and as a revolutionary has been a journey through Tehran, and it's that journey that I want to be remembered.

My name is Muhammad, my father was called Ghulam Ali and I was born on the fifteenth of Khordad 1326. I am 29 years old. My mother and father came from a village in the Talesh mountains, but I saw the world for the first time in one of the cardboard towns that dot the land between southern Tehran and the opening of the Kavir desert. Every summer I would go back to Gilan and stay with my uncle, but I belong to the slums.

I was eight when I began to study at school. Slum schools are modest. We shared books and pens. We were taught Farsi, Maths, Religious Studies and Arabic. Our teachers were those young clerics who want to spend their lives serving God's creation, rather than the court. On my twelfth birthday the fifteenth of Khordad movement began. The Imam denounced the shah as a 'vain and wretched man' and the seminaries at Qom were attacked by the police and the SAVAK. A generation of blacklisted clerics, from humble backgrounds like mine had decided to give their lives for Iran and Islam.

When I first met Ustad Karim I knew I wanted to grow to be like him. He taught us maths and Arabic. One day he took us by bus uptown to visit the Imperial Armoury. Three times on the journey from the bus stop to the museum we were stopped by police. In the north we could see that we did not belong. That nothing belonged to us. Not the bars, not the women, not anything else behind the vitrine.

We ate cheese and watermelon and bread under the Russian gates of the museum. American cars and French perfume breezed past us. After lunch the older boys tried to sneak away to buy single cigarettes. We queued to go into the museum, to see the ancient swords.

This first section of the text breaks off here. Like many it is creased and burned at the edges, suggesting it was on the author's corpse when found. When I was piecing these back together, I found a piece that partially fitted the tears of this first section of text.

In the early days of the Islamic Republic the interaction between Islamic Utopians and the challenges they faced from the secular left was performed in three squares in Tehran. In 1979, caught out by their leftist rivals, the Islamic Republican Party quickly moved to appeal to the working class. A pamphlet from Khomeieni appeared bearing the quote: 'Every day should be considered Worker's Day for Labour is the source of all things, even of heaven and hell as well as of the atom particle.' The challenge from the Marxists had been met with a slogan even more radical than the labour theory of value.

By the mid 1980s this utopian creativity, that had produced demonstrations of hundreds of thousands snaking their way from parliament all the way to central Tehran and the ministry of Labour, was over. The forced recantations of political views, collected under torture of members of the Tudeh Party's Central Committee, were broadcast as part of state celebrations of Worker's Day in 1983. Participation changed from large, outdoor, joyous demonstrations into solemn affairs; with the Revolutionary Guard bussing in workers for the afternoon, so factories did not lose a whole day's work. Since Khomeini's death, these events have been held indoors, at his mausoleum. Where in the Utopian Tehran, May Day shows the power and influence of the working class, Islamist or left, over the state, now it showed the power of the state over the working class.

I digress. Back to the text. Burned and charred, but still recognisably an extension of the previous section.

...Zulfiqar commissioned by Abbas the Great. I stopped and look. We pressed our faces against the glass until a museum guard slapped one of us with his guarding stick. Ustad told us all to stand back. After the guard had left, Ustad traced his finger over the glass. He looked at us and said: 'You can learn more about Iranian history in this case boys, than you can from a thousand of my classes. Look at it: The sword of righteousness, the sword of the lion of God, the sword of two swords clashing made of gold and jewels, may God forgive me, and kept in a case in a city where we have no meat to eat downtown – all to the glory of a Pharaonic regime.'

As we walked out of the museum, I saw a national service boy guarding the entrance. His sunglasses glinted orange in the evening sun, his rifle by his side. Ustad Karim spoke to him in his village language. The boy smiled. He bent close to us, so his officer couldn't hear and patted his rifle. 'This

is the Zulfiqar of our age', he said, 'and every man can have one'. He let
me touch it.

The Hosseinieh Ershad

*This next fragment describes the Hosseinieh Ershad which stands about halfway
up Tehran, from South to North, in the Zarrabkhaneh neighbourhood. Built with
the subscriptions collected by the newly university educated children of low
ranking bazaaris, the institute occupied a central place in the story of the Utopian
impulse of Iranian Islam. Ali Shariati, the famous philosopher, sociologist and
revolutionary, lectured here when he wasn't being detained by the SAVAK. Having
studied in Paris, he brought the ideas of Fanon, Cesaire and Sartre to Iran. His
response to these ideas was to radically re-imagine an insurrectionary left wing
Shi'ism that overturned the traditional concepts of Usooli Shi'ism, as it were, in
the same sense Marx overturned Hegel.*

*The cosmic tragedy of Hussein's martyrdom became a story of anti-imperialist and
proto-socialist martyrdom at the hands of a rapacious tyrant. Shariati developed the
idea of a 'nezam-e tohidi'; the society of monotheism, a social unity in which
idolatry and divisions of class would be abolished. His response to Sartre and the
disputes within Marxism led him to seek out the debates on the epistemological
break, and side with a young Marx whom he sought to 'free from himself'. From
Fanon, he drew the idea of the need for a violent break with the experience of
colonisation, and so he developed a theory of ideology, different to both the positivist
and critical definitions of the term.*

*Whereas for a Western radical, the struggle might be for a more democratic
articulation of the management of the polis, this would never suit the colonised
countries of Asia and Africa, for whom it would merely mean a more effective
management of the colonised. Against this Shariati posited revolutionary ideology:
the ideas that show the potential for social progress, reform and self-discipline that
could cut through the smooth surface of colonial oppression. As such his notion of
'ideology' was diametrically opposed to that developed by critical thinkers in the
Western traditions. The carriers of this revolutionary potential were, of course, to be
the revolutionary intelligentsia, the children of low ranking professional and bazaar
merchants, the mostazefin, who had recently acquired nationalised university
educations and national military training. After his early and suspicious death in
exile, his picture was hung at the demonstrations that led to the establishment of the*

Islamic Republic. Today a Tehran metro station, just into the northern part of the city, is named after him, in roughly the same lower middle class district as the Hosseinieh.

Jamal had been volunteering at the Hosseinieh for about a year when he was invited by one of the more senior brothers to copy tapes of the lectures of different revolutionary speakers. Jamal was a thin man, and his time in the Shah's jails seemed to have made him thinner. He was showing me how the machine worked, when something stuck out from the tape; the words popping out of the background noise and into my mind. A young guerrilla leader's voice. A New phrase: 'The Monotheistic Society'. Jamal knew what I would ask. 'Brother', he said, 'don't bring your little maktabi scowl into the Hussainia. This isn't the place for your courtly Islam.' I laughed. In the Hussainia, these words have become common currency. The youth who come here for the lectures are looking for an Islam that is cut off from the empty ritual and corruption of the mullahs who service the Pahlavi court. There's the smell of youth to the place – frustration mixed with cheap eau de cologne and new ideas.

Jamal loops the tapes into the machine carefully, tracing his finger lightly to smooth across the spool. 'Ninety-nine per cent of what we do has no reference to the Qu'ran.' I hold one spool for him. He carefully lays the other into the machine. By tomorrow night these speeches, recorded from radical clerics, student guerrillas and exiled intellectuals, will leave Tehran for cities all over the country. 'Our materials, these tapes, Kalashnikovs, they come from Europe. We bend them and shape them to the cause of Islam and freedom. Why should our ideas be any different? If those paedophile clerics want to sit in front of the shah pawing at 1,000 year old books let them. We will write our future in our faith, like the Imam says.'

A Prison Letter

Both of the sections I have presented so far appear to have been composed serially. They follow the form of prison biography, like the writings attributed to Khosrow Rouzbeh, the chief of the military branch of the Communist Party of Iran, in his final days before execution rather than the more meditative published form, pioneered by writer and novelist Bozorg Alavi in his Prison Scraps of Paper. *In this section though, our author does seem to move towards the latter style. In Bozorg Alavi's work, we can discern a conscious grappling with the limitations of the traditional prison poems of classical Persian literature. The Iranian genre was born in Iran's first modern jail, Tehran's Qasr-e Shah, converted from a late Qajar palace by Reza Pahlavi.*

Traditional prison poetry or 'sher-e habs' can be seen as a sub-genre of the Arab and Persian tradition of court poetry. The Islamic middle ages being as they were, with kingship and favour changing hands as quickly as one and other, a poet could find himself in a dungeon or exiled to some far flung village easily and frequently. In these traditional forms, the poet's imagination acts as a lawyer pleading clemency: a description of some object or moment of regal station, held by the king, is an appeal for clemency, as if an ekphrasis of power can bring the keys of the jailor to the dungeon door.

In the twentieth century, all of these formal qualities are inverted. Where the traditional poet wants to share his work with the king, the modern dissident has to keep it hidden in case of further punishment. Where the former writes to praise the powerful, the latter writes to damn him. Where one starts from a particular object outside of the cell to beg for their release, the latter uses studies of objects within their confinement to explain why they are there.

Yesterday morning, I was handed a letter. One of the Mojahed prisoners had passed it across to our block. All of Qasr-e Shah jail was talking about it. It was thirteen days before they transferred me here. They said everywhere in Tehran it was circulating, and the communists had copied it onto cigarette papers and got them into our cells. An open letter from a young guerrilla fighter, addressed to his father; the famous revolutionary cleric, Ayatollah Taleghani. His son is a member of the faction of the People's Mojahedin who have broken entirely from the faith of the Prophet (Oh God, Bestow blessings on Mohammad and the family and progeny of Mohammad), and embraced the Marxism of the Vietnamese and the Cubans. Where these two ideas have up to now been intertwined in our history and our struggle, more and more of our young people are choosing one over another.

Dear Father,

I hope you are safe and well. It has been two years since we lost contact. Naturally we have not heard much about each other. Of course I tried, without much success to get news about you. I am sure that you, for your part, have many questions to ask me about my recent life and the activities I have carried out. I will try, with all due diligence, to answer what I imagine are the questions that disturb you. Not because you are my father but because, and only because, for so long you were my teacher and for a longer while still, my comrade fighter in the war against imperialism and reaction. If I answer these questions adequately, I will have played my part, however modest, in the people's liberation struggle. I have found a new family. A family of young, committed, revolutionary intellectuals. This new family (if I can apply that term to The Organisation) is different to the one I left. My new family does not have constant comings and goings, fruitless get-togethers. Its air isn't close with the inertia of wasted time. A man can breathe. Father, you never silenced our voices, but you always stood out among (can I call you this?) the old men of our family. You wished for us to speak. But speaking isn't enough anymore. My new family spends every moment raising our consciousness, fanning the flame of liberty and preparing for the people's armed struggle. In my previous family, our attention was focused on resisting the establishment, growing up to become independent of the authorities, and all the time refusing to become mindless robots for the dominant class. In my present family, our attention is focused on actively fighting that class.

Father, I end this letter by stressing that I will resist the regime as you have done, and that I will follow your example to the end. I will try and write again soon, even though I do not know when, or even if, you will receive this letter.

Your son, Mojtaba

This letter struck me, I think, because in it I seemed to see a young man, not dissimilar to me, but moving in the opposite direction. Where I had recognised that only Islam could provide an answer to the problems facing my country, and had cut ties with the communists, this young mojahed, threw away the vestiges of his Islam and carried on further down the path of Marxism.

I am reminded of my own study. I remember Ustad lending me Jalal Al-e Ahmad's book, *Westoxification*. In it he explains how Iranian history is replete with revolutionary intellectuals who studied the ideas of the West, to deploy them in Iran. The liberals and the Marxists, the Democrats and the Communists, all are united in worship of foreign ideas. They go to the West to study. They lose themselves in ideas that never drew succour from their soil, or their soul. Every anti-imperialist knew the story of the three

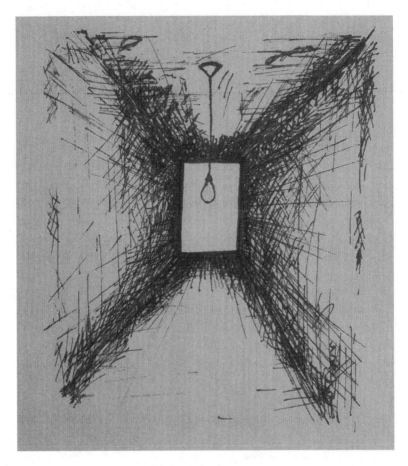

Illustration by Uzma Kazi

Shaykhs who had fought in the constitutional revolution against the British and the Russians. The Communists had told me how Shaykh Fazlallah Nouri had broken from the others and preached against the revolution, after the revolutionaries tried to force through unveiling and education for young women. They called him a traitor, a pro-Russian reactionary and executed him. The corpse of that great man dangling on the gallows was like a flag to me, raised to signify the triumph of this deadly disease – the plague of Westoxification.

I read the letter again and again in jail. My thoughts acquire a coldness towards young men who I once thought fought on the same side as me. I see a river of blood separating the people, as it separates the people from their oppressors. Marxist and Muslim factions have declared war with each other.

A rubbish tip, just into the desert, south of the Tehran slums. Children come out to play and look for firewood. Stumbling over an open dump they find a charred corpse. When the police arrive with SAVAK the body is recognised. It is that of one the leaders of the faction of the Mujahedin that remained Muslim. Killed by the Marxist faction. Over the next days more bodies, from both factions are found. The regime's newspapers crow: Now, when they want to kill a man, they burn his body and leave him in the desert. They tell the people his comrades killed him. All over the world tyrants kill rebels and dump their bodies where they can. But only Tehran can provide a setting like this. Where the slums of the south meet the breaking of the desert. For a century our jihad had moved closer to what the Marxists called class struggle, and that struggle became our jihad. In that place where grimy city and the humidity of human habitat meets the desert, the process had come apart. Burnt bodies in garbage dumps.

I presume when they're finished with me, that's how I will be found too.

A Khanqah in the Bazaar

The text becomes unreadable here. The handwriting is much more rushed. And difficult to decipher. There is a point where the meaning seems to break down entirely. One piece is simply filled in entirely. You can see the heavy strokes of pen embedded in the same way a child colours in the sky.

The psychoanalytic literature would see this as a 'foreclosure of meaning'. The medieval Iranian mystic Najm Kobra wrote about the 'nur-i siyah' or 'black light' which illustrates the supposed ending of the relation to the sensible world and the concomitantly alleged birth of the faculties that relate to the senses beyond it. In the case of our author we might start to recognise a certain kind of psychotic episode.

The Sheikhi sect that are mentioned in the passage below, represent a little known part of the history of Iranian Shi'ism. The school is one built on the practice of seeking visions of the hidden Imam, and through them ascending to visions of what in the Islamic tradition are called higher stations or 'maqam'.

Two points seem pertinent about the Sheikhi school for the purposes of the discussion of this text. First, the Sheikhi went on through the nineteenth and early twentieth centuries to play a disproportionately large role in the constitutionalist and nascent socialist movements in Iran. To take one famous example: in the revolt against the second Anglo-Russian partition of Iran in 1919, Sheikh Mohammad Khiabani, a young practitioner of the school, led an uprising which culminated in the fedayis and mojaheds of the Caucasian and Iranian Social Democratic Parties declaring the area around Tabriz as 'Azadistan'. Uprisings in Tehran were mounted in sympathy. Ultimately all were brutally put down by the Pahlavi state, supported by the British. Second, the visionary tradition of Sheikhism has a history that goes back much further in Iranian Sufism. We can trace a thread that goes back at least to the twelfth century: to Suhravardi and the illuminationist mystics, through figures like the twelfth century Sufi Ruzbehan Baqli and thirteen century mystic Najm Kobra. In this tradition, religious experience is prized above belief; indeed practitioners are exhorted to believe in only those things that they taste and see. It would be easy to see why such a practice could lead to the long periods of political quietism and withdrawal that characterise most of its history, but more difficult to see why it results in its occasional outbreaks of utopian emancipatory fever.

I remember walking through the gardens where the Sheikh's house met the corner of Ferdosi square. It must have been late into the night. As the Sheikh brought tea out to the garden, I could see the first stream of light leak under the gate, as I can see light illuminate the outline of the men who open my cell door when it is my turn in the interrogation room.

The tea sits between us. Offering a cube of sugar, the Sheikh asks me why I have come to see him. I tell him I have never thought of visiting before but the walls of my life seem to be falling around me, and that the letter I read has made me question everything. The Sheikh wants to know about the questions. So I pose them to him.

'I come from a part of Tehran where the only solidarity that was ever shown to us was from the young spiritual brothers who came to teach us. So when Shariati wrote his *Return to an Islamic Identity*, I was one of the first it spoke to. But the people who were trying to return to that have splintered. And everywhere I look for an identity or a return, I just see different adaptations to the new.'

'That's not a question,' said the Sheikh. He offered me a sweet. 'This house is a *khanqah* of the Sheikhi order.' I thought I had spoken out of turn.

'You should study the life of Muhammad Khiabani, the revolutionary martyr. He spent every day translating and preaching the newest communiques from the Social Democrats, and every night weeping with love for the most high.'

'Khiabani was a Sheikhi from a long chain of mystics who some scholars trace back to Suhravardi al-Muqtal. Suhravardi told a story about the sounds he heard – the songs of the tips of Gabriel's wings. Late one night, as morning broke, he went to a garden like this, and sat like this. An old man met him. He asked the old man where he had come from. "Nakuja abad," he answered.' The Sheikh explained: 'Na kuja abad, means the no-where-istan.

'In the west, philosophers and theologians have always sought, at radical moments, as we have too, to build a City of God. To return to their religious identity. But they misunderstand their own history. In Christianity the City of God, the first no-where place, which from Greek they call U-topia, is a model that is taken from a relationship between two social organisations. Like your slum teachers and your guerrillas, say. Their perfect city was an arrangement between the Vatican and the Empire of Rome. But for Shias the situation is different.'

'How can the aim of all politics be a relation between temporal powers, when Imam Hussein showed heaven through his two fingers?' I can hear crickets and car horns. 'The na kuja abad that we will build is a relationship between two kinds of time, not two kinds of space. The relationship between these two times defines the limits of the lives and cities we can imagine ourselves. On the one side we have those who want to celebrate and restore the purity and strength of the first of the believers; all they can do is look back. On the other side, those who look forward, and see the fulfilment of the end of time. When the seventy-two looked through the fingers of the Imam they saw both.'

'Na kuja abad is not in this city,' he says. 'Keep going north. Suhravardi called the ascent from time to eternity the journey to the cosmic north. Your trip is easier. Leave the city to the North, pass the villas and into the mountains. Go to the ruins of Alamut.'

I could no longer tell which sound was that of muscle and sinew against machine, and which was Gabriel's wings beating against the light.

From Tehran to Alamut

The final section of text seems even more broken up than the other sections. Thematically the author considers his journey to the assassins' castle, and undergoes a vision of the day that the fourth old Man of the Mountains, Hassan II, decreed the end of time. Rashid ad-Din Sinan, whose account is one of the few surviving contemporary ones says: 'On the seventieth of Ramadan, Hasan II, upon whose mention be peace, caused his followers to come to Alamut. They raised four great banners — white, red, yellow and green — at the four corners of the minbar. At noon he came down from the fortress and in a most perfect manner mounted the pulpit. Baring his sword he cried: O inhabitants of the worlds, jinn, men and angels! Someone has come to me in secret from the Imam, who has lifted from you the burden of the Law and brought you to the Resurrection. Then he set up a table and seated the people to break the fast. On that day they showed their joy with wine and repose.'

Circling the same visions and moments, the author's voice moves out onto a level that is ultimately recognisable, not necessarily to those who study theology or the history of utopia, but to psychologists and psychiatrists who recognise post traumatic stress disorder. In book three of the City of God, writing against accusations that Christianity had brought the fall of Rome, Augustine describes the 'edict of Mithradates, commanding that all Roman citizens found in Asia should be slain'. As a result of this massacre, a great madness descends on Rome, even on the animals of the city who, forgetting their domestication, bark and howl repetitively, echoing what Freud found in his grandson's game of peekaboo, and the shell shocked soldiers of the first world war. What Freud calls 'repetition compulsion', Augustine calls 'the cruel necessity'.

The fragments are quite difficult to piece together at this point.

I knew from the smell of damp and the thickness of the air that I had been taken somewhere else. I thought of the stories of flight and the night time visions that dot the history of the mystics and the Sufis, and I hated myself, because my religion is about fighting and struggling in this world, not smoking opium and dreaming of the next. I try and collect my memories of the night before. Leaving the old Sheikh's house I must have walked towards artillery square. Under the moon I walked. I was singing to myself. Feeling fresh and sober. And then I was grabbed.

Maybe, I am in the dungeons at Alamut, the place the old Sheikh told me about, but that would be stupid and depend on me believing in his tales of miracle. Maybe I am a peasant who didn't pay rent to the lords of Alamut. Maybe I am a Seljuk prince.

There is another break in the text here. The next fragment seems to be written on different paper, stuck to the previous pieces with some sort of homemade glue, a mix of decades old dirt and something else. The scholar in me wants to make the connection with the SAVAK's contemporary torture methods. The 'Chicago Tribune' ran a story about torture methods attributed to the Shah's secret police organisation including a detailed description of what prisoners and jailers nicknamed 'apollo', a macabre joke about the way it looked; a prisoner strapped into an electric chair, would have a large metal mask placed around their head to muffle their screams while amplifying them for the victim.

I wake in cold stone cells. The water running through the moss that lines the gaps in the wall is cool and refreshing, and I know the cells are carved out under a mountain. I am north of Tehran, in the air of the mountains - the ruins of Alamut. But the walls seem solid and the air seems cleaner than I have ever known. I smell the air of a different time, of different place. Of untime. Unplace. Nakuja. An active silence. Pierced only by the occasional sounds of a beating and a woman sobbing in pain. As my chains fall away I open the door or my cell, and look through the room next door.

The next passage is quite difficult to read so I preface it with a description of the tavoot-ha or 'graves' of Ghazal Hesar Prison, taken from the report Crime and Impunity from the Iran Justice Foundation. I presume this is what the author is referring to, but cannot see how this reference could be written in 1978. The Foundation report recounted how:

> In 1983, a group of leftist women inmates were taken to an unprecedented punishment ward in Ghezal Hesar Prison. From six o'clock in the morning until eleven o'clock at night prisoners were forced to sit, blindfolded and motionless, in small wooden cubicles — later referred as tavoot-ha (coffins, or graves). The head of this person called it his karkhane-ye-adamsazi (a human manufacturing factory). Covered in chador, with no movement permitted, the space was so tiny that there was no room to move anyway- while any sound, even coughing or sneezing, was punished by beatings — the inmates felt frozen in an eternal time. The overwhelming silence was broken only by the sounds of beating and the recantations, religious hymns or recitations of Qur'an broadcasted from the loudspeakers. Only a small minority of these inmates survived insanity, death by suicide, or falling into the abyss of collaboration (with prison authorities).

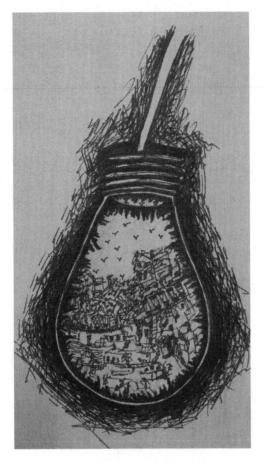

Illustration by Uzma Kazi

The peculiar thing is that the text seems to imply a knowledge of what came after the foundation of the Islamic Republic. The next section reads:

I see the room as a grid, with the grid containing nine coffins. Nine coffins each containing a woman, sit on the grid. The women are robed in black, their knees pushed up towards their chins, forced into a tiny wooden box. A radio on the wall plays the call to prayer. A woman sobs inaudibly. Too audibly. Three men crash into the room and drag her from the wooden coffin. Screaming, they push her chador away and beat her, the sound of the *adhan* bleeds out of a radio. It too fills the room.

I walked up the stair well. As I turned into the light the stairs seemed sharper, and harder to climb. At the top of the stairs the brown and grey dinge of the stones above me broke apart. Luminescent cobalt and mountainous sky.

In the courtyard the *fedayeen* gather. Outside the gates of the Garden of the Assassins. Roses and hashish stain the air. The courtyard grey, stone and metallic. An austere reflection of the sky above. In each corner a turret, on each turret a flag. Red. White. Black. Green. A central tower stands. On that tower, a door opens. A young man. Tall and thin. I can't see anything but his green eyes that light the courtyard and the mountains around it. He looks to the assembly. 'The Day of Resurrection is at hand.' Holding his two finger apart, and gesturing for us to look through them, he says: 'There is no other heaven than this, and no resurrection but this. The chains of the law have been broken.'

An army of children, the boys I was at school with, marching through minefields, towards tanks and gunfire. A plastic man on a white plastic horse has shown them green plastic keys to heaven. They know he is waiting for them. And on the horizon an army gathers. Black flags are hung. They prepare a path that brings the desert into the city. Aridity. The end is coming.

From the slum to the museums and villas of the north, through the bazaar, *Khanqahs*, mosques and Hosseiniehs, there is the crushing sound of the beating of wings. Tehran is born again.

THIRD SEX LAHORE

Nimra Khan

Sex and violence go hand in hand for Nazuk. 'Is there any other way to have intercourse?', she questions, punctuating with a deep, manly laughter as her Adam's apple bobs up and down, almost as if enjoying the flummery of the question. 'I think by beating me up, men feel they are in turn atoning for the sins they are committing. It's like inflicted retribution.' Her name Nazuk, which means delicate, stands in grand contradiction to her broad, burly frame. Tall at six feet, accentuated by strong shoulders, Nazuk is physically anything but delicate; almost like a big oak tree emulating a dandelion. Behind layers of a chalky mixture of water and white powder caked on her face, Nazuk has strong, defiant features adorned by a hooked nose and deep-set eyes. Her thin lips have been painted a bright pink, with a darker lip liner extended beyond them to appear fuller. She wears a tight-fitted *shalwar kameez*, with breasts made of foam as she coyly confides in me and prompts me to verify with the jab of my finger on her foamy bosom. Her hair, long and braided, is flung to the side and she has a habit of playing with her mane instinctively before answering a question, almost as if providing her with the strength to delve into her painful past. She tries to appear unaffected as we continue with our talk, but her sporadically glistening eyes give away her inner turmoil. 'My family didn't disown me. In fact, it was I who disowned them,' she states with proud defiance. 'Them not accepting me for who I was, was tantamount to them rejecting God as it was He who willed me to be with this. We are born out of humans, why must we be treated as any less?' Her growing aloofness with each question made her façade even more apparent. It revealed years of practised strength she had garnered from building a big wall around her – one brick at a time, one rejection at a time. Nazuk was indeed very *nazuk*, if not by her physical self but the frailty of her heart. 'I was born after a long line of sisters, and my father could not have been more jubilant about the final arrival of a boy. I just wish someone had recorded his expression when he learnt that I was physically far away from being a normal one,' she replies giddily. A dark expression overtakes the smile on her face as she adds, 'He was never a real man himself. Having a functional penis does not make you a man. He wasn't even human.'

Nazuk belongs to the historic city of Lahore, the second largest in Pakistan and the capital of its bustling province, Punjab. Once known as the 'Paris of the East', Lahore is steeped in rich culture and traditions while also maintaining the relative height of liberalism in the country, when compared to the smaller cities and villages. Acting as the cultural heart of the country, Lahore hosts much of its arts, cuisine, music, cinema and intelligentsia. Despite the growing modernity of the city, many factions of the society continue to spiral downwards in their regressive path of intolerance. 'I feel I was lucky to have been born in Lahore, rather than a city like Peshawar, because we live like princesses here compared to the harrowing stories of what happens there to people like us.' By 'us', Nazuk is referring to the population of over a million and a half in the Third Sex community, also called *khawaja siras* and derogatorily, *hijras*, in the country. A significant number for a highly marginalised section of society, in which almost every member is either forsaken, abused or assaulted.

The Third Sex community includes transgender, transsexuals, intersex and transvestites. The term transgender is used to describe people who do not agree with the gender they were assigned to by society, and may thus look, feel, act or think different from their ascribed sex. Transsexuals may change their sex through medication and/or surgery, but generally it is very expensive to do so and many live their lives feeling trapped inside their bodies. Intersex is a medical term for people who are born with reproductive or sexual anatomies that do not seem to fit the conventional definitions of male and female. Whereas transvestites are those who are born to one sex but sometimes prefer to wear the clothes and act like the other sex, also popularly known as cross-dressers.

It is indeed ironic that the plight of the Third Sex community is probably the worst in Peshawar, where no one bats an eyelid on affairs pertaining to homosexuality and sodomy, despite the fact they are openly condemned in conservative Islamic interpretation. But to be a *khawaja sira* is tantamount to being a pariah at best and a non-human duly deserving all forms of debasement at worst. Lahore has been in the front line of Pakistan's cities that have worked diligently towards changing the societal perception of the community, along with providing them an iota of respect and normalcy to lead their beleaguered existence. A good example of the initiatives taken by the city is the Khawaja-Sira Rehabilitation Programme in Lahore, which started in 2010. It was initially meant to provide support to *khawaja siras* above the age of fifty through monthly stipends, literacy, psychological treatment and free medical assistance. Due to the programme's success and growing support, it now also helps the younger community by encouraging dialogue and providing skills and opportunities, paving their way towards a dignified future.

Khawaja siras have a special place in the South Asian version of Islam. People believe that God gave them two genders, so they must be His special, chosen ones. Historically speaking, *khawaja siras* were highly respected and trusted as caretakers and guardians of royal harems, masters of art and culture, and at times the king's advisors as well. In the Mughal era, they were very influential and worked at high positions, garnering substantial wealth and treated as distinguished servants to the royal families of the emperors throughout the eighteenth and nineteenth centuries. According to historians they were given this position due to their lack of proclivity of making advances on the queens and princesses, and were thus trusted. They were organised in a hierarchy, with a senior or chief *khawaja sira* directing the community. During the nineteenth century, the British outlawed sodomy and cross-dressing, and brought with them a wave of conservatism that still shudders the foundation of the society today. They were discriminated against under the Criminal Tribals Act in 1871, which lumped the *khawaja sira* community with 'habitually criminal' groups like thugs. The community was deliberately marginalised and reduced to legal non-existence after 250 years of reverence and prestige. After colonialism, they were continued to be treated like outlaws and animals, which over time slowly embedded itself in the fabric of the Indian subcontinent even when it was torn in half. Pakistan may have gained independence in 1947, but colonialism and its stigma never ended.

Nowadays, the community lives on the margins of society, making their livelihood on the behest of those who shun them and still use them as entertainers, beggars and sex workers. Despite mostly being cast out by their very own family members, they still yearn for a semblance of a family life and thus have formed very close-knit communities with *gurus* (experienced elders in their community) and *chelas* (disciples). Ironically enough, by forging the same sorts of familial connections that they left behind, *khawaja siras* create a social order that mimics the very society from which many of them fled but can at least survive in with acceptance and love instead of disgust and disdain.

'Here everyone has some sort of a family tie,' says Salma. I find her humble house by making my way through the crowded, narrow streets of a dilapidated part of Lahore where open drains and human waste line the streets. Her front door is neck-laced with different wires hanging from the second storey above and she greets me with a wary smile infused with the aromatic smell of *masalas* wafting out from behind her. Dexterously slicing up green chillies with a sharp knife held between her long fingers and even longer nails, 'we have mothers, aunts, uncles and even daughters', she says, pointing the knife to a girl sitting in the corner of the room smoking an opium laced cigarette. Throwing the green chillies in a pan of oil and stirring somewhat shyly, the multitude of colourful bangles on her arm jingle merrily as she adds, 'Chutki even has a father,' referring to her proclaimed daughter. Seeing the confusion on my face, 'Not her biological one! That good for nothing bastard tried to sell her for a few measly drugs after having beaten her till her nose had no bones and her teeth were all lying in her stomach.' Chutki continues smoking. 'You forgot the part where he tried to play the role of my pimp as well,' she adds expressionlessly to the biographic account being given of her life. 'No, Chutki's father now is a good man. He gets us medicines and takes care of us. He might be married to someone else, but he loves me,' says Salma with a proud smile. Not wanting to talk much about her prior life, she states it is more or less the same for everyone in her community; their similar histories unite them together in a bond that is unspoken yet deeply understood. 'Most of us will probably have the same story of losing our virginity, as it's mostly at the hand of some relative or family friend who comes to know about our condition or is smart enough to notice something is amiss. Could be an uncle or a cousin, or maybe even a couple of them at the same time. And if you're beautiful, then you are pretty much doomed. Once we get used to this abuse and blackmailing, then we're forced to work as sex slaves and then ultimately rejected by the same society who comes and uses us for their needs. Think about it, the only reason why we even have jobs as dancers or sex workers, is because there is and always will be a need for it in society. People will always come to us no matter how much they spit in our face the next morning.' She stops for a moment to laugh throwing her head back, 'Ejaculate at night, spit in the morning!'

Continued discrimination and repulsion for the *khawaja sira* community has sucked them in a quagmire of destitution and other chronic social evils. It is not that discrimination against them is structural in Pakistan; rather it is largely rooted in how they are perceived as members of Pakistani society. In general, they are widely ridiculed and grossly mocked at even if they try to make efforts towards a decent living for themselves. 'If the society started accepting us and allowing us the same working privileges as a normal human being, we could surely help the economy and fight the tribulations of poverty that cripples us as a society and nation,' adds Salma, shrugging her shoulders at the preposterousness of the situation, along with its simple and easy solution.

In most parts of Lahore, decked with relentless traffic and roadsides advertisements, you can find many *khawaja siras* cat-walking at traffic signals, adding colour to the already vibrant city with their dramatic make up and flamboyant attire. They go from car to car begging for money sometimes through flirtation and sometimes through promises of the inundation of blessings through their prayers. Some donors even end up giving money to save themselves from the superstitious wrath of the community, as many believe that God pays attention to their curses. Which, in itself is quite a paradox. Many Pakistani also believe that they cannot be classified as Muslims and thus must be ostracised.

The position of the Third Sex in Islam is somewhat ambiguous. Although the Qur'an does not make direct references to the Third Sex, there are some verses that may be portrayed as such. Take, for example, 24:31, which speaks of some men who are 'without the defining skills of males'. This is possibly a reference to men with female gender identity, therefore acknowledging their existence in the society. Or consider, 42: 49-50: 'To Allah belongs the dominion over the heavens and the earth. Allah creates what He wills. He prepares for whom He wills females, and prepares for whom He wills males. Or Allah marries together the males and the females, and makes those whom He wills to be ineffectual. Indeed, Allah is the Knowing, the Powerful'. This verse has been interpreted by many in relation to bearing an offspring, but some scholars believe the term 'ineffectual' refers to people with a transgender identity. It has also been suggested that the verse describes diversity in sexual orientation and gender, 'which Allah, the All-Knowing and All-Powerful, creates as Allah wishes'; the 'females' and 'males' for 'whom He wills' being counterparts or objects of desire, and 'whom(ever)' being male or female. Commentaries on 13:3, which refers to 'every kind of fruit being made in pairs', also acknowledge that there is a third sex in plants, which can by analogy take us to the conclusion that there may also be a third sex, a unisex, in animals and humans.

While the intricacies of Qur'anic interpretation may escape *khawaja siras*, they do tend to observe the basic rituals of Islam. Most are keen to perform the hajj; and Ramadan is observed with great fanfare.

Salma recounts a story one Ramadan from six years ago. 'It was *chaand raat* (the night when the new moon is sighted to mark the end of the fasting month) in Lahore, and after having spent a month of dutiful fasting, we were all very excited to partake in the upcoming festivities,' she says. 'I had decided long ago I was going to wear a magenta *sari*, embellished with sequenced work. I even knew how I was going to make my hair and make up, and had planned to especially splurge and go to the beauty parlour for that.' Little did Salma know at that point that she would be half bald before the sun rose the next day. She went out with her friends to shop for bangles and have *mehndi* applied on her hands, where they came across a group of rowdy men marking an end to their holy abstinence by dousing in cheap, local alcohol. 'In hindsight, it would have been better to stick to the two paths we are instructed to employ when dealing with these type of men - either ignore or just plain surrender,' continues Salma. 'But I think the excitement of the night got to my head and I haughtily told one of the men his mother was waiting at home with her legs spread for him. And that was it. Somehow when it comes to their own mothers or daughters, these men go into a frenzy of respect and protection, no matter how much they manhandle someone else's daughter or mother.'

The men beat, kicked and slapped Salma and her friends around till the police intervened. They were taken to the police station instead of the hospital, even though they were battered and bleeding, while the men were left scot-free. 'But the night had just started for us,' Salma proceeded with a deep, melancholic sigh. 'At the station we were all stripped, not just of our clothes but also of our tattered pride for the amusement of the police. With our cheeks red from slaps and aching bones from the incessant punching and kicking, we were made to dance as tears trickled down most of our faces. Those who expressed no grief were hurled more abuse. It was obvious our misery and harassment was their joy, and boy did they languish in it.' After physically abusing them, they cut off everyone's hair as a sign of degradation and finally let them go. The next day, none of the *khawaja siras* in her neighbourhood and close communities celebrated Eid. They have a code: if even one of them was not happy, no one was to celebrate. After that incident, the only happiness they could remember on Eid was the howling laughter and dastardly mirth the policemen had so enjoyed.

The *khawaja sira* community has suffered this kind of brutish and degrading behaviour for decades. The Pakistani society has low tolerance and acceptance of anything that contradicts rigid belief systems, be they based on societal norms, cultural traditions, moral traits or religious teachings. When it comes to sexuality, the matter turns even graver. In Muslim societies pillared on a patriarchal structure, where gender discrimination runs asunder, the *khawaja sira* have little or no place in the social make up of society. They have survived without any form of identity or the most basic human rights.

However, their plight received special attention in 2009, after a harrowing incident in Taxila, near Islamabad, where local police reportedly attacked and raped a group of transgender wedding dancers. Muhammad Aslam Khai, an attorney specialising in Islamic law, filed a private case in the Pakistan Supreme Court. Khai's persistence and diligence finally gave *khawaja siras* official recognition and stature as third gender under the Pakistan Constitution. The Chief Justice of Pakistan, Iftikhar Muhammad Chaudhry, now hailed as a hero of the Third Sex minority, took the revolution forward and the Supreme Court, for the first time in the history of the country, granted the community their own gender category under Pakistan's National Database and Registration Authority (NADRA). As a result, *khawaja siras* can now have male transgender, female transgender or intersex written on their national identification cards. This catapulted a series of successful rulings in favour of the *khawaja sira* community by the Supreme Court. These included the formation of various judicial, law making and enforcing committees on a provincial and national level that work towards safeguarding the newly acquired rights of the third gender community. They now enjoy many of the rights of other citizens in Pakistan, including inheritance and employment rights. The police, who have been notoriously involved in the maltreatment of *khawaja siras*, have been especially warned to cease all forms of harassment under threat of serious prosecution.

The Supreme Court went further. It recommended that qualified *khawaja siras* now be given 2 per cent of the jobs in all sectors. According to the ruling, a Third Sex applicant with a tenth grade education is now deemed to have the same qualifications for government work as another citizen with a bachelor's degree. Moreover, in 2010, *khawaja siras* were also appointed as tax collectors. Using their special skills of persuasion, it has been reported, they have successfully collected hefty amounts of unpaid dues. Thus, the past few years have seen much official progress for the rights of the Third Sex, and what is more notable is the fact that they have been galvanised in a retrogressive and conservative country like Pakistan.

But, will the change in law usher in change in society's perception of the *khawaja sira* community?

Has the new legislation changed lives in the community, I ask Khushbu. She lets out a big snort from her powdered nose and guffaws at the apparent asininity of my question. 'You really think all these measures have currently helped us in any way possible or will in the near future?' Her belly laugh encourages laughter from her group of friends who have also joined our conversation, as they all live in a tiny, shabby house in a squalid neighbourhood of Lahore. Despite all the efforts and headway that has been made thus far, the actual assimilation of Third Sex empowerment has been lost in the murky waters of bureaucratic lassitude, institutional failures and indifference on the government's part. 'The government can't even provide basic necessities to entities they regard as individuals here, you think they would care for non-entities like us? We're not people to them. We're not even human. So while the common man has no electricity, gas and water, you think us lesser beings are going to fare any better?' says Khushbu with visible insouciance.

Since the Supreme Court ruling on identity cards, less than ten per cent of the *khawaja siras* have been able to obtain them stating their preferred gender designation. Most are still listed as male because they failed to submit the necessary documents such as birth certificates. 'Since we are worse than maggots in the eyes of others, our families have also had no qualms disposing us off like plagued vermin, you think we can go back and obtain our birth or school certificates?' Khushbu questions the idiocy of the situation. Some Muslim *khawaja siras* chose against getting their gender changed, as by doing so, they would be forbidden from performing pilgrimage, as Saudi Arabia does not recognize the Third Sex. The two percent quota allocation of jobs has only seen one province out of the four employing *khawaja siras*. The right to vote emboldened five members of the community to run for political office during the 2013 general election, but all failed to obtain a seat. The real impediment is the internal perception of bureaucrats and law enforcers. New laws and regulations are not easy to come about as it is, but what is harder is changing a mindset that is so deeply brainwashed with years of bigotry and rigid intransigence. The new laws may take a while to have actual impact, but at least the ball is now rolling instead of being kicked around.

'We came into this world with a *thumka* (a dance step), and we are going to *thumka* our way to the grave!' retorts Soniya, one of Khushbu's housemates, shimmying her hips and thrusting them to one side repeatedly to visually express her point further – which meant they will die doing what they do now and live the same quality of life. 'We have all long ago ceded to the plight of our fate', Khushbu explains. And then as an after thought adds, 'plight is the wrong word. Yes, we are cursed both literally and metaphorically, but we have gotten so accustomed to that part of our lives – which is a major chunk – that we had not only hardened ourselves to the bitter truth by internalising it, but our strength lies in managing to find happiness in the deepest abyss of our misery as well.'

Khushbu and her friends are all dancers; although that is not enough to sustain their livelihood. So they resort to more dire measures as well. 'When we're dancing in a room full of sweaty, horny men whose sexual desires are heightened by the thought of indulging in lewd perversions with "people like us", I close my eyes and imagine I'm on a stage in a land of the *goras* (Europe) where my rhythm mesmerises the audience and my beauty intoxicates them senseless,' Khushbu finishes with a dramatic flip of her hair and turns to look at my reaction with a smile. Soon the seriousness clouding her eyes takes away from the gaiety of it all as she continues her next thought. 'The brain is a very powerful organ,' she continues with her eyes narrowed. 'Once you learn to control it, you'll be surprised at how much you can really deceive it as well. Yes, I know; control and deception don't usually work for the same favour, but this world is a farce and deception your opium,' explains Khushbu. 'They all cease to exist. Their smell. Their laughter. Their brashness. And even though I am actually imprisoned in a derelict cage with my wings clipped off, I am still soaring inside. Even if just for a few moments, and that's one thing no one can take away from me irrespective of all the physical abuse and emotional trauma, of all the undue rejection and unconditional hatred.' A heavy silence fills the room, only to be broken by one of her comrades. 'Yeah, you soar till you get a rod plunged so far up your backside that it comes out of your mouth and smacks you back into reality!'

They all laugh. An orchestra of deep, effeminate, throaty and high-pitched laughter. The symphony sounded genuine, and completely free of shackles.

RANKING CITIES

Jeremy Henzell-Thomas

If you had a choice, which city would you like to live in?

There are a host of options. A web search will rapidly provide a list of the World's 'Greatest' and 'Best' Cities, the most 'Liveable', the most 'Loveable', the 'Smartest', the 'Best for Arts and Culture', the 'Greenest', the 'Deadliest', the 'Most Populous', the 'Noisiest', the 'Most Polluted', and, let us not forget, the 'Most Expensive'. More focused searches come up with such things as the World's 'Top 10 Halal-friendly Holiday Spots', the 'Best Cities for Muslims', the 'Largest Cities in OIC Member States', the 'Highest Muslim Population' in Cities in the EU, and so on.

We might start with Muslim population. There are an estimated 1.7 million Muslims in Paris and its surrounding area, by far the largest population of any city in the EU. Some demographic forecasts predict that Marseille will be the first Muslim-majority city in Western Europe, and alarm at this projection is often sounded by far right Islamophobes, with one website claiming that the 'French City with 40 per cent Muslim Population is the Most Dangerous City in Europe' and that 'Muslims have now set up unofficial checkpoints in various parts of Marseille'. Even this, however, did not sound the false alarm as loudly as the risible pronouncement of a self-proclaimed American terrorism expert in January 2015 on Fox News that the city of Birmingham in the UK (with an estimated Muslim population of around 25 per cent) was a 'no-go area', where non-Muslims dare not enter for fear of the religious police who beat people who do not dress according to Muslim dress codes, and where even the police keep away. Other European cities with around a quarter of the population estimated as Muslim include Brussels, Amsterdam, and Rotterdam, and in the UK, Luton, Bradford and Blackburn. Stockholm, Malmö and Leicester weigh in at around 20 per cent, with Berlin, Vienna, Copenhagen, Cologne, London and Paris between 9 per cent and 15 per cent.

The category of 'Most Liveable Cities' is one example of how problematic rankings can be. Different ranking systems with different concepts of 'Liveability', and different factors or criteria for measuring it, inevitably come up with different rankings, and such variability will always be found in rankings which are not simply based on raw statistics such as population, number of homicides, or other relatively objective measures. International Making Cities Liveable (IMCL), discussing 'the Value of Rankings and the Meaning of Liveability', points out that every city wants to be rated highly on the 'Liveability' Index because such status can 'attract new business and investments, boost local economies and real estate markets, and foster community involvement and pride.' The rankings are 'a powerful tool for economic development', and there is 'cut-throat competition and lobbying by world cities' to achieve a high position in the most prestigious rankings such as the Economist Intelligence Unit's (EIU) 'Global Liveability Ranking', the Mercer 'Quality of Living Survey', or *Monocle* magazine's 'Most Liveable Cities Index'.

In 2015, as in the previous year, cities in Australia and Canada occupied seven of the top ten positions out of 140 cities in the EIU's 'Global Liveability Ranking'. Given the dominance of English-speaking cities, this ranking has been criticised for being overly anglocentric. The EIU notes that the most liveable places tend to be 'mid-sized cities in wealthier countries with a relatively low population density', which explains why megacities like London and New York do not make it to the top rank. Unsurprisingly, cities with major conflicts are ranked lowest, including Damascus (140), Karachi (136) and Tripoli (132). Dhaka and Algiers are also ranked in the bottom 10, although major hotspots, such as Kabul and Baghdad, are excluded. The EIU also flags up those cities experiencing the biggest decline in standards of living over the past five years, and concomitant problems with unemployment, violence and civil unrest. These include (in addition to Damascus and Tripoli) Athens (69), Moscow (73), Muscat (88), Tunis (103), Cairo (120), Caracas (126), and Kiev (124).

Obviously, there has to be some preconception or operational definition to start with about what 'Liveability' is. The term is probably used more often to describe 'standard of living' than 'quality of life'. Standard of living is relatively easier to rank according to measures which are claimed to be 'objective, neutral and unbiased'. Criteria such as crime rates, health statistics, income growth, cost of living, sanitation standards, expenditures on city services, infrastructure, local transport, and even 'artistic and cultural opportunities' (as factored in by Forbes in their ranking of American cities) are generally more accessible than more elusive and subjective perceptions of quality which are not always bound up with functional considerations. It is also difficult to measure 'quality of life' issues centred on personal circumstances and states of mind which might include mental health issues, happiness, loneliness, social exclusion, and discrimination, although some measure of the latter might be provided by statistics on 'hate crimes'. As IMCL points out, 'standard of living issues are not directly correlated with happiness, with a sense that life is meaningful, that we are of value to others, and that there is much to be discovered and celebrated in the human and physical world around us.' Yet, it is also the case that these important aspects of well-being and quality of life are 'profoundly influenced by the built environment – by a city's liveability'. This comes more clearly into focus when we consider the most vulnerable and needy members of society, children, the elderly, those who are economically or socially disadvantaged or marginalised, refugees, asylum seekers and other categories of 'migrant'.

Such considerations figure strongly in the stated mission of IMCL, which includes the need to 'recognise and combat the negative impact of our built environment on physical, social and mental health'; to 'adopt planning and urban design decisions that will make our cities and suburbs more liveable for children, elders and the poor'; to 'emphasise ethical land use patterns to reduce extreme economic disparities'; to 'strengthen compact urban neighbourhoods to maintain diversity of ethnic and cultural identity'; and to build 'multifunctional' spaces that can 'regenerate civic engagement and democratic participation'. While important benchmark statistics are provided by Mercer to underpin the rankings from EIU and others, IMCL is surely right that 'a city may have to aim higher than to be placed top in these rankings to be truly "liveable"'.

To appreciate the potential difference between 'Liveability' and 'Lovability', we have to turn to the global life-style magazine *Monocle*. It identifies Palermo, Colombo, Tel Aviv, Chiang Mai and San Jose as the five 'Most Loveable Cities' (2013) which 'might not be slick or smart, might be a bit dusty in the corners or a nightmare to navigate, and they won't be making our top 25 most liveable cities list any time soon, but who cares? One thing they are not, is boring.'

While Palermo is here rated the most 'Loveable' city, a different story emerges from the European Commission report 'Quality of Life in Cities' (2013) which looked at perceptions of 79 European cities. Here, there is a relatively high level of dissatisfaction only in a few cities, of which Palermo is one. While Athens scores the highest level of dissatisfaction (52 per cent of respondents), Palermo (28 per cent) is amongst the other four badly rated cities, which also include Naples (34 per cent) and Marseilles (25 per cent). By contrast, there is an overall level of satisfaction of at least 80 per cent in all but eight of the cities surveyed. Of the 16 cities with a 95 per cent satisfaction rate or above, 12 are from Scandinavia, Germany, the Netherlands or Austria.

All of this shows how difficult it is to come up with rankings which can be reliably regarded as definitive in terms of how they factor in all relevant criteria. Anyway, relevant to whom?

The Global Power City Index (GPCI), a ranking of the world's top 40 cities by the Institute for Urban Strategies at the Mori Memorial Fund in Tokyo, aims to judge the 'comprehensive power of a city'. Pointing out that since half the world's population now live in cities, it affirms the need more than ever to create a liveable environment within attractive urban spaces so as to attract people, goods and wealth. The Index is based on six factors: Economy, Research and Development, Cultural Interaction, Liveability, Ecology and Natural Environment, and Accessibility. It also factors in the subjective preferences of five type of people considered to be important in cities: Managers, Researchers, Artists, Visitors, and Residents. In the 2014 rankings, London retains its place at the top of the comprehensive ranking from the previous year and further increased its score to widen the gap with New York at No. 2. Four Asian cities (Tokyo, Singapore, Seoul and Hong Kong) figure in the top ten, as well as four other European cities: Paris, Amsterdam, Berlin and Vienna. However, only two of the top ten cities in this ranking system are placed in the top ten 'Best Cities' in the *Condé Nast* World Readers' Choice Awards for 2015. They are London, at No. 10 (compared with the top spot in the

GPCI Index) and Vienna at No.3. Florence and Budapest are ranked the best. Kyoto is the only Asian city in the top ten, although Tokyo figures in the top 20, and Singapore, Hong Kong and Shanghai in the top 30.

Three cities with Muslim-majority populations are ranked in the top 40 in the GPCI Index: Istanbul (No. 21, between Los Angeles and Vancouver); Kuala Lumpur (No.34, between Taipei and Moscow); and Cairo (No. 40, below Mumbai). Of interest is the inclusion of a GPCI+ ranking, which emphasises the 'intangible values', the elements that appeal to 'human senses'. While Tokyo is ranked 4th overall, it comes in at No. 3 in GPCI+ because of its high scores in Sense of Safety in Public Places, Kindness of Residents, On-Time Performance of International Airport and Ease of Transportation, among others. Increased numbers of tourists also helped Tokyo climb from No. 8 to No. 6 in Cultural Interaction, previously not a strong feature of the city. Although the GPCI is widely respected as fair, one might still expect some lobbying for Tokyo to be involved in an Index produced by a Japanese institute based in the city, and this again raises the question of 'objectivity'.

If Istanbul is the top 'Muslim' city at No. 21 in the GPCI rankings for 2015, it is noteworthy that it comes in at No.3 in the 'Top 25 Destinations' for 2015 according to the ratings of travellers on TripAdvisor, the world's largest travel website. But what is even more striking is that the No. 1 spot is taken by Marrakech in Morocco. Other cities which appear nowhere in most city rankings also make it to the top ten: Siem Reap, the gateway to the Angkor region in Cambodia, comes in at No. 2, Hanoi in Vietnam at No. 4, and Goreme in Turkey at No. 14. London is still there in the top ten, but at No. 6, and New York City, the runner-up to top-ranked London in the GPCI rankings, is ranked at No. 11. Dubai is in 24th position, quite a few places below Ubud in Indonesia at No. 15. Award winners in the TripAdvisor ratings are determined using an algorithm that takes into account the quantity and quality of reviews and ratings for hotels, restaurants, and attractions in destinations worldwide over a 12-month period. Unsurprisingly, the priorities and preferences of tourists searching out 'exotic' or culturally iconic locations do not readily correlate with Indices of 'Liveability' based on standards of living or quality of life. This lack of fit is only too evident in the variable standing of Athens. It is rated at No. 20 in TripAdvisor's Top Destinations, above

Budapest, Hong Kong, Dubai and Sydney, but, as we have seen, it also scores the highest level of dissatisfaction (52 per cent of respondents) in the 'Quality of Life in Cities' 2013 rankings. The respondents consulted here are not tourists ticking off 'bucket shop' destinations, but are actual residents of the cities surveyed.

We might take a quick look at some other city rankings to demonstrate the extent of variability. Celebrating the 21st century as the 'Century of the City', the *National Geographic's* 'World's Best Cities: Celebrating 220 Great Destinations' (2014) surveyed perceptions of cities according to a range of criteria: Olympic, Festival, Silver Screen, Food, Haunted, Island, Happiest, All-American, Nightlife, Eco-smart, Oceanfront, High-Altitude, Canal, For Song, Walled, and Spa. The inevitable subjectivity of the judgements can be gauged from the introduction to this resource ('a must-have for all urban adventurers, on-the-go travellers and armchair travellers alike') which claims the reader will find 'a playful, informative mix of inspirational personal narratives, photo galleries, and fun facts, plus sidebars on oddities, local food and shopping, novels that offer a sense of the city, local secrets, and more'. In the 'Top Ten Happiest Cities', for example, Koh Samui in Thailand ranks the highest, followed by San Sebastian in Spain, and Auckland in New Zealand. Madison comes in at No. 4 because 'locals stay active all year round in the Wisconsin capital, kayaking, cross-country skiing, and jogging along landscaped lakeshores.' Kuala Lumpur is rated the 6th Happiest City. The position of Dubai as the 8th Happiest might arouse some variable reactions, including some sceptical or downright incredulous ones from immigrant workers in this much vaunted Gulf glitz-centre. Or as an article in the *Daily Telegraph* (dated 19 October 2015) asked: 'Who in their right mind would want to visit Dubai?' Referring to it as 'sterile and morally destitute', the article describes how 'Dubai's masters' treat guest like 'disposable slaves' and 'appear not to care if these people live or die'.

Moving from people excluded from the happiness provided by a decent meal, we might turn to the 'Top Ten Food Cities' in the *National Geographic's* 'World's Best Cities'. Louisville, Kentucky is rated as the top food destination, followed by Chennai in India, then Buffalo, NY and Ho Chi Minh City, Vietnam. In the more traditional Michelin rankings for the same year (2014), however, Tokyo kept its crown in surpassing Paris as the gourmet capital of the world with a record number of Michelin starred restaurants. Clearly there is a world of difference between *fugu* (the potentially deadly poisonous puffer fish, one of the delicacies which might be served up in a Michelin-starred restaurant in Tokyo) and the kind of fare which might contribute to the high standing of Louisville and Buffalo in the rankings of 'Foodie' cities. In the former case, the HotBrown, a midnight snack invented for revellers consisting of an open-faced Turkey sandwich on Texas toast with bacon, tomatoes and a cream sauce; and in Buffalo, what else but 'buffalo wings', the tangy chicken wings which are a favourite of bar-crawlers the world over? To muddy the waters further, neither Louisville nor Buffalo appear in the 'Top 10 Food Cities' on the 'ucityguides' website (the 'ultimate urban travel guide'); instead, it showcases the more orthodox and predictable destinations: New York City and Tokyo in top spots, followed by 6 European cities.

Such widely disparate rankings only serve to confirm the general point that ranking systems in many areas need to be taken with a large pinch of salt.

If you are confused about which city is the 'Most Liveable' (or 'Loveable'), the 'Happiest' or the 'Best for Food', we might not find any greater consistency in rankings of the best cities for 'Arts and Culture'. The *Condé Nast Traveller* Readers' Choice Awards for 'Best Cities for Arts and Culture' (2014) rated Krakow in Poland as No. 1, followed by Luxor. The rest of the top ten were mainly Imperial capitals of Europe, including St Petersburg, Budapest, Vienna, Prague, and Rome, but did not include London, Paris or Berlin. These three cities, however, followed top-ranked New York City in 2nd, 3rd, and 4th place in the 'Arts and Culture' category of Time Out's ranking of the 'World's Greatest Cities' (2009). In 8th place was Istanbul, between Chicago and Rome. 'Arts and Culture' is one of six criteria that make up the overall ranking by *Time Out* of the 'World's Greatest Cities', the others being Architecture, Buzz, Food and Drink, Quality of Life, and World Status.

As for the 'World's Smartest Cities', one ranking is provided by the IESE 'Cities in Motion' Index (ICIM). This is, according to the 'fastcoexist' website, 'one of the most comprehensive index of cities to date. While others look at "liveability", it attempts to include more or less everything.' We may all have our favourite cities, and our subjective reasons for loving them. They may make us happy, have a feel-good factor, give us a buzz, keep us entertained, look gorgeous at night, but the ICIM Index is not wedded to impressions. It is based on 50 indicators covering every facet of urban life, its 10 different dimensions encompassing governance, public management, urban planning, technology, environment, international outreach, social cohesion, mobility and transportation, human capital, and economy. It assesses technology by measures like broadband penetration; environmental performance by particle emissions; and international outreach by the numbers of visitors by aeroplane. In 2014, the top three positions were occupied by Tokyo, London and New York, respectively. Three Swiss cities (Zurich, Geneva, and Basel) ranked 4th, 6th and 7th. ICIM also identifies cities as 'high potential' (like Shanghai and Guangzhou), 'challengers' (rapidly improving cities like Toronto), 'vulnerable' (deteriorating cities like Athens), and 'consolidated' (maintaining an existing high ranking). The comprehensive nature of its metrics has the result of relegating some perpetually favourite places to uncharacteristically lowly positions. Rome, for instance, comes in at 54th and Istanbul at 75th out of 135 in this ranking of 'smartness', which, as 'fastcoexist' emphasises, is 'a catch-all phrase for a well-operated city that is pleasant to live in'. But of course, 'no city is perfect. Even the top cities have major drawbacks. Half the top-10 score poorly for "social cohesion", for example, with Tokyo coming in at 125th, London at 96th, and New York at 110th.' That said, one might want to question what is meant by social cohesion in this context, and how it is measured. New York also drops down to 37th for the environment, and Paris, which is fifth overall, has a ranking of 87th for public administration. ICIM reaches the inevitable conclusion that 'there is no single model of success'. City improvement depends on defining the model to be followed and identifying the specific areas in which the city needs to improve. Yet 'it is not enough for a city to stand out in a single area or dimension: cities should strive to achieve acceptable minimum rates overall, as areas tend to be interrelated.'

If ranking of cities as the 'best', the 'smartest', the most 'liveable' or the most 'powerful' attempt to factor in a large number of indicators, other rankings may be derived from more focused metrics. The ranking of how dangerous a city is may be based on homicide rates per 100,000 people compiled from criminal justice and public health systems, as in the UNODC (United Nations Office on Drugs and Crime) data for 65 of the most populous cities. The 2009 data from this source revealed the highest murder rates in cities in Venezuela and Central America. Mexico City, notorious for its drug violence, had a murder rate of 8.4 per year, but this might seem like a safe haven compared to Caracas, with a rate of 122 or Guatemala City at 118.3. New York City, where one might expect the rate to be high, came in at 5.6, one more per year than Amsterdam at 4.4, the highest rate in Western Europe. If Amsterdam seems relatively safe compared to those cities in the Americas where one is 25 times more likely to be murdered, its murder rate is, according to this index, still ten times higher than Tokyo's (0.4), and seven times higher than Cairo's (0.6). Glasgow's rate of 3.3 is just ahead of Brussels (3). London's rate of 1.6 indicates a 1 in 62,500 chance of being murdered, compared to 1 in 820 in Caracas, or 1 in half a million in safe Lisbon with its very low rate of 0.2. Men are far more likely to be homicide victims in almost every country. In Venezuela, Mali and Libya for example, over 90 per cent of victims are men. Women face a significantly higher risk of murder in just two of the world's countries: Nauru (where 80 per cent of all victims are female) and Malta (75 per cent).

As for the 'Noisiest Cities', a Citiquiet survey undertaken in 2014 judged three of the top four to be in India (Mumbai, Kolkata and Delhi), with Cairo in 3rd place and New York City in 7th. The noise level in Mumbai , the noisiest city, can reach over 100 decibels, caused by severe traffic congestion and overpopulation. Construction, loudspeakers, firecrackers, festivals, honking, rickshaws and taxis all contribute to the bedlam. Cairo is not only the largest city in both the Middle East and Africa, but also, according to Citiquiet, 'known for being alive 24 hours a day'. The average noise level at 7:30 am is 90 decibels, where the EPA (Environmental Protection Agency) proposes an acceptable level to be between 35 and 55 decibels. Perhaps surprisingly, Madrid is ranked noisier than New York, a ranking which can be partly attributed to a population which rarely turns in before midnight and a lively nightlife centred on roaring bars and clubs which usually do not close until 2 a.m.

The high ranking of Indian cities in noise pollution is matched by their prominence on the winner's podium in air pollution. Statistics compiled by the WHO on particulate matter for more than 1,600 cities for the years 2008-2013 rank four Indian cities as the most polluted on earth (Delhi, Gwalior, Patna, and Raipur), followed by three from Pakistan (Karachi, Peshawar and Rawalpindi). The WHO advises that fine particles of less than 2.5 micrometres in diameter (PM2.5) should not exceed 10 micrograms per cubic metre (ug/m3), but the top ten most polluted cities have 10 to 15 times this level, with top-ranked Delhi at 153 ug/m3 and tenth-placed Lucknow at 96 ug/m3. The *International Business Times*, reporting these findings in an article leading up to World Environment Day in 2015, points out that 'more than 200 million people worldwide are affected by air pollution. The problem is deadly – outdoor air pollution was estimated to cause 3.7 million premature deaths worldwide in 2012.' And it would be mistaken for cities in the 'West' to be too smug in the face of high pollution levels in the Indian Subcontinent and in other cities like Beijing which are synonymous with smog. A study carried out by researchers at King's College London, and reported in the *Guardian* in 2015, revealed that there are 9,500 premature deaths each year in London due to long-term exposure to two key air pollutants (fine particulates and the toxic gas nitrogen dioxide), more than twice as many as previously thought.

From pollution of all kinds, we might take a more inspiring look at cities judged to be the 'Greenest'. Ranking here can, of course, depend on a host of different criteria ranging from reduced carbon emissions to large open spaces, ample bicycling trails, and citywide recycling programmes. In the ranking of the 'Top 12 Greenest Cities in the World' by *Cities Journal* in 2014, the top two (Malmö and Melbourne) have made great strides in reducing carbon emissions. The Kyoto Protocol called for an international reduction of carbon dioxide emissions by 5 percent, but Malmö adopted the much more ambitious goal of 25 percent. One neighbourhood in Malmö, Western Harbour, gets all of its power from renewable sources. As for Melbourne, a persistent drought since the 1990s has necessitated a strong focus on sustainability, with the even more ambitious goal of becoming a city with net zero emissions by 2020. The 3rd and 4th most highly ranked 'Green-friendly' cities, Bogota and Minneapolis have both created miles of cycling paths within the city. In Minneapolis, these amount to a magnificent 84 miles of trails that wind amongst the city's many green spaces and parks. Chicago, in 5th place, has reduced greenhouse gases through its acres and acres of energy-efficient 'green' roofs. The Windy City is reported to have 'at least 359 vegetated roofs in the city proper which cover 5,469,463 square feet of the city's buildings. The rooftop gardens plant food for human consumption, house hives for fresh honey, and help stamp out pollution by dealing with excess carbon dioxide. There are no cities outside North America (the USA and Canada), Europe or Australia in the top 12 in this ranking.

While Malmö (at No.1) and Copenhagen (at No.10) both figure in the top ten of the *Cities Journal* 'Greenest' rankings, four Nordic cities (Copenhagen, Stockholm, Helsinki and Oslo) figure in the top 10 positions in the Global Green Economy Index for 2014, an in-depth survey of how 60 countries and 70 cities are doing in developing more environmentally friendly economies. In top place is Copenhagen, with a goal to be carbon-neutral by 2025 and with a city infrastructure designed to be conducive to bicycling and walking rather than cars. Amsterdam, another bicycle-friendly city, is 2nd, and Stockholm, the EU's first city to win the European Green Capital Award, is 3rd. Paradoxically, perhaps, New York, rated the 7th noisiest city in the world, is also rated the 7th greenest in this Index. The only other non-European city in the top 10 is Singapore at No. 9. This city, Asia's greenest, aims to have zero waste in landfills by 2050.

This cursory look at just a few categories for ranking cities can only scratch the surface of this highly complex field. We could go on to take a look at the 'Most Expensive Cities in the World'. In one measure in 2008, the top spot was occupied by the 'super-premium area of prime Central London', or at least according to some statistics on apartment prices per square metre in city centres. Even at that time, this area of London was leaps ahead of 2nd-placed Upper Manhattan in New York, though mere 'luxury property' in other swanky areas of London came in at No. 4. In 2015, another index of real estate prices, the Knight Frank Wealth Report, ranked Monaco in first place, followed by Hong Kong, London and New York. We might also look at the 'Cost of Living Index' published by Numbeo, the world's largest database of user-contributed data about cities and countries. The database for 2015, based on 2,054,546 prices in 5,465 cities, generates comparative indices for consumer price, rent, groceries, restaurants, and local purchasing power in 516 cities. Swiss cities are prominent in the higher echelons of this Index.

But rather than plough on in this way, always gawping at the 'top ten', we might turn our attention to Muslim communities, whether in Muslim-majority countries and cities, or in minority communities in predominantly non-Muslim cities. Looking back at the rankings we have already assembled, what do they tell us about any of this? Well, the dominance of non-Muslim-majority societies in Western Europe, Scandinavia, the USA, Canada, Australia and Asia is only too evident in so many rankings focused on the 'best', the 'most powerful' , the 'most liveable', the 'happiest', the 'best for arts and culture', the 'smartest', and the 'greenest'. There are some exceptions (not without their idiosyncrasies) with Kuala Lumpur and Dubai amongst the top 10 'happiest' in the National Geographic rankings, and most notably Marrakech as the top destination for TripAdvisor travellers. Istanbul hits the top ten for Arts and Culture in one ranking of the 'World's Greatest Cities', and three cities with Muslim-majority populations are ranked in the top 40 in the Global Power City Index: Istanbul (21), Kuala Lumpur (34) and Cairo (40). It is also worth noting that of 156 countries (rather than cities) ranked for Happiness by the Sustainable Development Solutions Network in 2012, the UAE was in 14th place and Oman in 16th. The UK was ranked 17th, just ahead of Qatar. Nevertheless, eight of the top 10 places were occupied by European countries, of which 5 were Scandinavian, with Denmark and Norway taking the top two places. Malaysia was ranked 56th and Turkey 77th. The Index was compiled using three main types of variables to measure subjective well-being: measures of positive and negative emotions, and evaluation of life as a whole. In the WHO Index of 191 countries in *Health Care in 2000* (the year the report was last produced), Oman is ranked 8th, Saudi Arabia 26th and the UAE 27th, all ahead of the USA (37). Nevertheless, European countries occupied 17 of the top 20 places, with France and Italy in 1st and 2nd place, and the UK in 17th.

Despite the positive ranking of some Muslim-majority cities and countries, the downside, though, is hard to avoid. As we have seen, in the EIU's 'Global Liveability Ranking' (admittedly suspected of being 'anglocentric') out of 140 cities we can find Damascus (140), Karachi (136), and Tripoli (132), with Dhaka and Algiers also ranked in the bottom 10, and then Cairo (120), and Tunis (103). In the field of Gender Equality, out of 130 countries listed in the *Global Gender Gap Report 2008*, 8 of the top 10 places were taken by European countries, 4 of which are Scandinavian. The USA ranked 27th, and Muslim-majority countries occupied 15 of the bottom 20 places. The variables selected were economic participation and opportunity, educational attainment, political empowerment, health and survival. Although these gender equality rankings relate to countries, they are clearly highly applicable to cities.

Of course, one can have reservations about all these rankings. The WHO rankings on Health Care, for example, have been criticised as depending crucially on 'a number of underlying assumptions – some of them logically incoherent, some characterised by substantial uncertainty, and some rooted in ideological beliefs and values that not everyone shares'. The existence of logical fallacies, uncertainties, and ideological biases exposed by complaints of this kind need to be taken very seriously and could be applied to any number of ranking systems. However, for all their flaws, rankings are unlikely to fade in importance as long as countries are concerned about how they stack up against each other and cities jostling for kudos and prestige. As always, we need to search for balance in how we draw useful implications and conclusions from the plethora of research available. To do so, we must guard against polemics driven either by one-sided advocacy or by intemperate criticism.

In an article posted on MuslimMatters.org, Youssef Chouhoud describes how, during a flight to Egypt, he came across an opinion piece discussing *Monocle* Magazine's annual index of the world's most liveable cities. 'After weighing about a dozen different factors ranging from school performance to the prevalence of independent retail stores and restaurants (what the magazine dubs the "Zara/Starbucks" quotient), *Monocle's* top ten sites with the "best quality of life" were decisively mid-sized and European.' What struck Choudoud was that 'the article noticeably lacked any meaningful critique of the list's methodology or ultimate results.' Later, he came across another *Financial Times* article that 'took to task *Monocle's* preconceptions and conclusions – and offered an alternate, equally valid perspective on what makes a city worth living in'. This prompted him to ask the question: 'What would a Muslim Liveability Index look like?' Recognising the complexity and scale of the research needed to undertake such a project, including how to decide on which metrics to use, he suspects that we won't be seeing such an index for some time. A ranking of the top cities for Muslims to live in would surely be fraught with contentious issues on several fronts, including 'controversial secular criteria' and 'religious sensibilities'. Nevertheless, he contends that if done right, 'this undertaking would likely be a watershed moment in global Muslim culture. It could, for instance, help clear up many misconceptions about living Islamically in the West. Conversely, the data could shine an optimistic light on Muslim-majority societies that are largely written off in this discourse.'

Whatever we might think about such an idea, it does raise the profoundly important question of how we give space to diverse and alternative perspectives in the manifold ways in which we are continually drawn into evaluating, grading, measuring and ranking so many dimensions of human life. By the way, according to *Arabian Business's* 'Top Ten Halal-friendly Holiday Spots', the winner is Bosnia and Herzegovina, followed by Singapore. Three European cities make it to this list: London (7th), Munich (9th) and Vienna (10th). And, of course, one can always go further in questioning alternative criteria themselves on the basis of other alternative principles, including ethical ones. Some Muslims may legitimately seek out not what is traditionally 'halal' but what is *tayyib* – in other words, food which has been reared under strict standards of animal welfare, usually 'free range' or 'organic'. How would that be factored into a 'Muslim Liveability Index'? How also would one factor in cultural preferences which some Muslims might have, but which might be forbidden, frowned on, or at least avoided, in some, or even many, Muslim communities? Would a Muslim's love of Western classical music, for example, be recognised in rankings of top cities for a Muslim to live in? Which Muslim, in any case? And what of a Muslim who practises yoga? He or she would be forbidden to do so in Malaysia, but a Muslim seeking a rich and varied vein of cultural activity might be happy to know that city liveability rankings had factored in some measure of intercultural richness and variety. And the same goes for any open-minded and inquiring citizen, whether Muslim or not, seeking to explore and engage with other cultures in a vibrant city.

That brings me to my closing personal perspective. I will not attempt to rank my top ten cities. Rather, I ask myself if there is one city which I rank particularly highly, one that has impacted me in a special way. Many cities I have visited, and in which I have studied, worked and lived, come to mind for all sorts of reasons, spiritual, cultural, architectural, academic, gastronomic, 'green', and, of course, romantic. In a sense I am returning to the 'Loveable' category, the one we briefly explored through the Monocle rankings, in which Palermo came first. Well, Palermo is not on my list, as I have never been there, and neither are Colombo, Tel Aviv, Chiang Mai or San Jose, the next most loveable in that list. High on my own list are some spiritually meaningful destinations and iconic sacred sites of pilgrimage and palpable *baraka:* Istanbul, where my wife and I committed to Islam; Mecca, where the awesome singularity of the Ka'bah enabled me to turn away from the obnoxious Makkah Royal Clock Tower Hotel and the brutalism of other mammoth developments catering for the superrich; and Chartres in France, where a sense of great mercy caused of mine and my wife's eyes to fill with tears as we crossed the threshold of the sublime Gothic Cathedral. We were touched also in Sarajevo, where we heard a multi-faith choir of young people singing *samo da rata ne bude* ('just let there be no war'). Important to me too are three places where I sought (and still seek) knowledge: London, Cambridge and Edinburgh, and two places which have fed my abiding love of music in the German tradition: Vienna and Berlin. I also rate Birmingham (not far to drive to from where I live), not because of its 'Muslimness', but because of the world-class acoustics in Symphony Hall and the salt and pepper squid I can find in its Chinatown. It is likely that this list is unique, as it surely should be if we are being true to ourselves and being always open to the unexpected rather than chasing after conventional 'bucket list' experiences or those judged to be compatible with a tribal affiliation, whether national, cultural or religious.

As a British Muslim with Welsh ancestors, the city that has a special place in my heart is one that is ranked first in one unlikely index: 'The Smallest Cities in the UK'. If the Vatican City is often ranked as the smallest 'city' in the world (though actually a country) with a population of 770, none of whom are permanent residents, St. David's in Wales is officially the smallest city in the UK with a population of 1,797. Like

Wells in Somerset, its cathedral gives it that 'city' status, irrespective of its size. I discovered St. David's a few years ago as I walked the 180 miles of the majestic and beautiful Pembrokeshire Coast Path over twelve days. It is named after St. David, the fifth century patron saint of Wales, whose emblem is a white dove. Later, I learned that he is reputed to have founded Glastonbury Abbey in Somerset. I lived in the small town of Glastonbury for many years, and it is there that I first encountered the heart of Islam. These small places perhaps remind us that the winner's podium need not be stacked with the biggest, the best, the smartest, the glitziest, the most expensive, the tastiest, or even the most liveable or the happiest. Meaningfulness has so many personal facets, and it can surely never be wholly encompassed by any list of rankings.

INSIDE THE VATICAN

Paul Vallely

The Vatican Bank is housed in a medieval tower that once served as a dungeon. Its lower floors have no windows. To gain admittance you have to leave Italy and go through the gate of the Porta Sant'Anna, be checked by two Swiss Guards, and pass through a two-door security kiosk inset in a plate glass window. Once inside you encounter, by the manned reception desk, a cash machine in the wall. The language which flashes up asking you to insert your cash card is Latin: *Insertio scidulam quaeso ut faciundam cognoscas rationem*. The semiotics of all this are clear: communication between what is inside this place and the outside world will be made as difficult as possible.

I was there by invitation. The email had come as something of a shock. The bank's new press officer – it had never before had such a person – wrote to invite me to enter what has been for generations one of the world's most secretive institutions. And not just to look around. Someone inside the bank had heard that I had begun work on a much-expanded second edition of my biography of Pope Francis. The offer was that officials would talk me through the financial reforms which were just part of the revolution in which the first non-European pope for a millennium was turning the Church of Rome upside-down.

Beyond the reception area, up a short flight of curved stairs, was a cream and brown marble rotunda. Round the edges stood eight highly-polished tellers desks at which representatives of religious orders, wealthy dioceses and Catholic charities deposit funds for onward transmission to pay clergy and build churches, schools and hospitals in the developing world. The official name of the bank is the *Instiutio per le Opere di Religione* (the Institute for Religious Works), known in Rome as the IOR.

Since much of its money came from collection plates, the IOR handled unusually large amounts of cash. And much of the money was wired out covertly to poor countries and failed states without functioning banking systems. Transparency and accountability have, therefore, never been high on the IOR's list of desiderata. Small wonder that, over the years, the Vatican Bank had become a byword for clandestine and dodgy dealing.

For such a small state the Vatican has a political and financial set-up which is unduly complex. This is, in part, because it consists of two administrations – the Vatican and the Holy See – entities that are in some ways separate and distinct but which also overlap in some key areas.

Vatican City is the last remnant of the territory once known as the Papal States. For more than a thousand years popes ruled as temporal as well as spiritual leaders over large swathes of central Italy. That came to an end in the mid-nineteenth century with the creation of the Kingdom of Italy and the retirement of the last ruler of the Papal States, Pope Pius IX (1846–78), to a tiny enclave where he became known as the 'prisoner in the Vatican'. The Vatican as it is today only came into existence in 1929 when the man who went on to become the Italian dictator Benito Mussolini signed the Lateran Treaty on behalf of King Victor Emmanuel III with a representative of the Pope. It created an 108-acre Vatican enclave within the city of Rome as an independent sovereign state whose territory, which includes St Peter's Square is distinguished from the territory of Italy only by a white line around the edge of the square. No passport is needed to cross from Italy into the Vatican and indeed the treaty grants a number of other Church properties around the city, and further afield, the same extraterritorial status enjoyed by foreign embassies. This sovereign territory is ruled by the Pope as a non-hereditary elected absolute monarch. In the person of the pontiff resides all legislative, executive and judicial power over the Vatican City State and its 594 citizens and the 2,400 workers who run its police force, fire service, post office and the highly profitable Vatican Museums. It has its own railway station and helipad and on occasions issues its own coins which are highly sought after by collectors. Its international reach is limited to membership of bodies like the International Telecommunication Union, Universal Postal Union and Interpol. The Vatican owns 18,000 works of art which would fetch billions if they ever went on the market but which in its books are valued at just one euro on the grounds that 'they belong to humanity'. The finances of the Vatican State, with its steady flow of tourists, are stable.

The Holy See, by contrast, is not a geographical entity but a spiritual, pastoral, administrative and political one. The Holy See is a term which refers to the body of universal government through which the Pope runs the global Catholic Church and its 1.2 billion members. By contrast with the Vatican City State, which dates back only to 1929, the Holy See can trace its roots back to the arrival of St Peter in Rome nearly two millennia ago. It is the oldest surviving juridical entity in human history. It does not fit the usual definition of statehood; it has not had a long-standing defined territory or population but it has had a continuing legal status in international law and has the oldest active continuous diplomatic service in the world, dating back to at least the Council of Nicea in AD 325. It is an independent sovereign entity which has diplomatic relations with 180 states. It is accorded permanent observer status at the United Nations. Its administrative body, known as the Roman Curia, runs the Catholic Church, overseeing forty ministerial departments known as dicasteries. It operates 116 diplomatic missions around the world, organising the Pope's overseas trips, and running the Vatican's radio station and daily newspaper. Its most prominent departments are the Congregation for the Doctrine of the Faith, which polices Catholic doctrine; the Congregation for Bishops, which approves the appointment of bishops worldwide; the Congregation for the Evangelisation of Peoples, which oversees missionary activities; and the Pontifical Council for Justice and Peace, which deals with social, peace and environmental issues.

The separation of roles between the Vatican State and the Holy See, and the overlaps between them, can be confusing to outsiders. The Swiss Guard – the military body responsible for the personal security of the Pope, following in the tradition of Swiss mercenaries historically recruited by popes – is resident in the state but employed by the Holy See and yet its members hold Vatican City State passports. Though it is the Vatican City State which is the recognised national territory under international law, it is the Holy See that conducts diplomatic relations on its behalf and enters into international agreements on behalf of the Pope. Foreign ambassadors are officially accredited not to the Vatican City but to the Holy See and papal representatives to states and international organisations represent the Holy See not the Vatican State. And though the Holy See uses Church Latin as its official language, its working language is Italian, as is that of the Vatican state, though the Holy See uses French as its main diplomatic language.

The finances of the Holy See, unlike those of the Vatican State, are unpredictable. It has income from the money it invested after Mussolini paid it 1.75 million lira in compensation for Italy's confiscation of the Papal States, covering much of central Italy, sixty years earlier; low interest rates have reduced the yield on this to between €15m and €25m in recent years. It holds some very expensive property in Rome and elsewhere, but this produces comparatively little income since the 2,000 palaces and apartments are largely used to house clergy. So the annual donation of around €70m from the Vatican Bank to the Holy See has been a significant element in its finances, exceeded only by donations from the faithful around the world which the US business magazine *Fortune* estimated to top $85 million in 2013. Until the advent of the recent financial reforms of Pope Francis all these funds were controlled by an impenetrable organisation known as the Administration of the Patrimony of the Apostolic See (APSA). According to a 2012 Moneyval report it has €680m on deposit with the Bank of England, the US Federal Reserve, the Deutsche Bundesbank, the Bank for International Settlement and others. A recent court case also suggests it may have more than €600m in more liquid assets. Its financial operations, like those of the Vatican's various other departments, have been so opaque that at the end of 2014 the Pope's new money-man, Cardinal George Pell – of whom more later – announced that he had found 'hundreds of millions of euros ...tucked away in particular sectional accounts [which] did not appear on the balance sheet.'

Vatican finances have fascinated historians for centuries but the Vatican Bank itself is a comparatively recent institution. Until 1887 Pope Leo XIII hid the Vatican's ready wealth – a trunk full of gold coins – under his bed. That year he decided to found the *Amministrazione per le Opere di Religione* to gather money to do good religious works. It was only in 1942 at the height of the Second World War that Pope Pius XII gave the organisation a new name and a clear banking mission. Its job was to protect Church assets from both Nazis and Communist threat. But it was also used to hide from the British and the Americans the deals that the Church in Germany was doing. Some reports suggest that the Vatican was dealing in German insurance policies which benefited from the fact that German insurers did not have to pay out on policies of Jews who died in the Holocaust but whose relatives could never certify the deaths. And one 1946 memo from a US Treasury agent reported that about $225 million in stolen Nazi gold had ended up at the Vatican.

The confidentiality which was built into the organisation from the outset has proved double-edged. In the 1980s Pope John Paul II used the IOR to send money to Solidarity, the Polish trade union movement which played a key role in triggering the fall of Communism in eastern Europe. With the Polish Pope's approval, millions of dollars of covert US aid passed through the Vatican Bank to Solidarity. William Casey, the director of the US Central Intelligence Agency, used to fly to Rome regularly to brief the Pope on the fight against Communism in Eastern Europe. There were suspicions too that the bank was also used to fund the Contras in Nicaragua, and other anti-communist guerrillas in Latin America as part of the anti-Liberation Theology liaison unit established between the Vatican and the CIA during the Cold War. Most recently the bank has been used to channel cash to vulnerable Christian groups in Egypt and Cuba.

A system aimed at getting money speedily and secretly to difficult places had obvious operational advantages. But it had a big downside too. It became an easy target for those who wanted to use it for criminal purposes. Around the same time the then chairman of the bank was an American, Archbishop Paul Marcinkus. This native of Cicero, Illinois – the one-time base of the gangster Al Capone – clearly got involved with the wrong people. In the 1970s Marcinkus started doing business with Roberto Calvi, president of the *Banco Ambrosiano* of Milan who turned out to have links with the Sicilian mafia and a Masonic Lodge called Propaganda Due (P2) which was also active in Argentina involving members of the military junta at the time.

What was going on might never have been disclosed. But then in 1982 the *Banco Ambrosiano* dramatically collapsed. In the revelations that followed it emerged that its main shareholder was the Vatican Bank. Behind the scenes Calvi had set up ten shell companies in Panama nominally controlled, via a Luxembourg subsidiary, by the Vatican Bank. He had borrowed $600 million from 120 foreign banks and lent it to the shell companies and used the money to manipulate the share price of *Banco*

Ambrosiano. Marcinkus was found to have been a director of Ambrosiano Overseas which was based in the Bahamas.

After the bank collapse a $1.3 billion black hole was found in the *Banco Ambrosiano* accounts. Calvi fled the country on a false passport. He was then found hanged under Blackfriars Bridge in London. Prosecutors in Rome saw it as a murder by P2 whose nickname was the Black Friars. The Vatican insisted it had no responsibility for the collapse of the bank but nonetheless in 1984 the Vatican agreed to make a $244 million 'goodwill payment' to Ambrosiano creditors. Three years later investigating magistrates in Milan issued a warrant for Marcinkus's arrest for 'complicity in fraudulent bankruptcy'. The warrant was never executed, because the archbishop hid away in the sovereign Vatican State.

The scandal came as a severe shock to Catholics around the world. It cost the Vatican hundreds of millions of dollars in a series of legal battles with the Italian authorities. But it did immeasurable damage to the moral authority of the Church. The shadow of shame which fell across the Vatican Bank has never fully lifted since.

The bank more or less kept its nose clean after the Marcinkus era, according to the leading expert of Vatican finances, Cambridge academic John Pollard, author of *Money and the Rise of the Modern Papacy: Financing the Vatican, 1850-1950*. 'The heavy Mafia-related activities took place in the 1970s and 80s, though I suspect that some money laundering may have gone on since then,' he said.

He was not the only one to think that. After the terrorist attacks of 11 September 2001 the world's financial authorities began to crack down on money-laundering which had ceased to be seen as merely a criminal matter and had become an issue of national security. The fear was that it disguised the financing of terrorism. International authorities steadily turned the screw on offshore havens which failed to comply with the new standards. The Vatican Bank, with 25 per cent of its business done in cash and so much of its dealings conducted in the shadows, was a classic suspect. A major investigation by the *Financial Times* showed that officials in the European Union persuaded the Bank of Italy, then headed by Mario Draghi, later President of the European Central Bank, to launch a crackdown on the IOR.

It did not take long. Soon afterwards a routine Bank of Italy anti-money laundering investigation at a UniCredit Bank branch, just down the road from the Vatican, found payment slips from unnamed holders of the Vatican Bank. But when the authorities asked IOR officials to identify the senders of the money they were told: 'Our laws don't require us to tell you.' The Vatican was a natural tax haven. It was an off-shore bank in the middle of Rome which Italians could enter merely by waiting for the traffic lights to change from red to green. In line with the Catholic Church's instinctive aversion to transparency the bank authorities adamantly refused to co-operate.

So the Bank of Italy switched its pressure to the forty commercial banks – known as 'correspondent banks' – around the world through which the IOR moved billions of euros a year. The banks, under pressure from regulators, asked more and more questions about IOR transactions. The 112 staff at the Vatican Bank, mainly Italians, couldn't or wouldn't answer them. In March 2012 American bankers forced the IOR to close the account it held with the US bank JP Morgan. The IOR had moved €1.5 billion through that one account in the previous eighteen months. In July the Council of Europe's Anti-Money Laundering body, Moneyval, announced the Vatican Bank was non-compliant on seven of its sixteen core standards.

The international bankers tightened the screw. The Bank of Italy forced all banks in Italy to close their IOR accounts. The crunch came when the German banking giant Deutsche Bank acted. Its Italian subsidiary managed the Vatican City State's eighty cash machines and credit card terminals. On 1 January 2013, Deutsche Bank closed them all down. With tourists only able to pay in cash the Vatican lost €40,000 a day. The Vatican Bank was on the brink of total collapse.

The world did not know that. In any case its attention was soon elsewhere. Just a month later Pope Benedict XVI dramatically announced that he was to become the first pope to resign for over 500 years. He was, he said, 'no longer physically, psychologically, and spiritually capable of handling the duties of office'. The turmoil at Vatican Bank – along with the dysfunctional nature of the Vatican bureaucracy known as the Curia, which had been laid bare in the Vatileaks court case – was high on the list of burdens Benedict felt he was no longer able to carry.

His resignation wrong-footed those in the Curia and the Bank who had been taking advantage of the old Pope's frailty and of his earlier inclination to turn his back on such matters in favour of theology. Benedict had been aware of the problems; he had just not known how to handle them. But he had tried. He had appointed a commercial banker, Ettore Gotti Tedeschi to take over the presidency of the bank in 2009. But the banker was out-manoeuvred by those who wanted no change. After three years of power struggles, the cardinals passed a motion of no-confidence in Gotti Tedeschi and he was fired two months later in March. Pope Benedict had been outwitted. But then he came up with the master-stroke which turned the tables on the old guard. Unable to sack them, he sacked himself. On 28 February 2013 Benedict became the first pope in 500 years to resign.

When the cardinals met to elect his successor discussion centred on the administrative and financial chaos into which the Vatican State and the Holy See had descended. Cardinal after cardinal stood up and criticised the 'dysfunction' of the system. The next pope was given a very clear mandate for reform.

When Jorge Mario Bergoglio was chosen as the 266th Pope of the Roman Catholic Church, taking his name from St Francis of Assisi, the great saint of the poor, one of the few things his peers knew about him was that, as archbishop of Buenos Aires, he had sorted out financial scandals and maladministration: when church officials had become embroiled with bankers who picked up their credit card bills in return for church endorsements Bergoglio had acted swiftly, decisively and transparently.

Within weeks of taking office, Francis set about tackling the problem of the Vatican bank and the wider finances of the Holy See in three ways. First, he moved swiftly to curb obvious excesses, scrapping the €1,500 bonus traditionally paid to Vatican staff between papacies, and stripping the bank's five supervisory cardinals of their €25,000 annual stipend. Second, he strengthened existing organisations and brought in no fewer than five firms of top-level management consultants to scrutinise every aspect of Vatican operations. Third, on 24 June 2013 he set up a commission of external secular financial and legal experts to work out what should be done with the IOR. A month later, in July, he set up a second group of outsider financiers to look at every aspect of the rest of the Vatican financial and economic portfolio. The two groups were told to think the unthinkable – including whether the Vatican bank should simply be shut down.

Meanwhile things were moving apace inside the bank. Four months after Francis became Pope the bank's new boss Ernst von Freyberg, who had been appointed by Pope Benedict just before he resigned, gave up his grand office. Its expensive leather furniture and fine oriental rugs were pushed to one side. Beneath its crystal chandeliers and heavy gilt-framed oil paintings, rows of desks were crammed in. At each place three individual computer terminals were set up for the team who were taking over. The baroque clerical drawing room suddenly looked like a city trading floor. This was the work of Elizabeth McCaul – a former superintendent of banks for the state of New York who had helped stabilise the banking sector after the 9/11 attacks. She had flown in twenty-five regulatory specialists from the United States and given them six months to trawl through every single one of the accounts of the Vatican Bank's 19,000 clients, some of whom held more than one account. The team began by sorting through computer scans of the passport of every account holder, which were painstakingly cross-checked against the names and faces of bank records. The activities were designed to make the bank compliant with Vatican law and align Vatican law to international standards.

At 6.30 on the morning of 28 June 2013 – just three months into the reign of Pope Francis – officials of the Guardia di Finanza, the Italian law enforcement agency for financial crime, pulled up in front of a rectory in Palidoro, a quiet seaside town west of Rome. When they rang the bell, the cleric who came sleepily to the door was informed that he was under arrest. A few hours later, wearing a well-cut grey suit, Monsignor Nunzio Scarano was shown into a cell in the Regina Coeli, Rome's most overcrowded prison.

Scarano, a suave, handsome priest known for his extravagant lifestyle was head of accounting at APSA – the body that then managed the Vatican's property holdings and controlled its purchasing and personnel departments. His nickname among other priests was Monsignor Cinquecento (My Lord Five Hundred) because of his habit of flashing €500 banknotes. His arrest made front-page news. He was accused of trying to smuggle €20m on a private plane across the border from Switzerland, in a money-laundering conspiracy involving the Vatican bank, an agent of Italy's secret services and an Italian broker under suspicion for running a Ponzi scheme.

Doubts about Scarano had first been aroused six months earlier, when he had reported a burglary at his apartment in the city of Salerno, south of Naples. Paintings from his art collection had been stolen, he claimed. When the police arrived at the seventeen-room apartment on Via Romualdo Guarna, in one of the city's wealthiest neighbourhoods, they were startled by its opulence. It was furnished with valuable antiques, and a spectacular display of art lined the walls in hallways divided by Romanesque columns. Scarano's collection included a painting attributed to Chagall. Police reports estimated the missing artworks were worth €6m. How could a bureaucrat priest on a stipend of €36,000 a year afford such luxuries? They were all 'donations', Scarano told the police. Investigators were convinced they were gifts – along with perks including trips, cruises and, reportedly, massages – from banks soliciting Vatican business. Scarano had €2.3m in his various personal accounts.

But the Scarano scandal had much wider implications for Vatican governance. Investigators suspected that he had been operating APSA as a 'parallel bank', through which Italian VIPs could avoid taxes and the mafia launder the profits of illegal activity. Scarano denied it all but, just a few days after his arrest, two of the Vatican bank's three top officials suddenly quit their jobs.

Cardinal George Pell is a big man. His physique – broad and 6ft 3in tall – is that of a priest who played professional rugby as a young man. An Australian, and the son of a heavyweight boxing champion, he has a personality to match: belligerent and blunt. He is conservative both doctrinally and politically. He is a climate-change denier who has been, at the very least, grossly insensitive to the victims of sex abuse in Sydney and Melbourne.

Yet, for all his conservatism, Pell had for years been a vocal critic of the Roman Catholic bureaucracy and its corruption under the previous two popes. He knew what he was talking about. The pugnacious Australian had knocked the finances of the archdiocese of Sydney into shape during his time in charge, leaving a legacy of nearly AU$1.2 billion after twelve years. It was not a one-off. He had done the same thing in the much larger archdiocese of Melbourne before that.

So, when the Pope's two financial thinktanks delivered their reports a year into the papacy, it was Pell whom Francis asked to lead the complete overhaul of Vatican finances. 'Francis has played it very cleverly,' said one seasoned Vatican diplomat. 'It was a masterstroke to get Cardinal Pell involved. He is a really tough nut. And it is far better to have him in the tent shouting out than outside shouting in.'

The Vatican bank was not to close, but it was to be stripped of its function of managing investments. The post of secretary of state – whose occupant Cardinal Tarcisio Bertone was much criticised after Pope Benedict resigned – was to lose control of Vatican finances. APSA was to confine itself to its original function of managing the Vatican's property, purchasing and personnel portfolio. A new overarching finance ministry, the Secretariat for the Economy, was established. So was a new Vatican asset management unit. Pell was announced as the new supremo over it all. He was also one of nine prelates Francis chose to be in his new cabinet of cardinal advisers, the C9.

The Pope was careful not to place too much power in one man's hands. Though Pell has been given unprecedented reach over all Vatican finances, he is overseen by a supervisory council chaired by another of the Pope's trusted C9 cabinet, Cardinal Reinhard Marx, the Archbishop of Munich. 'It's a separation of powers,' Pell told me over breakfast in the Domus Australia, the boutique hotel he established for Australian pilgrims to Rome three years before. It was just a few days after my tour of the bank. 'It's designed so there will be no unique focus of power.' Nor is it exclusively clerical. 'Half the members are lay people who have an equal vote with the cardinals.'

To add to the system of checks and balances that Francis has introduced, there will be a new position of auditor general, a non-cleric with powers to go 'anywhere and everywhere' in the Vatican to conduct spot checks as well as annual audits.

Pell has moved swiftly. All Vatican departments, for the first time in their history, have been told they must produce quarterly reports comparing actual spending with budgeted expenditure – standard practice in the secular business world. There was initial resistance. So, Pell sent out a forty-five-page manual to all 200 Vatican departments and allied bodies outlining the international standards of accounting and budgeting he is enforcing. 'The penny dropped after that,' Pell said. 'People realised the game has changed.'

The old guard inside the Vatican has not taken the changes lying down. Early on, the Pope placed an old friend, Monsignor Battista Ricca, inside the bank to be his eyes and ears there. When Ricca, who had been given authority to access all documents, got too assertive, dark forces within the Curia leaked a story about him to the Italian press. It claimed that Ricca had homosexual affairs while serving as a papal diplomat in Uruguay a decade before. One headline announced: 'Catholic bishop in charge of cleaning up Vatican finances got stuck in a lift with a rent boy.'

The Vatican denied the claims, but it was widely assumed that Ricca would have to resign. However, Pope Francis was not to be so easily manipulated. He saw the leaks behind the story as an attempt by conservatives to undermine his Vatican bank reform programme by trying to discredit one of his key reformers. When Ricca offered to go, the Pope refused to accept his resignation. When the press asked Francis about Ricca's gay past, he came out with the line which was to become the totemic phrase of the early part of his papacy: 'If a person is gay and seeks the Lord and has good will, who am I to judge?'

As Pell's reforms began to bite, similar dirty tricks were deployed against him. Stories were leaked to the Italian press, repeating Pell's more controversial attitudes on clerical abuse. (Some years before, he had claimed that the Roman Catholic church should be no more responsible for the abuse of children than a trucking company is for a driver who picks up and molests a woman while on the job. Pell's record on predator priests is currently under scrutiny by a Royal Commission in Australia.) More damaging to his role as Vatican finance supremo, fictions were put about that he was submitting extravagant expense claims. Pell shrugged his shoulders when I asked him about it. 'That's part of the game,' he said. 'It doesn't greatly cause me concern.'

At a consistory of cardinals earlier this year, attempts were made by old-guard prelates to curb Pell's powers. Pope Francis would not allow it. The Pope was clear that no compromise could be permitted in the pace of change. His watchword was the Italian *fretta*, meaning faster, stronger, more.

Francis has not just set the wheels in motion, he is following up. 'We speak every fortnight,' Pell told me — and more often, if the Australian prelate requires help or advice. 'He understands money and he's interested in it. Honesty, efficiency and transparency are his priorities.' The Pope has backed the reform effort at every turn. 'Whenever there were things we couldn't clean up on our own, he's been there to support us.'

Some might see an irony in that. The man who began his pontifical ministry demanding 'a poor church for the poor' has ended up establishing the Vatican asset management unit. But anyone acquainted with the Pope's track record from his time in Buenos Aires would recognise in this the combination of an audacious prioritising of the poor and a canny understanding of the politics of how change is achieved in this world.

Francis told his financier advisers at their first meeting in July 2013 that 'sound financial management was a pillar of his greatest mission: aiding the poor and underprivileged'. What that meant, said Cardinal Pell, is that 'the Pope wants to maximise the amount of money coming in so that it could be spent on the poor and the works of the church. Because we're trying to help people is no reason why we should be inefficient, or not transparent, or open to being robbed.'

As he rose from the breakfast table to head off to meet the Pope, I reminded Pell that he had once said he would only be happy when the Vatican bank was 'off the gossip pages'. Had he managed that? He smiled grimly: 'Not quite.'

MUSLIM LIFE IN SYDNEY

Irfan Yusuf

Sydney is a city made for postcards. Its gorgeous harbour is adorned by a giant steel arch bridge and an eggshell opera house. Locals affectionately refer to the bridge (which carries motor vehicles, trains, pedestrians and bicycles) as the Coat Hanger. The harbour has enough water to allow tens of thousands to travel by ferry. Each New Year's Eve, the Coat Hanger forms the backdrop to a spectacular multimillion dollar fireworks display. Within the city's greater metropolitan area are some of the world's finest beaches, at least three national parks and a host of rivers.

And over a hundred mosques. Perhaps the best known of these is located deep in the geographical heart of greater Sydney. The Auburn Gallipoli Mosque combines a stereotypically Australian name with an architecture perhaps better suited to the Ottoman Europe. It is named in honour of the peninsula where Turks, Australian and New Zealand troops (the latter known as ANZACs) met in battle for the first and last time during the First World War. The Turks were led by one Mustafa Kemal Ataturk. The ANZACs were misled by their British commanders into a colossal defeat. Last year, 2015, marked a century since that fateful conflict. Australians gathered on the Gallipoli Peninsula in Turkey and at memorials across Australia. New Zealanders did the same, though Aussies tend to forget the contribution their Kiwi cousins made at that battle. In the fog of war, Australia and the new Republic of Turkey forged a lasting friendship. Celibolu (the uncorrupted version of the place's name) is a place of secular sacredness, a battleground where Australians celebrate a military prowess born in crushing defeat, not to mention a tendency to fight other people's battles.

The Gallipoli Mosque is one of numerous managed by Turkish communities. It consists of a large shallow dome circled by smaller half-domes and seated on two square storeys. Two tall thin minarets stand either side. The interior is spectacular, with a plush red carpet and walls hand-painted with calligraphy. The structure is big enough to rate as a medium-sized mosque in Istanbul, but in Australia it is certainly something to write boastfully to Istanbul about.

By contrast, Sydney's oldest mosque (known appropriately as the Sydney Mosque), is a converted church purchased by the local Turkish community in 1975. The last time I visited, the floor was at a distinct angle. Facing Makkah, it felt like one was praying uphill; I almost slipped back.

Turkish mosques are dotted throughout greater Sydney in places where Turks historically lived and worked. Just south of Sydney (in Australian terms it is 'just south', despite being 90 kilometres from the city centre) in the suburb of Cringila sits the Bilal Mosque. Decades ago, Cringila was a hub for many Turkish migrants and their families. Generations of Turkish men and women were employed at the steelworks until the largest of these closed down. In place of steel, Wollongong now boast numerous kebab outlets. Turkish mosques are financially self-sufficient and usually named in honour of their locality instead of a Middle Eastern monarch or dictator. The imam is provided by the Turkish Ministry of Religious Affairs (*Diyanet Vakfi*) who pay his wages. Turkish imams generally deliver Friday sermons in Turkish and Arabic and often rotate between Turkish mosques.

That the Turkish Muslim communities are well-established in Sydney and in surrounding regional towns is largely due to a 1967 agreement between Australia and Turkey. It allowed for the mass migration of Turks. Anthropologist Liz Hopkins notes that under the agreement, Turks were deemed White Europeans notwithstanding their Muslim religious affiliation. This suited the self-identification of the migrants themselves and of their ancestral homeland which saw itself as European and white. These 'white' Muslims were not mere guest workers as was the case in Germany and other parts of Europe, but were eligible for Australian citizenship; which most took up.

The 1967 Treaty was one of a raft of radical changes made to Australia's immigration policy which saw the end of a system in which being deemed White was essential to be considered fit for migration. The Commonwealth of Australia was founded in 1901 as a marriage of convenience between existing British colonies. One of the first legislative acts of its Parliament was the Immigration Restriction Act 1901, popularly known as the White Australia Policy. Upon its enactment, Chinese workers were expelled as were South Sea Islander bonded labourers (effectively slaves). Indigenous Australians were not White enough to be considered anything, despite many fighting and dying in battle (including at Gallipoli).

Before the Turks arrived, white-skinned European Muslims from what was then Yugoslavia, Albania and Cyprus settled as part of a large wave of post-WWII migration. A small number of Lebanese and Syrian Muslims also managed to sneak in, perhaps pretending to be Greek.

During the mid-1990s, Yugoslav Muslims became known by the label of 'Bosnian'. Not much was known about these people, though I do recall one law professor named Alija Izetbegovic, who went on to become the first Chairman of the Presidency of Bosnia and Herzegovina, appearing on Amnesty International pamphlets as a prisoner of conscience. 'Actual' Bosnians did enter Australia as refugees. Many identified as Muslims, while others were deemed Muslim by default thanks to the ethno-religious assumptions and prejudices of the armies and militias they fled. Some found comfort living in Auburn, near the Gallipoli Mosque, while others chose to live near more established mixed 'Yugoslav' communities largely untouched by communal madness.

Turks may be a key feature of Sydney Islam, but I never knew much about them when I was growing up. My own family sneaked into Australia in 1965 when my father won a PhD scholarship at the Australian National University (ANU) in Canberra; and we eventually ended up in Sydney in 1970. When I was growing up, Muslim and Indian were synonymous. Muslims were brown-skinned people who watched long-winded Indian movies without the need of subtitles. A Muslim woman in my childhood imagination wore a sari or *shalwar kameez* and cooked very spicy food. Many Muslim men tied handkerchiefs around their heads when praying. Sofas were moved, white bed sheets were laid out on the floor, incense sticks burned and books in strange languages were read when a Muslim died.

Once a month, we Muslims would drive out to Bondi Beach to what was then Sydney's only Indian spice shop. It was managed by a friendly old couple. The husband wore an embroidered cap on his head and his wife wore a small headscarf. They spoke Hindi. Yes, they were Muslims too. At least in my mind they were until, years later, I was told Uncle Isi Moses prayed on Saturday and did not go to a mosque on Friday.

No doubt for many Muslim migrants Islam was part of a broader project in preserving ancestral language and culture. Religion often played second fiddle. The result was Lebanese Muslims spent more time with Lebanese Christians, Cypriot Turks all had Cypriot Greek accountants and lawyers and Yugoslavs were just Yugoslavs (apart from a small number of Croatian nationalist folk constantly chased by law enforcement and security agencies for being 'terrorists'). And half my 'Muslim' aunties sported red dots on their foreheads.

In their multiculturalism, Sydney Muslims are a microcosm of Sydney and broader urban Australia. Most Muslims, like most Australians, live in coastal cities. According to the 2011 census conducted by the Australian Bureau of Statistics (ABS), some 45 per cent of Muslims live in Sydney. They have migrated from over 180 different countries, many from nations (such as Lebanon, India, Fiji, Sri Lanka and South Africa) where Muslims live as minorities. Though multicultural, Sydney's Muslims are no longer just a migrant phenomenon. The largest group by place of birth are those born in Australia. And second in line are Muslims born in Lebanon.

For some strange reason, being Lebanese and being Muslim are considered by many Australians to be one and the same. It's as if your average Aussie imagines downtown Beirut to be full of bearded men and burqa-clad women. The irony is that most Lebanese in Australia are not Muslim. The ones that identify as Muslim come in all sectarian shapes and sizes. The *Ithna Ashariyya* (Twelver Shi'a) community is dominated by competing Lebanese religious and political factions. Their main mosque is located in the southern suburb of Arncliffe, close to the international airport. Surrounding the mosque are large blocks of units. Down the road is a small commercial district with shops, restaurants and the compulsory shisha outlets.

A short drive from Arncliffe is the village of Lakemba. In popular imagination, Lakemba is the Muslim heartland of Australia. According to the 2011 Census, 51.8 per cent of the population are Muslim. Roman Catholics are a distant second at 12.3 per cent. Nutty right wing journalists looking for shock and horror quotes and sound bites jump in a cab and head straight for Lakemba. Tim Blair, a columnist on Australia's *Daily*

Telegraph even took the 'risk' of staying overnight in a room above a pub. He found what he was looking for:

> Lakemba may be only 30 minutes from the centre of Sydney, yet it is remarkably distinct from the rest of the city. You can walk the length of crowded Haldon St and not hear a single phrase in English. On this main shopping strip the ethnic mix seems similar to what you'd find in any Arabic city. Australia may be multicultural, but Haldon St is a monoculture.

I have travelled far and wide, but I have never come across streets in 'Arabic' cities named Haldon Street. To those familiar with Lakemba, Blair sounds like Donald Trump describing parts of London. But Blair's assessment represents something close to the views of 'mainstream' red-top tabloid readers. I have, however, heard Lakemba locals laugh off the stereotypes with their own corrupted names – *Lakembanon* and *Lebkemba*.

The reality, however, is quite different. You'd expect a stereotypical Lebanese or Arab area to have an average household size of far in excess of 3.02 persons (we all know they breed like rabbits). But would you expect the largest ethnic group by ancestry of an Arabic city to be from Bangladesh? Or to have major communities originating from China, Greece, India, Pakistan, Vietnam and Indonesia. Indeed, Lakemba can hardly be describes as an 'Arab monoculture'.

But Lakemba has acquired a somewhat unsavoury reputation for specific reasons which have caused much grief and embarrassment. The Imam Ali ben Abi Taleb Mosque is located on Wangee Road, a residential street packed with blocks of units and the rear of a primary school playground. The mosque is managed by the Lebanese Muslim Association (LMA), a body whose representatives often appear in mainstream media (including Mr Blair's own newspaper) as representatives of 'the Muslim community'. Yet, according to LMA's own membership rules, the 'community' does not include women, who are barred from holding full membership; and men are ineligible for a Lebanese passport! (I am not sure anyone is actually looking for one.) The mosque's former imam, Sheikh Taj Din Al-Hilali, an Egyptian who spoke through an interpreter, often gave speeches which made headlines. Frequent targets of the Sheikh's speeches were Jews and women. In 2006, he made international headlines with a sermon claiming that women who dressed inappropriately were like 'uncovered meat' for cats to eat. 'Whose fault is that: the cat's or the uncovered meat's?' Some 500 persons were present in the mosque to hear his speech. Within weeks, millions more read about it on the web.

But Sheikh Hilali was no firebrand Salafi with a beard fit for a ZZ Top guitarist. Instead he was a mainstream al-Azhar educated Mullah. He established the Muslim Women's Association, spoke out against domestic violence and was very popular with young people. He was also very physically fit for his age. When he was in a tracksuit and sunglasses, you'd swear you were in the presence of Viv Richards.

The Shaikh has now retired, but his major Lebanese Sunni factional enemies are still active. They include a contingent of Salafi Muslims, some of whose imams have also made headlines of their own with colourful views relating female dress to sexual violence. One young Lebanese Salafi imam claimed women who dressed in an inappropriate manner were 'eligible for rape'. When asked to clarify, he said he was only referring to Muslim women who didn't wear hijab. My elderly Indian mother, who doggedly refuses to wear anything on her head except when performing the prayer or listening to Qur'an, was not impressed.

Amongst Sheikh Hilali's other enemies is a curious group from Lebanon who follow one Ethiopian cleric named Abdullah Hareri al-Habashi. Known as *Ahbash*, the group directly compete with the LMA on numerous Lebanese Sunni fronts. The rift between the Ahbash and LMA has split major extended families and village cultural associations. The irony is that, doctrinally speaking, there is little difference between the Ahbash and the LMA congregation. Both follow the Shafie school of law, reject scriptural literalism, celebrate the birthday of the Prophet and both are Lebanese (which, in Sydney terms, are essential articles of faith). Which often makes it impossible for an untrained non-Lebanese eye to tell the difference between the two. Until, that is, you mention Ibn Taymiyyah, the fourteenth century Syrian literalist theologian and jurist. The Ahbash cannot stand him and unambiguously denounce him as an apostate. The LMA crowd, Sheikh Hilali and his successors prefer not to regard ibn Taymiyyah as a traitor to Islam. In an Ahbash mosque, or indeed at a *mawlid* gathering, the very mention of Ibn Taymiyyah can lead to serious strife. The same goes for any of those recent hard-line religious scholars who take their inspiration from Ibn Taymiyyah – such as Syed Qutb, Hasan al-Banna or Abul Ala Maududi, the founders of Egypt's Muslim Brotherhood and Pakistan's Jamaat-e-Islami, respectively.

No doubt both Ahbash and the LMA band would have doctrinal differences with the followers of Abu Shu'ayb Muhammad ibn Nusayr, a disciple of the eleventh Shi'a Imam Hasan al-Askari. The followers of ibn Nusayr are known as Nusayriyya or Alawis. A small Lebanese Alawi community is present in Sydney. They operate a mosque, a comprehensive school and a youth centre. However, they have gone to ground since the beginning of the civil war in Syria. Occasionally anti-Shi'a and anti-Alawi violence has spilled onto the streets of Lakemba. A small group of Lebanese Sunni hotheads and thugs have also been prominent supporters of ISIS and have made their way to Syria. One Sydney thug, Khaled Sharrouf, made international headlines when a photograph of himself and his son holding a severed head of an ISIS opponent appeared in the press.

But competing factions, denigrating comments about women, and severed heads only tells a tiny part of the story of Sydney's Lebanese Muslims. The community has also made major contributions to public life. On the Australian Labor Party (ALP) side (for some reason the ALP uses American spelling for its name), two names are highly respected. Jihad Dib is a former high school principal, who transformed a troubled state high school in a disadvantaged area riddled with crime adjacent to Lakemba into one of the best performing schools in Western Sydney. Dib now represents the electorate of Lakemba in the Lower House of the New South Wales State Parliament, Australia's oldest Parliament. In the Upper House, Labor has lawyer Shaoquett Mouselmane who was the first person of Lebanese Muslim descent to be elected in any Australian parliament. Born in the village of Konin in Southern Lebanon, Mouselmane's family moved to Sydney in 1977.

Also on the Labor side in the Australian House of Representatives is Ed Husic who represents the large Western Sydney electorate of Chifley. Husic's father, Hasib, migrated to Australia from Bosnia some fifty-five years ago, part of the large post-World War Two wave from Europe. His father was a welder, his mother a stay-at-home mum of three children. After pursuing an Arts degree, Husic became active in the trade union movement and the ALP.

Both Jihad Dib and Ed Husic have faced problems with their names. Jihad has acquired unpalatable connotations; and Ed does not quite shield Husic despite his white European heritage. In his inaugural speech in May 2005, Jihad explained:

> In accordance with custom, I was named after my paternal grandfather as the first son of the eldest. That was a time when my name did not have the same connotations that it carries today, a time when the true meaning was clearly understood. My grandfather's name, Jihad, is an Arabic word that means to strive and to improve one's self, to overcome struggle and to help others improve their lives. Jihad is charity, jihad is service, and jihad is support of others. It is a name used by people of different faiths because they know its true interpretation. It is this meaning of 'jihad' that I want people to know.

Ed was given the name 'Edham Nurredin' by his parents. When he first stood for election in 2003, Husic's political opponent, a conservative and an active member of the Pentecostal Hillsong Church, questioned his Muslim identity. A number of her campaign workers frequently mentioned to voters that Ed refused to use his 'real' name. Husic was forced to defend himself. In a speech to the Sydney Institute in October 2005, he declared:

> The first time that many people knew I was Muslim was during the campaign. And many of these people had known me for 10 years...

> Just before election-day, I learned about the distribution of another pamphlet, this one claiming that I was a devout Muslim fighting for a better deal for Islam in Greenway. The sheet was a dummied version of one of my campaign ads, designed to mislead a reader into believing it was put out by me. I was also told there was a phone banking campaign that repeatedly rang voters with identified strong religious beliefs to let them know that I was Muslim. ... Obviously there was a big, organised effort to keep this issue alive. Was Ed a real dinkum Aussie? Could he be relied on? Would he be fighting for you or for Islam? ...

> I always considered myself as a regular Aussie, who happened to be Muslim. But when I woke up the day after the election I didn't completely feel like a regular Aussie any more. I actually felt – for the first time in my 34 years – that I had this brand stuck on my forehead. I might not have understood or appreciated what it was like to feel part of a sub-group that was treated differently – but I got a good sense of what it was like.

To the Left of the political spectrum, there is engineer and academic Dr Mehreen Faruqi who sits in the New South Wales Upper House for the Greens. Faruqi migrated from Pakistan with her family twenty-four years ago and has been a citizen for twenty-two years. She joined the Greens a decade ago 'because of the Party's strong commitment to supporting refugees, multiculturalism, human rights and the environment'. She too has faced a fair amount of criticism – but from the other side, the believers 'including Muslims and Christians for being a strong public advocate of LGBTQI rights and marriage equality'. How does Faruqi handle this? Australia's political culture does the job for her. 'Fortunately, we live in a secular state and in my view everyone has a right to practise their religion freely, but no one has a right to impose it on others,' she says.

Apart from issues of multiculturalism and identity, Muslims in Sydney – like Muslims everywhere – are also living in the shadow of terrorism. Around a hundred Muslim Australians have joined ISIS; and some thirty jihadis are reported to have been killed. To emphasise their connection to Oz, these characters (quite a few of them are converts), append 'al-Australi' to their real or assumed names – such as Abu al-Bara al-Australi!

There have also been two recent incidents in Sydney that have been deemed terrorist attacks. The first of these was the siege in Martin Place in December 2014 by Man Monis, an Iranian-born self-styled religious leader also known as 'Shaikh Haroon', who orchestrated a lengthy siege of the Lindt Café which ended when he and two of his hostages were killed during the storming of the premises by police. Evidence given by court-appointed expert witnesses has disputed whether the incident represented a terrorist attack, though media reports and statements by politicians and some representatives of law enforcement agencies have treated it as such. The second was the first allegedly Islam-related terrorist attack to be carried out by a minor, Mohammed Farhad Jabar, who shot and killed police worker Curtis Cheng outside police headquarters in Parramatta. Jabar, from a family of Iranian-Kurdish heritage, was fifteen years old and attended a local high school. Again, the incident is being treated by many as a terrorist incident with questions being raised about diverse issues such as mosques, Muslim leaders, and religious backgrounds of Muslim high school students.

Meanwhile, life goes on for Muslims in Sydney. They are like Muslims everywhere. Sunni, Shi'a, Alawi, Salafis, conservative, liberals, moderate, fanatics. All human life is there – as they say. Some are fighting over irrelevant doctrinal differences. Some are deeply misogynistic and cannot help denigrating women. But most are making an invaluable contribution to Australia. Though let's get some perspective, after all, more people in Sydney are being killed or wounded by great white sharks.

THE 'PEARL OF MOROCCO'

Martin Rose

Engraved view of Rabat by Braun and Hogenbergt, 1572.

For a short time in 1912 Fes was the capital of French Morocco, until it occurred to Maréchal Lyautey that the oyster-grey city, far inland below the heights of the Middle Atlas, was not a very secure location for an imperial capital. Apart from anything else, naval access was distinctly limited. The march to the nearest port was long and dangerous. In 1912, after two sieges of Fes in quick succession, his attention switched quickly to Rabat on the coast, 130 miles and a week's ride away through the Marmora forest. Rabat was eventually declared the new capital of Morocco, after a long bout of slightly mysterious arm-wrestling with Paris. It was – for the purposes of colonial government – a much more sensible choice.

Rabat was an 'Imperial City', which is to say that it was a habitual stopping place for the sultans on their royal progresses around their possessions, and that it boasted a royal palace. Indeed it boasted two, the great enclosure of the Mechouar with which we are familiar today, and the Qubaybat, the 'Little Domes', as the summer palace down by the sea was known, lost as it now is beneath the oddly Gormenghastian remains of French military and medical buildings. Like Salé across the river, it was a way-station on the only secure north-south route between Morocco's two chief capitals, Fes and Marrakech, and thus strategically important in its own right. Lyautey described it as lying 'at the intersection of the three major axes of Morocco, one towards Taza, one towards Marrakech, and the third one along the coast ...' and in the light of this strategic centrality it is surprising how small a part Rabat had actually played in Moroccan history in the preceding millennium.

But it had another feature too, which made it extraordinarily suitable for development as a colonial capital, a feature that was the product of Rabat's strange, episodic, history. The little city on the southern tip of the Bouregreg estuary occupied only a tiny portion of the walled area that Sultan Yacoub al-Mansour had enclosed in the twelfth century for his new capital: al-Mansour's city walls still stood tall, but they enclosed smallholdings and rough pasture and a good deal, too, of waste land between the marshy edge of the river and the Mechouar. Like Rome in the early Renaissance, the city had shrunk to a tiny fragment of what it had been – or, in the case of Rabat, had been imagined as becoming – and much of it lay empty, protected by high walls, open and inviting to the French architect of empire.

To understand why this was so requires a quick gallop through the history of Rabat. It is a rich history, but not one of steady and incremental growth like that of so many modern capitals. It has had very different shapes, names and characters at different times. Today it is on the verge of another, perhaps cataclysmic, transformation from a quiet, green and gentle city into a noisy metropolis little different from the other agglomerations of 'contemporary' architecture and shopping opportunity that are the capital cities of the modern Middle East.

***

But let's start with geography. Rabat occupies a strategic spot on the Atlantic coast, well enough placed as late as the turn of the nineteenth century to serve Fes as its principal port, and at the same time on the 'safe' corridor between Fes and Marrakech. At the mouth of the Oued Bouregreg the river broadens out between two headlands, offering shelter from the ocean, and an anchorage. The estuary had one very particular feature, a sandbar across the opening which caused a violent and often dangerous turbulence. This bar helped to define the usefulness and history of Rabat: in early modern times it prevented the passage of large-draught ships, so that the shallow pirate vessels could run for harbour across the bar, at least at high tide, leaving European warships helpless beyond it in the Sally Roads. The bar made of the estuary between the two cities a secure base for corsairs preying on the traffic of the Atlantic coast and further afield, helping to define the city's character. It remained a constant feature of Rabat until 1755, when the 'Lisbon' earthquake, with its epicentre 200 kilometres off Cape St Vincent and an estimated force of 8.5-9.0 on the Richter Scale, shook the two towns of the Bouregreg estuary (as well as damaging most of the other major towns of Morocco). The quake also raised the sand-bar significantly, making the estuary even more difficult of access for larger ships, and more dangerous for smaller ones. This probably didn't matter greatly at once, though in bad weather ships would sometimes have to anchor for a week and more in the roads waiting for the bar to become passable for the lighters which went out to unload them. As Mercier observed in 1905 of smaller ferry-boats, 'the current, of which the direction varies according to the tide, is often very strong and pushes many boats off their course. It even happens, if the boatman doesn't know his trade, that a boat is driven onto the bar and capsized by large waves. In this sort of case, many passengers don't make it back to shore.'

In the nineteenth century, as merchant ships grew larger, and as Casablanca began to offer a livelier trading centre only a little to the south, the port of Rabat went into long-term decline. With the opening of the magnificent new port at Casablanca in 1921, Rabat's fate was sealed. Today its main shipping, apart from the remaining ferry-boats that try in vain to compete with the new bridge between Rabat and Salé, is a large, plywood dhow built on the quay below the Qasbah des Oudayas, and used as a restaurant.

***

In the forecourt of one of the motor-car dealerships on Avenue Hassan II there is a large chunk of stone, which I have failed on several occasions to find, but which a reliable friend assures me – he is a *wali*, so it must be true – exists. It is the last fragment of the *limes*, the southern boundary, indeed the bottom left-hand corner, of the Roman Empire. It marks Rabat's position at the very end of the civilised world, Rome's *ne plus ultra*. Pliny reported in the early first century AD that the banks of the river Sala, as the Bouregreg was then called, had a serious elephant problem. Rabat was right on the very edge of the wild.

Even its name is a bit of a muddle. The older and once much richer town on the north bank of the estuary is called Sla, which the French frenchified into Salé and the English englished into Sallee or Sally, illustrating their shared inability to wrestle successfully with the vowel-free Rabat colloquial. Though the two cities have very different histories and characters, their fates were bound up with one another. 'Sla' seems to relate to the name of the old Roman settlement, Sala Colonia, which is also the etymological starting-point for Chella, the great walled enclosure outside the Bab Za'er, sitting on the site of the Roman (and perhaps an earlier Punic) port of which it incorporates the excavated forum. The observant reader will already have noted that modern Salé is on the north, and ancient Sala on the south bank of the river. The migration of names is confusing and at times seems almost wilful. The city of Rabat was often (for example by Richard Simson on his 1637 map) referred to as New Sally or *Sala Nova*, and sometimes even (in another engraved view by Braun and Hogenbergt, of 1572) as *Sala Vetera*, or Old Sally. It is hard to resist the impression that these two cities, which on the whole detested each other (as an old proverb has it, 'Slawis can never have affection for Rbatis, even if the river were to become milk and the sand raisins'), lived grumpily together like an ill-matched old married couple, sulking for long periods, exchanging blows on occasion, but muddling along in an inextricable, resentful embrace.

But whatever it was called on maps, Rabat had a perfectly good name of its own, *Ribat al-Fath*, of which 'Rabat' is just another un-euphonious francophone approximation. It means something like the Convent of the Victories, and reflects the first foundation on the south bank of the estuary in the tenth century, a sort of dervish garrison facing into the territory of the truculent pagan Berber tribes to the south. By the time of the Almohad conquest and the reign of al-Mansour (1184-99) it had shuffled round through 180 degrees, focusing its belligerent attentions northward to face Spain and serve the imperial ambitions of its Almohad sultan.

Al-Mansour, 'the Victorious', had an ambitious vision for making Ribat al-Fath his imperial capital, and he built to scale. Most spectacular was the great stone-and-*pisé* enceinte, the 'Almohad Wall', on the two land sides of the city, enclosing a vast area of some 400 hectares. The two other sides were protected by the sea and a cliff along the river. Into this space were built a number of monuments, most notably the Hasan mosque whose enormous tower still dominates the Rabat skyline. It is built to echo two other great mosque-towers in al-Mansour's transcontinental empire – the Giralda at Seville and the Kutubiya in Marrakech – but had it been finished would have been larger than either, just as the mosque itself would have been larger than any on earth apart from Samarra's Al-Mutawakkil mosque. Its unfinished colonnades stood until 1755 when they were felled by the 'Lisbon' earthquake. Other remnants of that great building spree are two magnificent gates – one, the grand entrance to the Qasbah above the Souk al-Ghazel; the other, the Bab al-Rouah on the Marrakech road. The mosques of Salé and the Qasbah des Oudayas date, too, from this moment of architectural energy.

There must have been other less important buildings, but most of the land within the walls was never built on at all and al-Mansour's Rabat remained a vast, empty enclosure overgrown with wild vines and brushwood where it was not cultivated. When the sultan died in 1199, the restless attention of his successors moved on, and Rabat subsided into sleep. Such settlement as there was concentrated on the tip of the point, where the medina now stands, along the Alou ridge and the slopes down each side of it; but nothing of great moment actually happened for 400 years. Every view that we have of the city shows an empty circuit of walls with a village on the tip and a half-built tower, all set in a green field, with Chella in the background.

Chella (the French transliteration leads English-speakers to mispronounce it as though its 'ch' were the 'ch' of chocolate rather than the 'sh' of sheep) is testimony to another, even more glancing, if slightly more protracted, moment of interest in Rabat from the powerful. The Almohads were defeated in Spain and in North Africa by the mid-thirteenth century, and their Merinid successors took understandable umbrage at Rabat's having cast its lot with the Christian Spanish invaders: the Merinid sultans favoured Salé over the rapidly disappearing ghost-city on the south bank. They did however take the site of old Sala Colonia in hand, walling it and making of it a royal necropolis where sultans from Abu Yusuf Yaqub to Abul Hassan are buried. In time, it too fell into decay, although it remains a place of great beauty and not inconsiderable superstition, where quiet fertility rites take place, marabouts are revered, sacred eels propitiated and the Merinid sultans are remembered through the misty filter of wonderfully baroque folk-tales. Through it all, Rabat continued to sleep.

***

During this long sleep, Salé, the 'City of Saints,' was the dominant partner, a bustling, conservative place of commerce and handicraft, and scholarship on an industrial scale, where farmers came to buy shoes and sell sheep, and students came to sit at the feet of the famous teachers in its *madrasas* and mosques. Both cities of course were deeply marinaded in the cultural and political tides that washed to and fro between Spain and Morocco, and the consequences of Muslim decline in Iberia. An Andalusian exile like Lisan al-Din al-Khatib, poet and vizier, spent his banishment from Granada at Salé in 1359-62, studying Sufism and absorbing the aesthetic of Salé's Merinid madrasa, recently built by Abul Hassan. Ibn Khaldun, born in Tunis to a family from Seville, spent his career in Granada, Fes, Tlemcen and Tunis, dying in Cairo in 1406. Other Muslims migrated southward individually, and in groups, over the centuries as al-Andalus was squeezed and dismembered by Christian armies; but it was only with Philip III's expulsion after 1609 of the *moriscos* – those Muslims who had converted to Christianity and remained in Spain, but whose sincerity it was prudent, or useful, to doubt – that a new impetus was given to Rabat by mass migration from Spain to Africa. The emigrés went first to port cities along the North African coast, and the number of them who eventually reached Rabat was small – fewer than 6,000 at most. But all of them had burning grievances against Christians in general and Spaniards in particular, for the pillaging and expulsion they had suffered. Some of them carried the keys to Spanish houses and gardens that are still lovingly preserved today as symbols of a violent, heart-scorching loss. Most of them wanted revenge and recompense, and the already prosperous business of piracy was a very attractive career option and investment opportunity.

Once in Africa, these *moriscos* were referred to as Muslims, and while their religious practice was often at first considered wild and even heterodox, they seem on the whole to have slipped off their Christianity like a coat on a hot day. The Slawis regarded the Spanish incomers as no better than wine-bibbing heathens; but a captive friar in Salé wrote that 'though manie of the Mores of this place were brought up in Spaine, and are therefore of a well-tempered naturall disposition, yet the great infection which this place receives from the Alarabes or wild Arabians … hath brought a general corruption into their manners …'. They were curiously intercultural, in fact, speaking the language, and wearing the clothes, of their Spanish home; suspected of Christianity by Moroccans as they had been of Islam by Spaniards. Their women went about the streets with heads uncovered and they themselves planted vines for wine-making – both behaviours that scandalised the orthodox. Even at this late stage though, migrants from Muslim Spain were travelling within a cultural zone that had been continuous and coherent for almost a thousand years – and many had families and business associates south of the straits. Rabat became a crucible of cultural fusion.

The Spanish Muslims who came to Rabat were from two very distinct sources. First were the *Hornacheros*, the Castilian-speaking Muslims of the small hill-town of Hornachos in Estramadura. They were a cohesive band of armed hillsmen with a fearsome reputation for lawlessness, independence, fighting spirit and solidarity. By the time they left their home town in January 1610 they had made themselves such a violent nuisance to the Castilian authorities that they were allowed to march out of Hornachos to embark at Seville with their arquebuses on their shoulders and their coin and their chattels carried between them – like a garrison that had surrendered with full military honours. Their first port of call was Tetouan, where some settled and where Spanish-derived family-names like Bonito, Blanco and Carpintero testify to their passage. Many moved on to Salé, where they weren't much welcomed, and soon crossed the estuary to Ribat al-Fath. Here they took over what is now the Qasbah des Oudayas, the walled fortress within the town that occupies the high point of the promontory's tip, and which had been the site of the very first *ribat*. They were already well established when the second wave of refugees arrived, attracted perhaps by the magnetic idea of the *morisco* city that Rabat was rapidly becoming. This second wave was for the most part a ragbag of penniless Andalusians, expelled without arquebuses, capital or house-keys, piecemeal from the ports of the south coast. They were not enormously welcome at first, but settled below the *Hornacheros'* walls, in a little warren of houses across the Souk al-Ghazel from the Qasbah. In a fairly obvious division of labour the *Hornacheros* provided the business capital, the pirate ships and perhaps the ship-masters too; and the Andalusians, the fighting crew, for the pirate fleet.

The next half century, until the Alawite sultan captured both towns in the 1660s, was a jumbled confusion of three-cornered fighting between the *Hornacheros* (sometimes in control of the Qasbah, sometimes not) and the Andalusians (the same, but alternately), one side or the other frequently allied with the town of Salé, generally ruled by a sanguinary saint, and when possible with the naval forces of any visiting European power. The three towns, Rabat, Salé and the Qasbah made up a pirate republic sometimes over-dignified as the 'Republic of the Bouregreg,' which must in reality have been rather like Captain Jack Sparrow's Tortuga. 'The alliances shifted in unpredictable fashion, the game of *tertius gaudens* was played with consummate skill, and the external powers often entered at the invitation of one of the players, only to seek their own goals in turn,' as Janet Abu-Lughod nicely puts it. It was a time of chaos and bloodshed as all parties battled over control of *la course* – the lucrative corsair business of capturing Christian shipping and turning its ships, cargoes, crews and passengers into cash. It may have been a defining moment of economic growth and political semi-independence for Rabat, but in the end all the squabbling parties lost out to the renascent Alawite sultanate which nationalised the business of piracy.

This was the period when Rabat took its premodern form. The medina became a walled city in its own right, with a new stone-and-*pisé* wall – the 'Andalusian Wall' – built across the tip of the point from the Bab al-Had in the old Almohad enceinte, to the cliffs above the river at Burj Sidi Makhlouf – the line of Lyautey's Haussmanesque Boulevards Gallieni and Joffre (now Hassan II). The rest of the great enclosure was left outside the new inner wall, and despite its tall defences was not altogether safe for townsmen to walk or ride through unarmed.

Rabat also began to develop its own very particular culture. The little city on the Bouregreg was, and is, the only city in Morocco to be founded by Moriscos, and so to distil into itself an Andalusian essence (of a very particular late Ibero-Andalusian texture) that is still perceptible – largely because it has become characteristic of a broader Moroccan high culture. In the late twentieth century there were still some 50 or so Rbati families of Andalusian lineage, and along with the *hnifiin*, the almost equally clannish old Moroccan Arab aristocracy who to a great extent followed the Andalusian ways, they occupied the heights of Rbati society. Fair-skinned, inward-looking, inward-marrying and sophisticated, they developed an attractive Spanish-impregnated culture of their own, while shaping many of the tastes and attitudes of Moroccan society, and eventually taking leading places in it. As a nineteenth century chronicler put it, 'They are unequalled through their pure, noble Andalusian descent from the ancient ancestral ... civilisation, which is evident from its remaining in Rabat and the people from Rabat ... how they are distinct, Splendour of the Sun, in their knowledge and their letters and their arts and their crafts.'

Rabat itself, as the medina grew and became more organised in the seventeenth century, took on a most un-Moroccan plan of straight-ish streets and well-segmented quarters. The houses acquired classical architraves around their doors, today buried deep in many layers of paint, and the material culture took a characteristically Andalusian form, with embroidery that echoed the floral patterns of Spanish women's *mantones*, and painted woodwork tending to flowers, vines and curlicues rather than the sharp geometries of Fes and Marrakech. Music too remained highly traditional, with the Andalusian arts of *'oud* and *rebab* cultivated and practised amongst Andalusian Rbatis, along with the sung poetry of the Andalusian *muouashat*. Their cuisine had, and has, its distinct features, most obviously the *bastilla* (once Spanish *pastilla*), the overpoweringly rich sugared pie of pigeon and almond paste that is still so enthusiastically eaten across Morocco. Above all, though, it is visible in the people. Many of the leading families of Rabat have names that if scraped only a little reveal their Spanish origins, names like Berrado and Bargash, Belafrej, Kilito, al-Ronda, Krisbu, Karaksho, Guedira, Guessous, Al-Madur, Al-Qistali, Sabata and Marino: one list has almost 100 Rbati family names, extant and extinct, that are Spanish in origin.

This was the Rabat that drifted on through the eighteenth and nineteenth centuries. Integration into the Alawite realm began to chip away at the Andalusian uniqueness of the city, with Arabic replacing Spanish as the lingua franca, and European dress fading away in favour of 'Arab' dress, albeit of a startling whiteness that was often commented on as Andalusian. Rabat scarcely grew, confined within the Andalusian wall of the medina, and it scarcely changed – though the earthquake of 1755 began the long, slow commercial decline of the port, hastened by Moulay Ibn Abdallah's decree of 1781 ordering all commerce and all foreign representatives to move to his new port of Essaouira, far to the south. 1829 saw the formal end of the business of piracy. By the mid-nineteenth century the port of Casablanca was beginning to attract migrants from Rabat and Fes, while European manufactured imports were undermining the traditional artisan economic base of Rabat and its sister city across the estuary. Rabat was isolated, a quiet, stable island of a very particular, syncretic culture in a sea of change, and the history of Morocco seemed to be passing it by.

***

All this changed in 1912, of course, when the victorious French decided to fix the capital of the Protectorate in one place, and chose Rabat. The little city was cracked open to the world and began the dynamic course of development and internationalisation that characterised its twentieth century. Fortunately, the French Vice-Consul, Louis Mercier, wrote a detailed topographical account of the city in 1905 and through his eyes we can see the city, innocent on the verge of huge changes, a sleepy and beautiful backwater on the Atlantic coast of Africa.

One immediately striking feature of Mercier's Rabat is the insecurity prevalent in the countryside around the city – country much of which was within the walls, and today is well inside the city centre. The problem was armed and predatory tribesmen, Za'er and Zemmour, who preyed on anyone vulnerable, native or European: of Bab Za'er, Mercier writes that 'according to a local tradition reported to us, the name of this gate comes from the fact that the Za'er killed a great many townspeople here in continual ambushes. Nowadays it is the gate through which you must never pass unarmed, advice which is taken seriously;' and of the Hasan Tower, that 'very few citizens dare to venture as far as the Hasan Tower, because of its position close to the Oued, on the edge of which there is no rampart at all, [which] means that one can all too easily meet there Za'er or Zemmour tribesmen with hostile intentions.' Only on the walk down the coast from the Bab Alou towards al-Qubaybat, the sultan's summer palace, could walkers 'be fairly sure of not being troubled by the audacious enterprises of the Za'er: they call this stretch of coast *Madreb El-Aman*, which means "the Place of Safety".' Much of the rest of the little city's surroundings were not *Madreb El-Aman* at all.

Rabat's inhabitants were well protected behind the Andalusian Wall. Mercier reports that the Sultan had forbidden foreigners to travel by boat up the Bouregreg past the wall's end at Burj Sidi Makhlouf, though wildfowlers did brave the centre channel of the marshy river, and occasional expeditions with armed guards made pleasure-outings to the orange groves of Souissi Pasha (where the first navel orange, *bi-sur'*, is said to have been grown) and to the Hasan Tower, where a tennis court was maintained in the courtyard for picnickers, though by Mercier's time it was not deemed safe to play there. This insecurity helps explain Mercier's detailed description of Rabat's walls and gates, which were far from simply decorative, all locked and guarded at night with only the little Buwayba allowing the possibility of late entrance under certain circumstances. The walls were poorly but adequately maintained, if not as well built as those of the Qasbah. In addition to the outer Almohad circuit already noted, they included another wall further out to the south – the Alaouite Wall - running up from the coast at the Qubaybat and enclosing in a long strip the

summer palace and the Mechouar and part of the Aguédal, which would
become the suburban quarter of Agdal. These walls were consumed in the
southward expansion of the city during the Protectorate, and now the sites
of the gates are marked by big road-intersections two of which — Sahat
Bab-Tamesna and Sahat Bab-Marrakech — preserve the names, while the
Bab al-Qubaybat (or Bab Dar al-Baida) has disappeared under the old
Casablanca road where it meets Rue Qubaybat.

Otherwise the Vice-Consul describes a town that was — superficially at
least — not much changed in centuries. He enumerates the quarters and
their gates, the places where trades clustered, and the places of pleasure
like the Alou, the breezy ridge at the top of the medina, and the

> very large space which borders the northern edge of the town, sloping steeply
> down to the sea. It is enclosed on two sides, the north and the west, by the
> walls of the inner circuit; on the south by the town itself; and on the eastern
> side by the *Qaçba* of the *Ouidiya*. Here one can enjoy a splendid view of the city
> of Rabat and the area immediately to its west, a view that extends across the
> Atlantic, the sandbar and part of Salé. This area is the destination of idlers, and
> all who like to dream, of whichever race. All this precious space remains
> unbuilt upon, because it is covered in tombs, forming several cemeteries made
> holy by the numerous *qoubba* of local marabouts. You see there too, on the
> ridge, a small battery of old cannon, next to the *Qaçba*. The three or four
> bronze pieces, mounted on wooden carriages, are aimed towards the city and
> are used to fire salvos at times of public rejoicing.

He accounts for the water-supply, brought in by aqueducts from Ayn-
Atiq and Ain R'eboula, and the fountains that they feed. And he tells
interestingly of some of the city's more particular localities, including the
Mellah, the Jewish quarter,

> formed by a large central street off which lead many cul-de-sacs. At the end of
> this main street, on the west side, there is a large open space, up against the
> southern and eastern faces of the inner walls. This is where the great rubbish
> heaps of the quarter, which is remarkable for its cleanliness, are located. Here
> too blow the foul stenches of various local industries, the drying of bones after
> butchering, of animal waste and of skins. A large breach opened in the walls on
> the eastern side very close to the south-east angle gives onto the river and Salé,
> offering a magnificent view. This breach has never been sealed up again,
> undoubtedly through the negligence of the Makhzen, and perhaps also because

the cliff here constitutes an adequate natural defence, overlooking the waters of the river with an almost vertical drop of about 15 metres. At the entrance to the Mellah are to be found the butcheries for kosher meat and the spice and vegetable merchants. All along the main street there are the shops of tailors, shoe-makers, silk-workers, embroiderers on leather, tinsmiths and so on.

The city's Jews were of Andalusian and of Berber origins, and although active in many trades, worked the gold that Muslim men were forbidden to wear, as well as pickling in salt for public display the heads of the Sultan's decapitated enemies. They were not always well treated, Mercier noting that Jews and Christians were particularly abused on the street

> called *Ridjal Eç-Çoff* or 'the Saints of the Throng,' because it encloses a large number of sanctuaries and venerated tombs … The whole street's character as *horm* means that Jews can't risk walking there except in bare feet: they are still often roughed up when passing under the pretty arbour which leads from the tomb of *Moulay El-Mekky Ould Moulay El-Tehamy* and crosses the road about halfway along. As for Christians it is not uncommon for them to be insulted and jostled in this place, and invited to turn round and go back the way they came.

Modernity intruded, particularly along the Alou, the ridge on the north side, where a tarmac road and, for a time, a small railway led from the port below Bab el-Bahr, along the Alou, out through a hole blasted in the wall (and later re-sealed) and on to the quarries close to the Rothemburg Battery. The road had been built a decade or so before Mercier wrote, to transport the two 24-ton, 26cm Krupp guns destined for the battery, for which a huge crane had been installed, and a quay built, at the port. The whole thing was a shemozzle typical of the times, a gigantically expensive military folly foisted upon Moulay Hassan by the Germans, with no obvious defensive use, though it doubtless made a good show next to the Sultan's residence at al-Qubaybat. It took thirteen years to build (1888-1901) and never fired a shot in anger, humiliatingly failing even to salute the Sultan successfully at its inauguration. Indeed the biggest bang it ever made was in 1911, when its magazine was accidentally ignited and an enormous explosion rocked southern Rabat, killing several members of the garrison and wrecking the heavily rusticated Balmoral-like building of the fort.

Rabat, though, was changing more than appeared on the surface. The growing import of European manufactured commodities and luxuries was undermining the traditional artisanal crafts of Morocco's cities and the delicate social structure that rested on traditional employment, education, administration and religious practice. Meanwhile other port cities, primarily Casablanca, were fast taking away the business of Rabat's small port. The commercial city that Lyautey declared Morocco's capital in 1913 was already living on borrowed time: its new status as capital city would be its salvation.

***

The development of colonial Rabat has been well chronicled and explored, perhaps above all by Janet Abu-Lughod, to whom any writer on the city must acknowledge a great debt. She analyzed the development of French Rabat with unblinking clarity, seeing in Lyautey's apparently benign planning policies for Morocco's cities, 'a system of cultural and religious apartheid, segregating Europeans in new cities laid out on vast open spaces and "following a plan aimed at realising the most modern conditions – large boulevards, conduits for water and electricity, squares and gardens, buses and tramways," while confining Moroccans to the oldest cities which, he decreed, should be touched as little as possible.'

Lyautey's town planners began in Rabat with an almost empty canvas on which to work, in the 'vast open space' enclosed by the Almohad walls. The decision was taken early, and was fundamental to Lyautey's vision of the Moroccan protectorate, that the medina would remain the Muslim town and that the French *Nouvelle Ville* would be built on the empty ground, and would be French. Separating them was a crucial part of the plan, but it became clear quickly that because of aggressive land speculation by Europeans in the area immediately outside the Andalusian walls, there could be no dramatic spatial separation as at Fes and Marrakech where the European towns were built well away from the medina. Nonetheless the broad boulevard and a 250 metre zone in which building was forbidden, between the Andalusian Wall and the *Nouvelle Ville* served much the same purpose – a *cordon sanitaire* in both hygienic and security senses.

An arch-conservative, romantic royalist and ruthless imperialist with a deep fascination for oriental culture, Lyautey saw and seized the chance to mould Morocco into something very different from other colonies – it was technically a Protectorate, with the Sultan maintained as a figurehead, but behind every decision stood the French colonial administration, and behind that administration, until 1923, Lyautey. With his Director of Planning, Henri Prost, he set about building what has been called 'a masterpiece of successful town-planning and architecture'. It is indeed a very beautiful city, and although the medina and the *Nouvelle Ville* remain stylistically and architecturally distinct, the racial and cultural lines of division between old and new blurred and vanished with the end of the Protectorate. Under Lyautey the French administration built the regime which Abu-Lughod calls 'urban apartheid', by which each legal device designed for the development of the city, 'became a tool not only for city planning but for the systematic transfer of Moroccan resources to the French colonists and their new and elegant urban quarters'. This was done through a legal framework of land-registration that was designed, and abused ('the opportunities for fraud were spectacular'), to ensure that prime land was concentrated cheaply in French hands. It was underpinned by an entirely unscrupulous system of land appropriation from the royal domain and the *habous* (or *awqaf*) which allowed the authorities to fund infrastructural development with the sale-proceeds of lands for which they had not paid. And a system of building regulation was designed to make effectively impossible the conversion or refurbishment of buildings in the medina that Europeans would be prepared to live in, and the construction in the *Nouvelle Ville* of houses that would be acceptable to Moroccan Muslims.

This is of course vastly to oversimplify, but in early twentieth century Rabat we face the contradictory spectacle of a truly lovely city – and Rabat is still the loveliest of all Arab capitals – built on the systematic spoliation of its native inhabitants. Prost and his colleagues set aside the medina, but nothing else south of the river, for Muslim Moroccans. Europeans, who made up at no point more than a third of Rabat's population, had a land area ten times the size of the medina reserved for them. The medina itself was hemmed in on all sides either by water or by European areas, so that it could not expand: Océan, immediately beyond the south-western wall of the medina on the coast, was built for lower-middle and working class southern Europeans; Agdal was reserved for the university; the southern area of Qubaybat, where the Sultan's summer palace had stood, became the Quartier Militaire taking in Fort Hervé, as the Rothemburg Battery

was re-christened by the French, and Camp Garnier; and adjacent, the
Institut Pasteur and the Hôpital Marie Feuillet. Within the Almohad Walls
was the Quartier des Services Administratifs du Protectorat centred on the
French Residency, and conveniently close to the Touarga and the Mechouar
which formed the royal precinct. A little further down the hill lay the
commercial zone, its spine the Avenue Dar a-Makhzen, now Mohammed
V, its centre the crossroads where the PTT, the Mairie and the Banque du
Maroc would stand.

The result was that the medina became a pressure-cooker, its population
but not its land-area ballooning. Immigration fed dramatic growth (the
Moroccan Muslim population of Rabat-Salé quadrupled between 1926 and
1947 alone, and a full half of the Muslim population lived in the medina by
the end of that period), but zoning-laws made it impossible to expand. So
population densities rose dramatically as migrants from the countryside
arrived, fleeing the disastrous effects of land enclosure and privatisation,
looking for day-work on the vast building-site that Rabat became in the
1920s and early 30s. They crammed into the medina until it was saturated.
Gardens were built upon, houses sub-divided, and gradually the medina
became poorer through a blend of inward migration by landless labourers
and the relocation of the rich. Middle and upper class Rbatis moved when
they could – and there was never a law actually forbidding them – to the
new suburbs that grew up after the war and to which their access became
more readily accepted: Agdal, Souissi and Aviation in particular. When the
medina could hold no more people, poor migrants began to settle in
bidonvilles, shanty-towns, along the coast beyond Océan and in the hills
above the river outside the Za'er Gate. It was a problem that the French
only began to address in the last decade of the protectorate, and one which
persists to the present.

One consequence of this was that the richer inhabitants of the medina,
which meant predominantly the Andalusians, settled in more commodious
villas in the new suburbs (and there is a suggestion that Hassan II positively
encouraged this exodus, in the interests of homogenising the city). Rabat
expanded southwards into Agdal, and then on into the estates of Souissi
Pasha which became the Quartier Souissi, recalling the family which had
provided the city of Rabat with several generations of *qa'ids*. Aviation grew
up around the aerodrome, and slowly but surely the frontier of gentility

pushed further out into the countryside, consuming the lands of the Oudaya *jaysh* and other tribes to build first Hay Riyad and then the newer Hay Riyad Extension. Meanwhile some of the *bidonvilles* became surreptitiously more formal and ultimately even legal, like Darb Akkari; and others, particularly the eyesores of Douar Doum and Yacoub al-Mansour (the Almohad Sultan again, drafted in to make of one of the poorest zones of Rabat a celebration of past grandeur) were veiled from the sight of motorists with high walls, and gradually cleared and replaced, or moved, a process still not complete today. But rather than follow the intricacies of town-planning through the twentieth century, I shall change tempo a little, and turn to the Rabat I knew myself between 2010 and 2014, a city in which the distinctions of race had been almost entirely erased – but in which those of class and wealth remained acutely visible.

***

In 1922 a French resident wrote of Rabat that 'for the moment, Rabat still guards its special character … that of a small, elegant provincial town where one is always happy to recover in the calm of privileged nature, green, and still full of poetic memories of past ages'. Amazingly, this seemed still true enough in the summer of 2010 when I first arrived in Rabat with my family. The twin cities of Rabat-Salé had in the 1920s a combined population of perhaps 50,000: today Rabat alone has 580,000 people and the combined greater metropolitan area, some 1.8 million. But in a strange way, Rabat has kept its magical green calm, its perfect scale and its touching beauty, despite this enormous growth. The medina and the *Nouvelle Ville* have grown together, interpenetrating comfortably enough, with the streets between the worn green square in front of the old Mairie and the city wall periodically filling up with African traders from Boulevard Hassan II, and then emptying again like a rock-pool at the ebb as the police re-impose their authority on the city's pavements.

For four years my office looked down onto Avenue Allal Bin Abdallah, a narrow street that leads from the Septième Art, that famous old cinema and garden café by the Banque du Maghreb, down to the Bawayba, the smallest gate in the Andalusian Wall. The street's buildings were a pleasantly shabby Art Deco, with plant-filled balconies and swags of washing drying in the sun. On the scuffed green space opposite, overlooked by the coffee-drinkers at the Majestic, where the bees buzz in swarms about the pastries, regular demonstrations gathered. Once a week they would be the *chômeurs diplomés*, the graduate unemployed, marshalled by stewards in stencilled tabards, hopelessly chanting their demands for non-existent jobs in the civil service. From time to time the police would break up a demonstration, and a stream of young men and women, pursued by gendarmes with batons, would race up the street as the patrons of the Majestic and the Fine Brioche languidly uncrossed their legs and folded their newspapers. They took the same precautions, with half-closed eyes and quietly benign clucking as the overspill of worshippers and mats from the Molina mosque choked the side-streets for Friday prayers at noon. Coffee and sticky buns continued seamlessly, and the bees buzzed on.

There are three or four bookshops in the streets around, full of promise until closely examined, but capable of the occasional serendipitous surprise; and newspaper vendors who often deal in dog-eared books too; seductive 1950s shop fronts, vanishing fast; an ice-cream parlour called, irresistibly, the Tagadirt; shoe-cleaners who, until technology rendered them less useful, were all paid by the police to listen to the conversation of their polishees; and restaurants of varying degrees of pleasure. Most days, I'd have lunch at the Septième Art, in the pleasant garden beside the cinema (which looks like a gaily painted nuclear bunker) where topiary peacocks and elephants sway above rattan tables and evilly unhealthy, cheese-fraught meals emerge from a small kitchen, to be eaten with resentful pleasure on sunny afternoons.

This is the *NouvelleVille*, M Prost's *chef d'oeuvre*, and if you half close your eyes you can still see the wasteland of the Almohad enclosure rising towards the outer walls, the ghosts of narrow paths winding up through the scrub, small ruins and shabby cottages. The vines and oranges are gone, but there are other, surprising delights in the white-walled city that has displaced them. The cathedral of St Pierre, tall and white and curiously constructed of vertical planes like wafers, was inaugurated by *le maréchal* in 1921 and sits in the middle of a refurbished piazza of rattling trams: from it can often be heard the strains of energetic singing in African languages (including, at one Christmas mass, an offertory hymn with the unexpected refrain 'Wonga wonga wonga.') To the right are the great public buildings of Rabat, aligned along the Avenue Mohamed V – the Parliament, the faded Hotel Balima, the Post Office, the PTT, the Bank and the beautifully restored Art Deco Gare de Ville where the trains stop below ground level in a deep cutting, and leave by tunnel for Fes, Casablanca and Marakkech. On up the hill, beneath the fiercely pruned shade-trees on the pavements, one comes to the French cultural centre, and the city's last bookbinder, M Tazi, who is rich in goodwill but has much still to teach his apprentices about book-binding; and the ministries, not least Defence where in the cool of the morning brass bands practice zealously but not always accurately behind the brown walls and the orange-trees. The Sunna mosque stands at a forking of the ways, a great white building, stately and tall, built in the 1960s, the Muslim counterpart to St Pierre. Here the funeral of Sheikh Abdessalame Yassine, the Islamist leader, took place in December 2012: Thousands of mourners paralyzed the city centre for hours, unreported in the press, ghosts as much as the smallholders and herdsman who lived here before Prost. Then the road runs up the wall of the Mechouar to the Bab Za'er. Little danger of being caught by tribesmen there today, but a breath-taking view across to Chella on its promontory, the rich green hillsides covered with unexpected dairy cows among the *marabouts'* tombs, and the drop to the Oued Bouregreg beyond. Behind you the Mechouar, the great palace compound, a huge open space of lawns and avenues, and neat buildings. The palace itself, with its golden doors, glitters in the distance, and all the ministries that need to be kept well under the eye of the King are neatly lined up, while guardsmen, boiling alive in red serge uniforms, march grimly to and fro.

Outside the Bab Za'er you can turn left for the Hasan Tower with its long-vanished tennis court, and the Royal Mausoleum where a Sufi sheikh sits cross-legged night and day on his sheepskin reciting the Qur'an. Also on the valley's edge is the British Residence where mosquitoes the size of golf-balls rise malignantly off the evening river to eat your ankles while you make diplomatic conversation in the garden. Turn right, on the other hand, as I used to do on my way home to Souissi, and you are heading south towards the plush suburbs, along the Avenue des Za'ers (there's nothing like defanging these impossible tribesmen and then celebrating them). Above you on your left is Yusufiya, once a worthy project for rehousing the inhabitants of the Douar Doum slums, now a solidly middle-

class neighbourhood which offers discreetly, from the wasteland at its
summit, one of the loveliest views I know, down onto the Oued Bouregreg
with the *laqlaqs*, the storks, circling well below you on the thermals, above
a chequerboard of rich greens and duns, returning home towards Chella
at dusk.

Rabat is rich in views of extraordinary beauty. When you have feasted
your eyes from the high place in Yusufiya, you can turn to Chella itself
where the storks are returning. At evening they fly home in their hundreds,
great flapping, clacking raggedy-winged *cadis*-of-the-air, to nest amongst
the trees which they share with thousands of egrets. The best-known and
most photographed stork in Morocco nests on Abul Hassan's minaret, but
Chella is not just a resort for birds and tourists: it has a life of its own. On
Fridays in good weather it is packed with a colourful throng of families
from the medina with their picnics and push-chairs and noisily playful
children. Women make fertility offerings of hard-boiled eggs to the ancient
eels in the water-tank, where, remarkably, an official sign declares the
eel-pond a *lieu de culte*, (and Nina Epton records, in the 1950s, that 'a
queenly eel is said to rule over all the creatures of Chella that share her
small, watery domain ... a queenly eel with long hair and earrings'). Cats
swarm everywhere. The fluorescent-green tombs of marabouts demand
prayers and the lush vegetation of the Andalusian garden spills over its
crumbling wall above the fecund black earth of the small farms running
down to the river. And all is surrounded by high, crenellated walls that
march tawny up the hillside surrounding this rough and lovely crucible of
Rbati history.

For the next glorious view of Rabat you must go to the point, to the
Qasbah des Oudayas, ancient *Hornachero* stronghold with its masonry held
together by iron bindings and its cannons, the same that Mercier saw,
poking mutely from the walls. Here, crossing the Souk al-Ghazel, you are
faced with the astonishing Almohad gate, reached today by a majestic, long
flight of steps that continues the line of the old rue des Consuls, where
nineteenth-century dips hung their ostrich-plumed hats. You enter, dog-
legging through the crooked passageway into the main street. Today the
Qasbah is a maze of tiny, stepped alleyways and blue-painted walls
reminiscent of a Greek island, but there was a time not so long ago when
apart from the ancient mosque and *madrasa*, it contained 'nothing but

shacks of poor appearance or even simple *nouail* (huts) which shelter the
Ouidaya contingents and their swarming families'. From the top, known
as the semaphore platform, the view is overwhelming. In front of you the
Atlantic beats on the town beach and the mole; to your left are the
fortifications and bastions that run down the coast to the lighthouse and
the smelly, squatted remains of Fort Hervé, behind them a hillside covered
with thousand upon thousand of Muslim graves, a mosaic of colour and
sun-warmed repose running up the slope to the Alou ridge. To your right,
perhaps the most wonderful urban view you will ever see, across the deep
blue Bouregreg estuary and the site of the once-dreaded bar, to the walls
of Salé. Beyond the water and beyond the salt-flats on the Salé shore is
another enormous cemetery where centuries of *salétins* and their saints
have been interred, with the walls of the city rising behind them, an
unbroken chain of towers and curtain surrounding the medina of Salé. The
city rises above the lip of its walls to its great mosque and the streets and
squares where once a year the pirate and mariners' guilds still parade with
vast 'candles,' each the size of a Fiat Cinquecento. There are very few views
in the world to compare with Salé seen across the estuary, and it is a very
fragile sight-line. A heliport control tower in front of the walls already
gives Rabat the finger.

From the Alou I used to enjoy walking down through the medina, a *bain
de foule* in which all the senses are overloaded – smell, sight, hearing and
touch. The road along the Alou remains the only through-road for traffic
in the medina, heavily parked and noisily thronged. On one side of it are
the cemeteries, still wonderful for meditative walks, falling away to the
shore (Mercier's 'destination of idlers, and all who like to dream, of
whichever race'); on the other, also falling gently, the quieter residential
streets of the medina, where tall, blank walls still hide islands of
traditional, even Andalusian, life, and tiled doorways with clumsily
classical architraves offer small glimpses through beaded curtains of
courtyards and corridors. You can still walk down the *horm* of Ridjal
Eç-Çoff – now called Sidi Fateh for one of the Throng in a process of saintly
synecdoche – though you won't get roughed up under the pretty arbour
once feared by Jews and Christians.

Eventually you reach the Souaika, the long, disjointed cross-street that
forms the core of the markets, roofed in palm-mats, floored in God-only-

knows-what and selling everything you could imagine wanting, from fake
Mancunian teapots to the olive-oil soap that looks like axle-grease; from
straw hats to tortoises and from *babouches* to bundles of mint, pirate DVDs
of every film ever made in Hollywood or Casablanca, and counterfeit
sunglasses. You can stop outside the mosque and try a sliver of braised
cow's face or ankle, or you can stock up with pastries, underwear or
painted woodwork. Eventually you will tumble out, perhaps through the
Bab el-Bahri by the old Mellah, down to where the Customs House stood
in Rabat's trading days; or out of the Bab Chella (named for those very
distant times when you'd set out from here on your pony, perhaps in a
solar topee and escorted by a pair of soldiers, to cross the wild, Za'er-
infested country to the outer wall and the necropolis of Abul Hassan).
Outside the Bab Chella today is the wide expanse of Prost's *cordon sanitaire*,
its railway long ago transferred into tunnels further up the town, now
called Avenue Hassan II, frantic with buses, taxis and pedestrians, cyclists,
sans-papiers and shoe-cleaners; and beyond it once again the *Nouvelle Ville*,
that pleasant, green-and-white city in which, just occasionally, I am
tempted to see echoes of Celesteville, capital of the elephants. Which
brings my wandering mind back, once again, to Pliny.

***

It was a fascinating and very emotional time to live in Rabat. Politically, it
was the moment of the so-called 'Arab Spring', and the hopes and fears of
Morocco's clever, passionate but often unhappy people coursed up and
down these narrow lanes and broad boulevards, sometimes pursued by
gendarmes with batons – but that is another, and different, story. As for the
city itself, it stands on the edge of a precipice of change. Very soon after I
first reached Rabat, three big urban projects were completed and
inaugurated. The Pont Hassan II, a great arc of concrete, not unlovely in
itself, linked Rabat and Saleh, changing the dynamics of the region
dramatically. No more ferries, and no longer the old bridge designed to
take traffic round, rather than through, Salé as it headed for Fes – suddenly
the two old sparring-partners are drawn firmly together by this new
umbilical cord, and their long-running open marriage is being – as it were
– concretised. Commuters pour over the bridge in the morning and the

evening, many of them in the new tram – *al-tramway* – that is the second of the great urban projects. *Al-tramway* was not without its problems. Priced, like so much of the new Rabat, for the middle class rather than the poor, it was also an alarming novelty to Rbati pedestrians, and a warden with flags had to be posted at every intersection and crossing for several months after it opened, to avoid as many as possible of the inevitable collisions. Teething-troubles overcome, it functions well, though taxi-drivers grumble at the loss of road, and sensitive souls at the wraparound Macdonald's advertisements that it drags through the city.

The third of the great projects was the tunnel under the Qasbah des Oudayas, a huge road diversion that takes the honking, roaring traffic away from Souk al-Ghazel and the thoroughfare it had become, and pipes it under the Qasbah, and out onto the coast. This of course brings blessed relief to the medina, though it makes it almost impossible to get a taxi there at night; and forms the completing link in the coast road that runs along the edge of the estuary and down the sea-coast to the lighthouse and beyond.

These three signs of change pale into insignificance beside what is now being built and planned. It is said that King Hassan II was stern in his determination to preserve the view across the valley to Salé, and his grave in the family mausoleum looks out across the valley. But by the time I left Rabat in 2014 there was little but digging and building in the Bouregreg valley, and Phase 1 of the new development, made up of marina and shopping opportunities and pastel-coloured housing, was already in place on the flood-plain. Marshes gave way to fields in the twentieth century: now the fields must give way in turn to concrete, and great placards read smugly 'Where Rabat meets Salé.' The planning is ambitious and involves the infill of much of the valley with housing, 'leisure facilities' and public buildings.

There is to be a new cultural centre for Rabat, centred on a Grande Théâtre by Zaha Hadid. In a 3D maquette of the whole development, Ms Hadid's theatre looks like an enormous marshmallow that has been sat upon by a careless, perhaps Plinian, elephant. The developers are as pleased as punch with the whole thing, which is budgeted at 9,000,000,000 dirhams, and will take shape between 2014 and 2020: 'Phase 2, which will cover about 110 hectares, is located on a site already exceptionally well served by the tramway, the road and motorway network, and only ten minutes from Rabat international airport.' Which is to say that the project fits into the logic of cultural and touristic attraction. Rabat-Salé intends to attract 4 million tourists a year by 2020. To service their needs there will be not only Ms Hadid's Grand Théâtre, but a new museum of archæology and earth science, 'thematised promenades' by the river and lots of hotels. As well, of course, as another marina ('it is hard to imagine the refurbishment of the Bouregreg valley without a marina ...'), 105,000 square metres of office space and a house-building programme 'which combines futuristic and traditional buildings with typical touches of the old medina.'

This new quarter will be 'a real hyphen between culture and the general public. That's the principle mission for the five cultural centres in the Bouregreg valley'. I'm not entirely clear how this rhetorical hyphen will operate in joining culture and the general public, but I suppose the latter will pour down from both banks to throng the facilities provided by the former. And of course they will. It would be churlish to question the appetite for a 'proper' capital city – after all, the glories of old Rabat, the 'calm of privileged nature, green, and still full of poetic memories of past ages', are probably more valued by presumptuous birds of passage like me than by many Rbatis (though I know quite a few who squirm at what is happening to the 'Pearl of Morocco'). More disturbing, given the failure of the French to address it under the Protectorat, is the segregation of rich and poor, the chasm of affordability that bisects Moroccan society – and its cities.

I very much hope it works well and gives real satisfaction to Rbatis of all classes, because the price that Rabat is paying is a high one, in the permanent loss of the almost inexpressibly lovely views of Salé's walls across the salt-flats, and of the slow-moving river flowing gently through the patchwork of small green fields with the *laqlaqs* clacking in the trees and the fishermen languidly casting their nets from their fishing-boats as they have for so many centuries.

ARTS AND LETTERS

FESTIVE BRADFORD

Syima Aslam and Irna Qureshi

What do you think of when you think of Bradford? Bradford is a city where a number of small, but hugely impactful, events have led to the creation of an urban myth embedded in the British and international consciousness. Carefully crafted by the media, every new story emerging from Bradford adds to this legend.

When journalist Yasmin Alibhai-Brown tweeted from the inaugural Bradford Literature Festival in May 2015, she referenced an event dating back a quarter of a century, that marks the point from which all Bradford myths stem: 'The city that burnt *The Satanic Verses*'. The event defined our city as the absolute centre of conservative Muslim culture in Britain. The ideal place for fleeting visits by journalists to pick up horror stories, and to measure the pulse and gauge the temperature of collective Muslim feeling.

But it was the second part of Alibhai-Brown's tweet that is of significance: 'Hosts a fab @BradfordLitFest.' Bradford is a city of many stories. And the Bradford Literary Festival is creating and telling new ones.

That the 1989 Rushdie affair still looms large is significant. Not only did it mark the first time a post-Windrush 'racial' minority community redefined itself according to its faith, it was the first time a minority Bradfordian community had catapulted the city onto the media world stage. Bradford wasn't the first site of protest in Britain over the publication of *The Satanic Verses*; the book had already been banned in several countries including South Africa, Pakistan and Bangladesh. Nevertheless, images of bearded men denouncing Salman Rushdie, and setting fire to his book in the centre of Bradford, were seized on by the media and beamed around the world. This one event, and the media response to it, has shaped all subsequent narratives about the West Yorkshire city over the intervening twenty-five years.

Paradoxically, the event also marked a moment of new confidence among Bradford's Muslims, who felt invested enough about their lives in the UK to seek a voice and representation in a way the previous generation never had. The generation before belonged to the pioneer phase of migrants, hailing mostly from rural Pakistan, who regarded their stay in Britain as temporary, clinging instead to the idea of Pakistan as a spiritual and cultural homeland through their belief in the 'myth of return'. Thus campaigning for change or civic rights had seemed irrelevant to them.

For the second and third generations of Pakistani Muslims in Britain, the Rushdie affair represented a coming of age. For the first time in their lives, they realised the power of collective voice. The ensuing global protests and Ayatollah Khomeini's fatwa, imposing a death sentence on Rushdie, felt like victories in which they had played a significant role. It evoked a connection with other parts of the Muslim world – a sense of brotherhood – where all stood united against one common enemy.

What the Bradford Muslim community failed to recognise at the time was that the impact of the image of a burning book, unprecedented in Britain and evoking as it did uncomfortable memories of the Nazi bonfires of 1933, symbolic of the repression of freedom of expression, as well as a death sentence on a writer, would cast a long shadow into the future. It would seal Bradford's reputation as being full of backward, violent, religious fanatics.

The stigmatisation of British Muslims, which had its precursor in the Ray Honeyford affair that had rocked Bradford's education system in the mid 1980s, accelerated at a national level and the perception of Muslims as the inherently subordinate, if not pejorative, 'other' began to gain ground. Up to this point, everyone hailing from the Indian subcontinent was referred to as 'Asian'. Now, in order to distance themselves from Muslims, some in the Hindu and Sikh communities began to differentiate themselves either by faith or nationality.

The Rushdie affair led to the proliferation of Muslim organisations at both local and national levels. It also produced the community leader phenomenon in the media, whereby representatives of these institutions were sought out and groomed as spokesmen – assumed to be trusted figures, authentic in religious practice, and empowered to be the bridge between communities. This become a double edged sword used both by those within the Muslim community who wanted to give their voice an authority it may not necessarily have, and by the media to represent views that fitted their storyline rather than the reality. It also contributed to Muslims misleadingly being viewed as one bounded community; impenetrable without the help of mediators. Thus there arose a unitary narrative representing Bradford's 129,041 Muslims as one homogenous group, which not only obscured individual complex realities, but ignored the different ethnic, sectarian and doctrinal approaches, differences, contradictions, conflicts of interest and changing motivations. This skewed approach to Bradford's Muslims epitomises how Muslims across Britain are now regarded.

The next chapter in the tale of Bradford came in 2001– a year marked by disturbances in a number of northern towns, including Burnley and Oldham. However, predictably, it was the unrest in Bradford involving around 1,000 youths from across the city's different communities that entered the national consciousness. Due in part to earlier riots in Bradford in 1995, and compounded by the post-Rushdie narrative, the events of 2001 were reduced to simplistic reporting that played on the unforgettable televised pictures of the Rushdie book-burning, bolstering the image of a loutish and intolerant community of Muslims. Even though it was widely accepted that the northern riots were triggered by social and economic factors and provocations by the far-right, analysts, quick to explore a religious motive for the disturbances, identified Islam as the principal driver.

The 2001 riots occurred just three months before the 9/11 attacks in the United States. Whilst unconnected, the proximity of the two events generated a watershed moment; the collision of an international event with a local one. 9/11 resulted in Muslim allegiance coming into question, and merged with the heated debate sparked by the riots about the alleged lack of integration of Muslim communities and the incompatibility of their cultural beliefs with British values. This led to increasingly intense scrutiny of British Muslims and Bradford again became the natural choice for the media and policymakers to gauge the temperature of Muslims nationwide. That the perpetrators of the London bombings of 7 July 2005 hailed from Beeston and Dewsbury, both located on Bradford's doorstep within West Yorkshire, and one of the bombers being Bradford born, served only to reinforce this focus.

In the new national narrative about home grown terrorism, Bradford is, as ever, conspicuous. In June 2015, Zohra Dawood along with sisters Sugra and Khadija abandoned their husbands, and travelled with their nine children to join their militant brother in 'Islamic State' in Syria. A few months later another Bradford family, including five children, also disappeared, allegedly making the same trip. Now Bradford was being associated with the Islamic State. However the fact is that Bradford actually has very good race relations. Although the far right English Defence League continue to make an annual pilgrimage to the city, in the hope of sparking violence, the only response it has received are thoughtful counter-protests organised by all the communities working together. The riots may have put Manningham on the national map, but the disturbances also marked a turning point in community relations, with all communities in Bradford determined to ensure that the events would not be repeated.

Bradford rose to prominence during the nineteenth century as one of the greatest manufacturing cities of the Victorian Empire. It was the city's industry that made it a popular destination for immigrants; for over 150 years, it has embraced diversity. Bradford was nicknamed 'Worstedopolis' for making 'worsted', a fine wool fabric used in top quality clothing. Although the British textile sector fell into decline from the mid-twentieth century, the different communities in Bradford are a living testament to the central role immigrants played in creating the yester-year might of the British economy. The Bradford population swelled from immigration initially by Irish workers and Jewish merchants in the 1800s, followed by South Asians in the post-war boom period of the 1950s, to Eastern European workers after expansion of the European Union and now includes the largest Roma community in the UK.

Although numbers have now dwindled to 299 according to the 2011 census, during the 1820s and 1830s Bradford was a focus for Jewish German immigration and, in the early nineteenth century the Manningham area was known as the Jewish quarter. In 2013 when the 133-year-old Bradford Reform Synagogue, a Grade II listed building and the oldest Synagogue in the north of England, was faced with closure it was rescued by donations from the Muslim community. Bradford's Synagogue Council has recently appointed its first Muslim member.

The Bradford Literature Festival, of which we are the founders and directors, has deliberately sought to wrest back control of the city's identity by highlighting these bonds of faith. That is why we programmed a Jewish strand as part of its Bradford Heritage events. It is also why we decided to hold the festival's very first Sacred Poetry occasion, in September 2014, at the city's last remaining synagogue. The Sacred Poetry event offered an uplifting celebration of divine music and verse from across the religious spectrum. It featured Islamic spiritual poetry, *taizé* (a form of Christian meditation) and musical *shabad kirtan* recitations from the Sikh holy book, the Guru Granth Sahib. Rudi Leavor, chair of the synagogue, was invited to recite prayers to open the event, along with participation by Atar Hadari, a renowned local Jewish poet.

This is not to say we have completely freed ourselves from the past. The Bradford Reform Synagogue is in the Bradford West constituency that garnered national headlines after electing the radical left-wing politician George Galloway during the 2012 by-election. Just weeks before the inaugural Sacred Poetry event, following a spate of violence between Israel and Palestine, Galloway declared Bradford an 'Israel-free zone' where not only Israeli goods but also Israeli citizens were unwelcome. Although Galloway's comments ran contrary to Bradford's reputation as a City of Sanctuary, and led to the politician being questioned by police after complaints that his remarks incited religious hatred, the media's attention threatened to yet again reinforce the negative image of Bradford's Muslims. While Atar Hadari had been contracted by the festival long before, these developments threatened to pull the festival and the Israeli-born poet into the media maelstrom that Galloway had created. In the event, the Sacred Poetry event succeeded in generating positive headlines for Bradford.

The Bradford Literature Festival, now regarded as the city's flagship event, was created as a response to the lack of relevant cultural offering for those who wished to step beyond the lazy racial stereotyping of Bradford as a mono-cultural city. It also stemmed from a desire to re-write the Bradford narrative and showcase the richness that a genuine melding of cultures creates. The festival therefore celebrates Bradford's cultural, architectural, faith and literary heritage; the city's status as the world's first UNESCO City of Film and its designation as a City of Sanctuary.

We are also building upon a proud tradition of cultural innovation. Bradford was one of the earliest centres of Indian film screenings for the South Asian community in Britain. During the 1950s and 60s, immigrant mill workers travelled from as far away as Newcastle and Sheffield to Bradford to catch an Indian film on their day off. During the 1980s and 1990s, Bradford was one of the few cities to host the revolutionary *bhangra* day timers; club events where thousands of young Asians whose conservative parents disapproved of mainstream British nightlife, would dance to live *bhangra* music during the afternoon – when they were thought to be at school or college.

Bradford also spearheaded the European Mela scene thirty years ago. The Bradford Mela was feted as one of Europe's largest multi arts festivals, attracting international audiences of over 200,000 in its heyday and is still talked about. The mela was symbolic of, and synonymous with, the first generation holding onto the 'myth of return' in which life in the UK was viewed as an extension of life 'back home'. The mela prioritised the preservation of cultural identity over promotion of social integration, and this was reflected in the cultural programmes it hosted.

Bradford today remains at the forefront of pioneering cultural movements. This time, however, the cultural context has changed. The second, third and fourth generation have a different identity to the first generation. Their identity, unlike that of their parents, is no longer rooted in South Asia. Instead their roots are British but they remain culturally attuned to South Asia, and this is reflected in the culture they want to experience. Any new cultural movement therefore requires programming that creates events acknowledging the fluid and shifting nature of this multi-layered identity. A celebration of this shift in identity politics is also important given the rhetoric around immigration and otherness now present across the UK as a whole.

Therefore, the latest cultural innovation to come out of Bradford is a festival, which while it reflects and responds to the different communities that make up the city, also brings all the communities together. With cultural literacy at its heart, and a distinct, diverse and dynamic brand of programming, Bradford Literature Festival offers an exploration of race, faith and culture through a celebration of literature, history and the arts. The events inspire civic and community pride and act as an important reminder that migrants – whether settled or newly arrived – along with the indigenous community, have a role to play in building a city. The festival is unique in that the voice of each community is viewed as being equally valid and relevant and it has therefore successfully reached audiences that traditional literature festivals do not. As such it is relevant not only to Bradford's different communities but also to Britain.

This is the first literature festival, out of the 250 held in the UK, to be programmed by two British Muslim women. The unique cultural space that the festival occupies, and its ethos, is a reflection of this. Previously cultural programming by the South Asian diaspora has in the main focused on heritage, while programming that is deemed to be for all communities has come from mainstream white middle class arts professionals. Thus programming where the cultural leadership comes from a minority community and yet represents all communities is a new concept, and a reflection of the energising transformation in South Asian cultural identity.

The festival can address cultural literacy because we, the festival directors, to use anthropologist Lila Abu-Lughod's term, regard ourselves and thus programme the festival as 'halfies'. This enables us to focus on both the cultural fusions and the richly distinctive cultures that make Britain the country that it is today. It means that we bring the same cultural confidence to curating events about the Brontës or Byron as we do to Ghalib or Iqbal. This position, perfectly balanced at the cusp of two cultures, and equally at home in both, also enables us to confront the ethics of representation. The Arabic word for trust, *amanah*, also has a deeper and more profound meaning; it is the moral responsibility to fulfil one's obligation to both God and other people. This cultural background, and the lived experience of being 'othered', also brings an awareness of inequality. Having seen how the Pakistani Muslim community is represented, and British Muslim people are talked about from without, we are committed to delivering authentic experiences that reflect from within the different communities we work with.

We want to create a neutral ground where people can discuss differences and engage in open, honest, unfettered dialogue about the challenges faced by society. The festival's current affairs strand enables discussion of emerging contemporary issues in ways that are constructive, provocative and insightful.

The 'war on terror' is just as much a war of ideology as of weapons. It is a war whose ramifications have reverberated through Bradford society. As festival directors we felt that this was a narrative that Bradford, and its Muslim community, needed to own rather than issue an apology for. The festival, therefore, has unflinchingly addressed the key issues pertaining to this debate.

The 2015 festival coincided with the ten-year anniversary of 7/7 and a strand of events related to 7/7, radicalisation and ISIS was programmed. These addressed the current discourse through events such as 'The War on ISIS Explained' and 'Sectarian Warfare in the Middle East and its Global Consequences'. They also asked open and searching questions about what lessons, if any, had been learnt in the last decade by the Muslim community and the government.

One of the greatest national concerns of our time is whether or not Muslims can be trusted. With each new atrocity committed in the name of Islam around the world, this question grows louder. In response, the festival brought together leading writers, commentators and politicians in events, such as 'Muslims and Trust' discussing can the state trust Muslims and can Muslims trust the state and 'Religious Intolerance in Contemporary Britain: How do rising Islamophobia and Anti-semitism reflect on British Values?' This enabled issues to be discussed in the open rather than in closed groups, either within communities or bureaucracies.

We also devote an entire strand of programming to spirituality and mysticism. Encapsulated within the Sufi Poetry weekend is a core message of universality. Contemplative and inspirational in tone, the strand melds and explores eastern and western spiritual influences using mystical poetry as a cornerstone. From the *Mathnavi* of the thirteenth century Iranian mystic Jalal ad-Din Muhammad Rumi to the eighteenth century *Songs of Innocence* by William Blake, it focuses on the commonality of religions and influences that transcend national borders. It also incorporates Sufiana Kalaam, a form of mystical Sufi poetry in Punjabi and Urdu recited at the shrines of Sufi saints. The oral transmission of this has remained strong, and is part of the everyday idiom and proverbs of the Punjabi language still in use in Britain today. Used as a form of oral intercultural literature, Sufiana Kalaam resonates with much of the South Asian diaspora and offers great potential to build community cohesion and impact on literacy and engagement in Bradford's Pakistani community.

The festival uniquely employs culture to address education, economic engagement and cultural regeneration. More than a quarter of Bradford's population is Muslim and amongst school children this figure rises to 40 per cent. With a growing population, and every other live birth in the district now of Pakistani origin, this demographic is set to change even further. Bradford schools have been consistently poor in their performance with two communities being disproportionately affected – white working class boys and Pakistani families, both from the poorer, deprived areas of the city.

One of the drivers behind creating the literature festival has been a passionate belief that education has the power to change people's lives; that literacy holds the key to empathy and compassion, health and wellbeing, and economic and cultural engagement. So a main aim of the festival is to engage children with books by creating excitement around reading and literacy in a manner that is relatable and accessible. The other imperative is to take literacy into the home by showing parents that literacy does not have to stop at the classroom door. Creating appropriate content to enable this to happen, across all communities but particularly for those from a deprived background, is one of the cornerstones on which this festival has been built.

The other key issue in the city that has affected every community has been that of economic regeneration. Bradford has been trying to regenerate for years but each time it has stumbled. At this moment in time there is a sense of renewed hope that the city is on the cusp of a fresh economic start. The launch of the long anticipated Broadway Shopping Centre potentially heralds a renaissance for Bradford. After much of the area was razed to the ground more than a decade ago to make way for development, the proposed shopping centre was abandoned amid the recession. With the loss of the city's nerve centre, and the subsequent proliferation of pound shops, the derelict site poignantly become known as 'the hole in the heart'. From this a new £260m shopping centre has now emerged. The development comes on the heels of Bradford's new public space, City Park, the largest urban water feature in the UK boasting one hundred fountain displays, transforming the heart of Bradford.

Economic regeneration, of course, is not viable if people refuse to come into a city because of fear or the myth that has built up around Bradford.

Bradford is a rich district; what the city needs is a mechanism to pull people back in so that they can see that beyond the myth lies a beautiful, vibrant and, most of all, welcoming city. Inspired by one of the world's most successful literature festivals, we wanted to create a Hay of the North, a destination festival that would facilitate cultural restoration to complement the economic regeneration. The richness of the communities in Bradford, hailing from so many different parts of the world, enables the creation of a truly international festival that can attract people from the district, the Yorkshire region, the rest of the country as well as internationally.

The nineteenth century literary siblings, the Brontës (Anne, Emily and Charlotte), are one of Bradford's major attractions. Their novels, such as *Wuthering Heights* and *Jane Eyre*, are synonymous with Yorkshire's unspoilt, dramatic moorland. The festival celebrates their legacy and influence in the Brontë Heritage Weekend. In doing so it aims to attract an international audience and promote the idea of the home tourist thereby furthering the city's tourism agenda. This is also an opportunity to re-engage local audiences with their literary heritage, including the South Asian/Pakistani diaspora, who may not have engaged with the Brontës and the environment in which they wrote. Ironically, the lived experience of the Brontë sisters is not dissimilar to that of Pakistani girls living in Bradford today. Therefore, even if language may at first seem a barrier, in fact the novels are culturally relatable.

The festival was created from the desire to realise a vision. As Bradfordians, as mothers bringing up young girls in the city, as women experienced in dealing with the media, we were acutely aware of the Bradford narrative. We wanted to shatter its stranglehold. We know that unless we are seen we are invisible. We thus want to create a different narrative to be seen and heard. Literature – open and uncensored – is the ideal way to address this. There is no idea that is espoused that does not find itself into the written word. There is nothing in the world that cannot be found in a book – therefore, there is nothing that a literature festival cannot tackle. Literature encompasses the world; it covers every culture, every creed and is always at the forefront of progress.

The Bradford Literature Festival is the new thinking for Bradford.

THE MIGRANT WORKERS
OF DUBAI

VMK

A #RealTrouper is anyone whose life is a revealing story of a thirst for success, a responsibility to provide for a family, an ambition to make a change from what seems destined because of the 'accident of birth'. They are at crucial moments in their lives, trying to enact some kind of change, and being hopeful while chasing their dreams and fulfilling their expectations. They go through experiences that we can all relate to in some way or form and are universally shared. Every city has its RealTroupers.

The United Arab Emirates has expats from all over the world – living in segregation, within their gated communities and well as their own social systems and traditional cocoons. It is an ideal place to challenge prejudices and phobias, isolation and alienation, and the existing definitions of cultures and labels used in societies.

The purpose of #RealTrouper is to draw inspiration from different communities and showcase shared aspirations and emotions that unite us all.

THE TENANT

Maria Chaudhuri

In the earlier part of 1929, when her father Sajjad Ali passed away, Lily was nine years old. Later, she remembered more of her mother's screams and howls, day and night, for weeks after the death. No one really bothered to explain to Lily why her father suddenly disappeared. One day it seemed he was resting in bed with a cold, wearing his white cotton kurta, blowing his nose into a creamy white hanky, a tumbler of ginger tea resting on a white crochet doily on the bedside table and a book on his lap. Lily had been playing at the foot of the mahogany four poster bed with her old rag dolls and from time to time Sajjad Ali would look up from his book and share from it, an odd line or two: '*I believe that on the first night I went to Gatsby's house I was one of the few guests who had actually been invited. People were not invited – they went there.*' And the next day: '*I wonder where in the devil he met Daisy. By God, I may be old-fashioned in my ideas, but women run around too much these days to suit me. They meet all kinds of crazy fish.*' Lily hardly ever understood any of his quotes or any of his peculiar remarks for that matter but there was something comforting about his mild presence, something reassuring about his fragile attempts at communication, disjointed as they were.

Lily also loved the story of how her father had named her. Her father's mother, Lily's grandmother, had been married over the phone to a man who was finishing his studies in Bilayat; one of those matrimonial 'trunk calls' that senselessly required the bride to place a veil over her head and keep her eyes on the floor while muttering 'kabul' three times into the receiver. One year later, when her husband returned to Bengal from Bilayat, i.e. London, he brought for her an English perfume called Lily of the Valley. She had never smelled anything so sweet, and in fear that she might never again acquire one of its kind, Lily's grandmother placed the fragrant bottle inside a locked glass cabinet in the living room, where it still stood in the same spot, half a century later, except that the musk had long evaporated. When Lily was born, the first daughter after two sons, Sajjad Ali immediately knew what to call her.

So, after three days of cosying up with her father, watching him nap and read and slurp his ginger tea in contentment, when Lily was told that he had been found dead near the outhouse in the middle of the night, she was understandably confused. Adding to the confusion was an uncharacteristic madness that emerged in her mother in the wake of her husband's sudden demise. About twenty years old at the time and mother of three, Nargis seemed to have lost her stately elegance and calm disposition overnight. She pulled out fistfuls of her long black hair and beat her chest like a gorilla and if one of her four children happened to be in her way (which they tried their best to avoid), she pounced on them with renewed vigour, drowning them in her tears, terrifying them with her maniacal screams. In the days that followed, Lily felt that she could not even grieve as the fond memories of her gentle and bookish father were not only at odds with his unexpected death but were brutally tarnished by her mother's inconsolable mortification.

***

The only thing that Lily felt sure of, after her father's death, was that she had never quite seen or known her own mother for what she was. She had thought of Nargis as a beautiful woman with a long, thick braid in which she routinely stuck a jasmine or a marigold just before sunset, when it was time for her husband to come home. She was always surrounded by a gaggle of aunts and ayahs and other neighbourhood women, but she never failed to keep a watchful eye on her children. She made them delightful treats of pithas and parathas at the end of each week and took them to the Big Bazaar with her on Sundays where she gave them a coin each to spend as they chose. Oh, the pleasure! Lily always bought sweets of various shapes and colours while her brothers picked up odd items like spindles, marbles and once even a goldfish in a little plastic bag of water. It was impossible to find any of that grace or mirth in her mother anymore. Now, Nargis had lost her beauty, her grace and even her voice from screaming at everyone, and she had stopped cooking and caring for her children. If Lily and her brothers cried or fell sick, Nargis pounded the walls until her fists bled and one of the neighbours came running. But after six months of providing for Nargis and her children, even the kindest relatives and neighbours grew tired. Accusing her of an incurable affliction, they tied Nargis by her wrists to the four-poster mahogany bed and threatened to put her children in an orphanage if she showed no signs of recovery soon.

For about a week, Nargis lay motionless on that bed, blood drying on her bruised wrists, spitting out every bit of food and water anyone gave her. Lily was sure that her mother would die of starvation, if nothing else, and in a strange way, the thought relieved her. She was afraid of this madwoman who had replaced Nargis and if she couldn't have the old Nargis back then she wanted this new one gone. On the seventh day, when Nargis's delicate lips started to turn into a pale blue and her breath grew faint, someone felt compelled to bring a doctor to Nargis's bedside. In truth, young Rajat was not even a doctor yet, but a local medical student who made house calls for those who didn't have much money to pay a real doctor. Rajat accepted payment in the form of a chicken, fresh fruit, a new kurta or anything else he considered useful for his hand-to-mouth existence. At that time, he lived in a men's dormitory in the filthiest part of town, but after paying the five coins for his narrow bunk bed, Rajat had nearly nothing left for his food and clothing.

Lily remembered that afternoon well, even though she wouldn't dwell on it for several more years to come. It was the beginning of the rainy season and the sky had that indecisive grey pallor that could either burst into a downpour or diffuse into golden sunlight. The first thing that young Rajat ordered was to open wide the wooden shutters of the window by Nargis's bed. 'This room has no oxygen! Let some air in, now!' At the sound of his sharp, commanding voice, Nargis jerked her head towards him, the biggest sign of movement she had shown in days. Later, Nargis would define that moment as the moment that she got a second lease on life, the moment when she had the epiphany that her life wasn't over after all. Though never once would she say that the moment had anything to do with Rajat's sudden appearance. Instead, Nargis would make it a point to emphasize that it had been her husband, Sajjad Ali, who had magically appeared in a chariot-cloud that stopped right outside the open window. Nargis had turned to him, silently pleading to join him, and he had said, loudly and clearly, that she must never harbour such thoughts again. She had to gather her strength for her children, and when it was time, Sajjad Ali would come back for her in that same chariot-cloud by that same window.

That Nargis was being visited by her dead husband in a cloud on wheels, – while Rajat untied her wrists and checked her pulse, – was not evident to those who were watching, certainly not to Lily. To Lily, it seemed as if Nargis was mesmerised by Rajat's presence, compelled by his every command. For a week, she had spat out every morsel of sustenance, and now, in Rajat's arms, she suddenly sank into immediate obedience, and like a thirsty animal, noisily lapped at the saucer of water he held under her chin. The madness of the past six months slipped away from her withered skin with each drop of water that she sipped. She sat up straighter and smiled and said with much of the sweetness of her former self,

'Why is everyone looking at me as if they've seen a ghost? Where are my children?'

'How is this possible? Less than an hour ago, she was nearly dead,' blurted one of the stunned onlookers.

'It was dehydration,' shrugged Rajat, 'Should be fine in a day or two. Make sure to put salt and molasses in her water for quick rehydration.'

But Lily wasn't listening anymore. She was watching her mother's expression. Nargis was looking at Rajat out of the corner of her eye and on her features was an odd mixture of serenity and excitement. Suddenly Lily's chest felt unbearably heavy. Heavier than it had at the news of her father's passing, heavier even than it had at the onset of her mother's manic depression and near-demise. Lily noticed that the murky grey sky had cleared up after all. A hesitant sun was peeking from behind riceball clouds but the light did not reach Lily's heart.

***

It was traditional for a widow to dress modestly and in white. But in the wake of what she referred to as her 'second life', granted to her by Sajjad Ali's benevolent spirit, Nargis somehow found a way to look as charming as she had before. She put away her bright saris and replaced them with creamy beige, pale lemon or icy peach ones – not a vibrant selection – but piquant enough to bring out the colour in her cheeks and demure enough for people not to raise an eyebrow. If she wore white at all, it was when she made public appearances, and even then, she chose fine white silks with sparkling silver borders that made her look more elegant than drab. All the white cotton yards that Nargis had acquired during her six months of grief were cut up to make kurtas for her sons and there was enough leftover to make one dress for Lily. When the dress was finished and Nargis held it up for Lily to survey, the plainness of the dress seemed so stark that neither of them could speak. That night, Nargis stitched the pattern of a small pink waterlily on the front of the dress but perhaps because it was done hurriedly, as an afterthought, the flower was a bit lopsided and had the look of wilting.

One early morning Lily woke up to an unusual lot of clamour. Following the sounds, she rubbed her eyes and walked out to the front yard to find Nargis standing in one corner of it, supervising a group of village hands to clean out the tiny tool shed, next to the small patch of a garden, that had remained locked for as long as Lily could remember. A curious array of objects were found inside the shed which had a tin roof, one tiny window and a creaky wooden door. Heavily rusted pots and pans, books that were so moth-eaten that they crumbled to the touch, ancient oil lamps and spittoons. Nargis permitted the village hands to take whatever they wanted of the loot except one item. It was an old, dried-up ink bottle and quill. Nargis held it against her chest for a minute before she turned to an intently-staring Lily and said, 'Your father and I used to write letters to each other before we got married. He would roll up each precious letter with a bit of string holding a small stone on one end and then throw it into my room from outside my window. This must have been the ink and quill he used to write those letters…why else would he have saved this one when he threw away so many?' And for a split second, Lily thought her mother's eyes grew moist.

Even though Lily was not directly informed, she soon picked up snippets of conversation between Nargis and other women from which she gathered that the tin shed in the front yard was being cleared out for rent. Though Sajjad Ali's teaching position at the local university had made him one of the most well-respected and educated men in the small town of Comilla, it had not allowed him to acquire much wealth. And while Nargis now owned the house they lived in and received a tiny pension from the university, it was nowhere nearly enough for her and her three children. Middle-class pride made it extremely difficult for Nargis to ask Sajjad Ali's brothers for help on a regular basis. Nargis's own brother had asked her to rent out the Comilla house and move in with his family but this too was unfathomable to Nargis. She suffocated at the thought of living on the dole, in cramped quarters, in a treeless, airless city like Dhaka. To leave Comilla at all, home of the red Mynamati soil, home to the best sweet-makers in Bengal and home to the memory of her parents and husband, was impossible for Nargis. And so, one of her well-wishers suddenly gave her the idea of finding a tenant for the little abandoned shed. At least it would bring in a small but steady sum at the end of the month and it might be useful to have a strong male hand around the house in times of need.

After about a week of toil, the tin shed was finally ready. A narrow, creaking chowki with a threadbare mattress was brought in from the main house along with a rickety wooden desk and an old chair missing one arm. But the walls and floors were tolerably clean albeit a little mouldy and Nargis placed a beautiful oil lamp with red-stained glass on the desk. She stood back to consider her work, stepping on Lily's toes. 'Why are you always at my heels?' she frowned.

Lily shrunk into the corner. She decided to use the room as her secret hideaway until the tenant moved in. She was not opposed to the idea of a tenant in their own front yard although she feared it might tamper with her endless hours of frolicking there with the neighbourhood children. Mostly though, she was relieved to hear that at least for now, they would not have to move to their uncle's house in Dhaka. She despised her cousins Nimmi and Minara who made it a point to put on Big City airs around Lily and her brothers. And when Nargis told her that she was looking for a tenant who could also be a tutor to her children, Lily felt lighter and happier than she had in months. She began to imagine the tenant to be a big, burly man with heavy glasses and a kind face, who, just like her father, would sit her on his lap and read her beautiful passages from heavy leather-bound volumes.

But when Rajat moved in on a cool November day, carrying a jhola – a not-so-sturdy hemp bag – with a few items of clothing, a bar of soap and a comb with a few of its teeth missing, Lily stared in disbelief and disgust. This man, whom she had never expected to see again, was hardly the kind, paternal tutor and friend she had hoped for. He was far too young to be fatherly and there was something overbearingly needy about his disposition.

Between the extended palms of his hands, Rajat clutched something wrapped in oil-soaked newsprint. 'Bhapa pitha for the children…a woman makes them fresh on a woodfire by the riverside….' His voice trailed off in embarrassment, as if it suddenly struck him that his description was not necessarily appreciated. But Nargis smiled and graciously accepted the offering. She arranged the pithas on a delicate white plate and insisted that Rajat stay for a cup of tea.

Rajat's eyes moved deliberately over every object in the room which he had visited once before but this time he took in the modest furniture, the muted colours, the slanted rays of sunlight across the grey cement floor and smiled inwardly as his eyes came to rest on what he considered to be the most beautiful object in the room: Nargis.

***

In his twenty-two years of life, Rajat had never had a room of his own. He was from a small village called Choddogram, bordering the town of Comilla, where his father Monsoor Mia was the local butcher. During Qurbani Eid, Monsoor Mia came home with big cuts of meat and enough money to fall back on for a few months but the rest of the year was not half as lucrative. But Rajat's mother was a clever and seasoned homemaker who somehow made more out of less. She dried and cured some of those special cuts of meat and sold them at a good value; she cleaned people's homes and used her modest earnings to make a lush little vegetable patch full of perennial vegetables. Then Rajat's mother died of a sudden, debilitating illness when Rajat was about twelve years old. One morning she was coughing up blood, the next morning she was unconscious and by dusk the following day, her frail body was as cold and grey as the River Buriganga in the distance. Within a week of her mysterious death, Monsoor Mia spent all the money his wife had saved for months; within two weeks, her vegetable garden dried up into a gnarly brown mess and within a month Monsoor Mia re-married. The new wife bore him three children in four years. By the time Rajat was seventeen, their little hut was a picture of squalor and hunger. No one had enough to eat and the new wife screamed at Rajat all day. 'You're seventeen! My God you're old enough to have a family of your own – why do we need to feed your sorry arse?' Rajat ate one meal of two rotis a day and slept in the barn with the cows but the vicious complaints continued, until late one night, when Monsoor Mia entered the roofless barn where Rajat slept. Rajat was lying on a stack of hay, using one arm as a pillow, staring up at the inky night sky. In the soft moonlight, Monsoor Mia's gaunt face looked ghostly pale. Hurriedly he pressed a dirty white pouch into Rajat's hand and whispered hoarsely, 'Take this. This is the only memory of your mother I saved for you. Take this and go – make your own destiny my boy.' 'But Abba, where will I –' Rajat started to speak then stopped mid-sentence. Monsoor Mia had already turned away and was on his way out.

Rajat left home that night, walking barefoot all the way to the train station where he slipped in, unnoticed, into one of the cars of a stationery cargo train. He had no idea when he had fallen asleep but when he awoke, the train was just pulling into Comilla railway station. Sitting amidst what smelled like bags of rice, Rajat pulled out the dirty pouch from his shirt pocket and emptied its contents. A small pair of sparkling gold hoops slinked out. Rajat stared at them for a while before putting them back into the pouch. Then he walked out into the crisp morning air.

Rajat never sold the earrings but they gave him something far more valuable than their monetary yield. Small as the baubles were, and probably not of great worth, those earrings, as if twinkling with the patience that Rajat remembered well in his mother's eyes, urged him to move forward and not look back.

***

At first, Lily's brothers Shobhon and Tokon adjusted well to Rajat's role as their tutor. Perhaps they had been hungry for a male presence in their lives or perhaps Rajat was by far the most soft-spoken and kind teacher they'd ever had, whatever the reason they grew fond of him overnight. The days and nights fell into a kind of natural pattern. Before the sun came up fully, Rajat, Shobhon and Tokon would rise and bathe together in the little pond in front of the house and bring in heavy iron bucketfuls of water on their way back for the daily household use. Lily and Nargis made a modest breakfast of warm rotis which they served with homemade raab (a sticky honey-like concoction of molten sugarcane molasses that Nargis loved to make) and piping hot tea. They all ate together, sitting on wooden stools around the clay hearth in the kitchen and even though those early hours were wrought with a sleepy silence, Lily never failed to sense an electric undercurrent between her mother and Rajat. She had no idea what it meant or what was the source of this undercurrent. She only knew that it made her feel something she had never felt before...a kind of heady tension that felt unseemly, untoward and even unfaithful to her father's memory. It made her rush to finish her breakfast and gather up the plates for wash, making everyone else stir and follow suit, breaking up the cosy little circle, a circle she did not feel part of.

Lily loved to go to school during those days. It was the only time she could forget about the strange new feelings that chased her at home. School was the only place where she caught glimpses of an outside world that was big and mysterious and fraught with the unfamiliar things that she had only come across in her father's thick old leather-bound books. Even though Lily was an introverted child with few friends at school, she still felt free and alive at school. The rest of the day went by quickly, in a flurry of lessons and daydreams and youthful laughter and conversation.

The evenings were harder to pass. Lily, Shobhon and Tokon were expected to sit down with Rajat for two hours before supper and work on their assignments. And even though Nargis entrusted the children solely to Rajat's guardianship during this time, Lily could sense that her presence was never that far. Lily might suddenly look up from her books to find Nargis hastily move away from behind the curtain or hear her dainty footsteps in the next room, her ankle-bells jingling in a fashion that suggested that she was simply walking around in idle circles. Midway through their lesson, Nargis would arrive with a tray of tea and snacks, but instead of leaving it there, she'd linger, quietly, lest she disturb the children, but the very silence spoke louder than words. Lily often noticed that Nargis had placed fragrant flowers on her snaking braid and a red bindi on her forehead before appearing with that ritualistic evening tea. She could have easily sent the servant boy in with the tray but she never did. It was not until a month had passed of Rajat's tenancy, that Lily started waking up to find Nargis missing from the large four-poster bed they shared. Soon after her father's death, Nargis had brought Lily into her bed as neither wanted to be alone. But now, a sudden soft movement or quiet rustle in the middle of the night would wake Lily and as she blinked to adjust her eyes to the darkness, she would slowly come to notice that Nargis's side of the bed was empty. She would notice too that the fine white mosquito-net was tucked back hastily into the mattress where Nargis must have lifted it to make her exit, as if she did not mean to return right away from a prompt trip to the outhouse or a quick drink of water for her suddenly parched throat. No, these nocturnal escapades were regular and long and clearly pre-meditated. Lily longed to stay awake to watch her mother return but she was far too young and always sank back into an exhausted slumber despite her best efforts. And when her eyes opened again at the first light of day, Nargis was always next to her, peacefully asleep, long dark hair spread out like a Japanese fan against the white pillow.

But a year later, when Lily turned ten, she demanded to return to her own bed in the next room. It was a much smaller room, with barely any furniture except Lily's little wooden bunk and a chipped wooden desk, but Lily loved that neither the bed nor the room smelled of her mother and the constant supply of flowers on her braid or her attar-soaked saris that left a trail of heady perfume long after she was gone. Nargis had grown more beautiful in a way that Lily did not recognise. There was something feral about her beauty now. Gone was the soft, maternal aura of her ways, replaced by a bold, restless gait. Nargis still cooked and cleaned and made sure her children went to school but Lily could not shake off the feeling that they – her children – had become part of a clockwork routine that needed to be completed before Nargis could shed her daily skin and escape into the night's adventures. To Nargis, it seemed, her children were no longer living, breathing creatures who grew and evolved every day and who might be watching *her* in turn. And even though Lily never spoke about any of it with her brothers, she envied them their close companionship, which seemed to carry them through. Shobhon and Tokon were 14 and 15 now and they came home later and later in the evenings after hours of playing cricket with the village boys. Their voices were changing and bristly hair was sprouting on their smooth faces. They hardly paid any attention to Lily or anyone else around them. It was as if they had already joined that unfamiliar outside world that Lily had only sensed and glimpsed at times. Even Rajat spoke more carefully with them, taking care not to arouse their increasingly hot young tempers. They were hardly interested in the lessons anymore and Rajat struggled to keep their attention on the books. Sometimes when the boys were downright insolent and disobedient, which they were frequently so, Rajat turned to Lily helplessly and it was the only time their eyes would meet and lock in a complete lack of comradeship. It was always Rajat who looked away first.

Around their mother, Shobhon and Tokon were slightly more tolerant, but only if she held her silence, served them food and never asked about their whereabouts or their school work. Still, Nargis remained commendably unruffled by the changing currents of her childrens' temperaments. Her facial muscles twitched or hardened when they acted against her wishes, and to young, unprotesting Lily, she might still administer some harsh words, but her eyes remained deadpan, as if it was a mere inconvenience rather than a deep concern for her child. In her short life, Lily had never witnessed such single-mindedness, such bold conviction and such dedication to a purpose (and what exactly was the purpose? A secret but overwhelming affection for Rajat?). And for the first time, Lily wondered if it was even love that Nargis was chasing or herself. Not that she ever found the answer to her question. Though one night she might have come close to it, when she overheard a conversation between Nargis and Rajat.

Lily was suddenly woken by the sound of not-so-hushed voices coming from her mother's room. This was a new phenomenon as Lily knew that Nargis's nightly visits with Rajat always took place in the tin shed outside the main house. Clearly, Rajat now had permission to come into Nargis's chambers at any time of the day or night. Fully awake, Lily stared up at the ceiling, filled with the morbid dread of having to listen to Nargis and Rajat's voices even if she didn't want to.

'Rajat, hush, keep your voice down,' Nargis was saying, as if she read Lily's mind.

'Oh never mind. How long will you hide this? Hide us?' Rajat said as he must've clasped her wrist because it was a followed by the jangling of bangles and a slight gasp from Nargis.

'You musn't speak that way. You know we must always remain a secret. You want the whole village to know? What will happen then?'

'What will happen Nargis? Don't be such a fool. People know. Your children know...everyone has eyes and ears.' There was a growing undertone of derision in Rajat's voice.

'You think I'm a fool?' Nargis's voice trembled.

'All women are fools,' Rajat retorted.

'Why are you taunting me tonight?' Nargis pleaded, 'I've given you everything, every bit of myself. Must you speak of me so poorly?'

'No, I've given you everything. I brought you back from the throes of insanity; I've given you back your youth, your laughter, your desires...' Rajat's voice trailed off and for a minute there was only the sound of rustling sheets and a faint moan.

Lily was surprised by the malice she heard in Rajat's voice. And even more surprised when Nargis spoke again in a voice that had gone from fearful and pleading to saccharine sweet.

'You're right, my love. Without you, I'm nothing.'

It was the first time Lily realised that perhaps her mother was not just a stranger to Lily and her brothers. It was entirely possible that neither Lily's father nor Rajat fully grasped the sudden flashing in Nargis's dark eyes, the unexpected shadows across her lovely face or the quick and unpredictable changes in her moods.

***

It was a bright and crisp August afternoon and Lily decided to take a walk by the river on her way home from school. It would add at least half an hour to her usual commute but she knew that her mother would never notice her lateness. Nargis enjoyed long siestas after which she awoke to take long, luxurious baths to prepare herself for the evening and Rajat's return. Lily and her brothers came from school and helped themselves to the rice and curry that Lily and Nargis prepared early in the morning, before sitting down for their lessons with Rajat. By the time they finished their lessons, Nargis would finally emerge, resplendent after her bath, eyes smudged with kohl, lips reddened suggestively from chewing paan. Lily often shuddered to think that her mother slept all afternoon in preparation for her wakeful nights.

But everything was different on that September afternoon when Lily took the long way home. As soon as Lily stepped on their front porch, hair tousled by the river breeze, arms full of the wild purple petunias she had picked along the river bank, she felt her heart lurch. Her mother's cousins, Parul and Farida, who had not visited them in years, were waiting to receive her it seemed. They were both dressed in heavy silk saris and the expressions on their pasty faces were both secretive and festive.

'Why are you so late darling?' they drawled in unison. 'Nargis said you'd be home an hour ago! Come now, the haldi-lady is waiting for you.'

'What's a haldi-lady?' Lily asked.

'Have you never been to a wedding in this town, dear child? The haldi-lady is the one who scrubs the bride with haldi and bathes her before the wedding.'

'Whose wedding is it today?' Lily asked with even greater surprise. This time Parul and Farida exchanged a furtive look.

'Come, come,' they said, 'There isn't much time.'

'Where's my mother?' Lily asked, desperation rising in her voice.

'She has gone to get the Kazi.'

In the end, Parul, Farida and two other women had to drag Lily, kicking and screaming, to the back of the house, where the haldi-lady waited with her unguents. She was an obese woman with thick, curly hair and her own hands were calloused from rubbing her salves on other women's bodies. She regarded Lily without sympathy and asked her to strip. When Lily didn't comply, Parul and Farida came forward. Despite herself, Lily started to feel better after the bath. The scrubbing had warmed her and the water had calmed her. She even started to think that perhaps her mother had the right idea in wanting to get rid of her.

After all, what was left of Lily's old life? Gone were the wonderful stories of her father's leatherbound books, gone were her doting brothers – replaced by two brooding brutes. And her mother, what to say of her mother? Her mother had managed to stamp out the very fire which ignites the warmth in a family. So perhaps it was better that Lily started a new life of her own. It was all happening a bit earlier than she had imagined and she would have to beg her new husband to let her continue her studies – but it was not unheard of to be married at her age. But where was Nargis? And who had she chosen for Lily? She wanted to hear it straight from her mother's mouth. She wanted her mother to at least do her the honour of giving her away. She wanted her mother to be fully present, at least on this day. Lily allowed Parul and Farida to wrap her in a red and gold sari and tie up her long hair in a bun, which they decorated with gold thread. Lily had never worn kajal in her eyes before and she was very pleased with the results. But as she placed the red bindi on her forehead as a last touch, Lily still didn't understand why neither Nargis nor her brothers were visible.

Lily had fallen asleep in the bamboo mat where Parul and Farida had left her, fully adorned as a bride. The commotion woke her but her eyes opened into a gathering darkness. One mosquito buzzed around her face insistently. Parul and Farida had burst in through the door with a hurricane, exclaiming loudly, 'Hai Allah, Lily, you've been sleeping! Your sari has come undone! Come, come, the Kazi is here.'

Farida dragged her to her feet and fixed her sari with a few deft moves. Lily started rubbing the sleep out of her eyes and her aunt swatted her hands angrily. 'Now you've smudged your kajal, you silly oaf!' Before Lily could say anything, two white figures appeared at the door. One was Nargis, regal and demure in one of her old cotton saris that she had not worn in ages and which Lily found to be an odd choice for a wedding ceremony. And the other figure was the Kazi, wearing a long white tunic and white skullcap. They moved forward like one large white iceberg and with which step that they moved closer, Lily felt her heart turning into ice. Why didn't Nargis smile? Why didn't she come forward and embrace Lily and explain to her what was going on? The Kazi opened his almanac and cleared his throat.

'Shall I start?'

Nargis nodded, as if in a daze.

'Do you, Lily Begum, take Rajat Mia, the eldest son of Monsoor Mia, to be your lawfully wedded husband?'

In later years, Lily would always remember that moment in different ways. Each time she would recall it, her brain would regurgitate a different scenario, would refurbish a different outcome. In her dreams, that moment would take on garish embellishments, such as a naked Farida in the background or her mother screaming like a banshee. Between her dreams and her constant replay of that moment, Lily's mind eventually managed in snuffing out the reality of what had actually happened.

In reality, Lily had looked on from one face to the other, trembling like a leaf, until finally, her eyes came to rest upon her mother. Nargis returned her gaze steadily. It was as if her very eyes had turned into stone. When she spoke, her voice was calm, convincing, conniving.

'Kazi Shahib, I know it is your duty to extract my daughter's consent for her marriage. But you must consider her tender age and the special circumstances of this marriage. She is with child. This man, her tutor and our tenant, has exploited her. Now it is up to us to help this poor child by giving her and her unborn child the right to live honourably. So please, allow me to answer on my young daughter's behalf. She has already endured too much.'

The Kazi nodded, reluctantly. 'Begum if I hadn't known your family for decades, I would never allow this. But I too have a twelve-year-old daughter and I cannot imagine this fate for her. I can empathise with your sentiments. You are a brave and strong mother.'

Nargis smiled, hauntingly, enchantingly. Lily's mind was soaring, soaring. No one made a fool of her mother. Neither grief nor pleasure. Neither life nor death. Nargis stood alone, unflinching in her demands, unfathomable in her expectations.

There were a flurry of documents that Nargis signed on Lily's behalf and the next thing Lily remembered was following Parul, Farida and Nargis out into the courtyard which was now alight with white paper lanterns. Someone had painted white and red floral patterns on the steps with an amateur stroke. A chowki had been placed in the middle of the small courtyard and covered with a red sheet and on either side of the chowki, two large pots with banana leaves had been placed. This was the stage for the bride and groom to sit and look at each other for the first time once the marriage had been conducted by the Kazi. Lily was led to the stage first and then Rajat. Someone flung a gold translucent cloth on top of their heads and held a mirror under their faces.

The customary merry making began. 'What do you see in the mirror, Rajat? The moon, the stars or your wife?'

Rajat didn't answer. 'And what do you see Lily? The moon, the stars or your husband?'

Lily didn't answer.

Someone pushed Rajat's head closer to Lily's. 'Come on, man! It is rude not to compliment your new bride!'

Rajat and Lily's eyes met and locked in the hand mirror placed under their faces.

Rajat spoke quietly, 'I see my future.' Lily saw in his brown eyes, the bewilderment of a man long lost. A man consumed by his confusion; ravaged by his need for love. With a heavy dread Lily realised that she was his last hope just as she knew that she could never love him either.

A group of women started singing wedding songs and a few young children started swaying and dancing. The aromatic scent of freshly cooked biriyani infused into the midsummer night's air. Somewhere, far away, the blaring whistle of the station master, signalling the departure of the evening train from Comilla station, the same train that Rajat had once taken to arrive there.

FOUR POEMS

Zohab Khan

I write

I write,
I write not to fight,
But to love.
I write not to fight,
But to love.

I write not to fight,
But to bring light to darkness.
I write not to fight,
But to bring sight to blindness.

I write to inspire an internal fire in those who
desire to fly higher,
For my feet were never designed for the ground.
I prefer to walk on the clouds.
Where my footsteps make not a sound
And I can twirl like a mystic insouciant dervish,
around and around,
          around and around.

I write to tell those who pose
                    not to pose
          because you can't pose
when you write prose, poetry.
Your mind,
          set it free,
And fall hopelessly in love with the love of
poetry.

But to some it seems,
that the only rhyme schemes be
A,A,B,B
and A,B,A,B,
and A,B,B,A.

But that's just not my way,
It's just that I prefer
A,B,H,N,A and A,B,T,Z,K.

And A,
dollar sign,
     question mark,
       SEVEN,
exclamation point,
   hash,
      star,
         FOUR,
equal sign,
  plus sign,
      SIX,
       SIX,
        SIX,
open bracket,
  closed bracket,
  X
   X,
   X,
smiley face,
   percentage,
   SEVEN,
    L,
      M,
        N,
          O,
            P,

SEVEN,
Q,
W,
E,
R,
T,
Y,
SEVEN,
A,
A,
B B A,
A,
B B
A.

That's why
I prefer not to confine my mind to prewritten
lines.
I prefer to set free my mind,
In a place where elastic lines,
Intertwine with mystic rhymes.
In these sadistic times,
It's hard to find oneself.
Materialistic objects should not define oneself.

That's why,
I write,
I write not to fight,
But to love,
I write not to fight,
But to love.

Evident

It's evident,
From our decadent,
    dividend driven,
      dollar dazed days,
That we always need someone new to blame.
Whether that be refugees,
                Aborigines,
           Television twerkers,
         Or Muslims in burqas.
It could just be,
          that the worst is in us.
            In God we trust,
        But maybe God trusted us
          just a little too much.
Cos we kill in his name.
Nah,
We kill *cos* we kill.
 We kill *cos* we can.
 We kill *cos*
     your Gaza homes
          are on my holy land,
    that my God gave to my chosen
                 people.
We kill *cos*
    warlords declare war holy on infidels,
When really they're killing
          for oil wells.
We kill *cos*,
     cops kill kids,
       cos colour lines
          somehow seem to define
             who is
             and
          is not equal.

We just people!
And Australia,
I know why you're afraid.
Because the last time boats came,
They carried terra nullius terrorists.
Who left heads slain like ISIS
And left a generation stolen,
Who now sleep on sidewalks,
        Trying to put back
                        broken
                            puzzle pieces
            At the bottom
        of booze bottles.
Boston bombs
    blew minds,
While Baghdad bombs
    barely make headlines
We live in interesting times,
Where geographical location,
        Somehow is an indication
            Of the value of a life.
Third world lives lost
            might as well be livestock.
For they are put in cost columns
                    of conglomerate company
spread sheets
    to see whether saving lives is
economically viable.
Tribal –
    mentalities have caused,
Geopolitical genocide of the most
        grandiose scale.
Question?
    When did human lives go on sale?
Riddle.
If multinational logging corporations,

slaughter Amazonian Aborigines,
and no one is around,
do their screams still make a sound?

See I've found,
    that most of us live our lives in
                boxes.
For we've built these boxes,
to block out external factors,
          like facts that,
        33% of the world's
       population is
      considered starving.
And it's hardly,
acceptable,
That we've got this conceptional idea,
That survival of the fittest
      means we leave our brothers
      behind.
But when did the fittest become the fat cats?
For I dream that
      we have leaders that'll lead us,
         rather than bleed us dry.
And I wish that I could tell that everything is going
to be alright.
But honestly,
   sometimes,
      I
        just
         don't
          know.

Faith

Faith,
I was always told faith was blind,
But I prefer to see mine,
Cos see I'm
                a dissident,
                discordant,
                devilish,
                disbeliever.
Who decisively decided that he's dazed and
definite,
        that religion could be,
                        maybe,
                                is,
                    a life prerequisite.
That's why I continually question it,
And lurk on cold pathways.
And wait for the right phrase,
For lyrical miracles.

I'm not a spiritual teacher.
Nor a empirical preacher.
I'm a Torah, Qur'an, Biblical reader.
A Siddhartha Gautama Buddha believer.

Faith is my love,
That's why I need her.
I need faith like I need to breathe.
I need to breathe like I need to eat.
I need to eat soul food.
Food for my soul.

As I grow old,
I seek to start meditating,
                levitating,

        elevating up above.

Yo bruv,
Where's the love gone?
Bring back the days of the true love songs.
Bring back the days
     when we used to play,
          used to pray,
           used to say
            what we *wanna* say.
Nowadays,
it's all power games.
I miss the days when
        Mumbai was still Bombay,
Back before that terrible September day,
       When those two planes,
Forever changed the New York skyline.
I long to take back what's mine.
I long to take back what's mine.

I long to take back what's mine.
My freedom of speech.
My freedom to preach.
My freedom to roar
       at the top of my lungs
          till my mouth gets sore.
For I,
     Only know one holy war,
And that's to love more and hate less.
      And for some jihad means terrorist.
But jihad means struggle,
    And I jihad on the daily
         to be the best me
         that I can be.
Cos terrorism, knows no religion.
Was it not terrorism,

When terra nullius was claimed
        and people were slain in the name of
the all mighty British Empire.
That's why,
        I long to inspires you to view religion from
the other sides eyes.
For I am not Muslim, nor Jew,
I am not Christian, nor Hindu.
I am me,
I am you.
        We are us,
        We are one.

He Said

He said,
"Go back to where you came from,
        YOU
                DIRTY
                        TERRORIST!"
He called me,
A dirty terrorist.
But,
To be honest,
This isn't the first time I've heard this.
So I've become used to such abuse,
And I've learnt to pick and choose
what I listen to.

But this,
        this was new.
This time,
This middle aged man,
        Held in his hand,
The hand of his ten year old son.

And I'm not one to tell someone how to
                  raise their seed,
  But this,
This made my soul bleed,
    black, boiling, blood.

For when I have a son,
Ima teach him love,
Ima teach him respect and acceptance,
For all creatures in existence.
But this man,
He didn't seem to understand,
    That his
        Wicked
          Words,
            Would manifest,
              In the chest,
              Of his son.
Leaving him with a hate filled heart,
He'll go to school with,
    Thinking its cool to,
        Act
          just
            like
              dad.
And call that kit kat brown kid a dirty *Ayrab*.
And trust me,
You should stay back,
When I'm in a mind frame,
    Where *Ima* name and shame
        a racist terrorist.
        And,
    for the next 4 minutes
I waged war with my words.
My lyrical jihad was heard,
Down every street in Wagga Wagga.

My poem of mass destruction,
  Caused destruction of
Hiroshima and Nagasaki proportions.
People,
  Please,
    Proceed
      with caution.
For I,
Rock no suicide vest,
But I assure you,
   A bomb
   Lies
    inside
     this
      chest.
Ready for love explosions of the most poetic
kind, I am a terrorist –
     of the mind.
  Spreading extremist ideals of
  Peace,
  Love,
  Harmony,
One
 poem
   at a time.
So when I rhyme,
  I rhyme
Not to be heard.
  But to be heard.
      Word

REVIEWS

TIMBUKTU THROUGH THE LENS

Zina Mamouni

It is a city of mystery and mythology. The mystery of Timbuktu is essentially the mystery of a highly developed city which flourished south of the Sahara in the desert. Not the sort of place in the middle of the 'Dark Continent' associated in history with extensive urban centres. The unknown origins of the city and its early development adds to the mystery. The mythology surrounding the city is a product of European imagination: Timbuktu is the fabulous 'City of Gold' located at the furthest corners of the world – nowhere is 'as far as Timbuktu'. But beyond the mystery and mythology, Timbuktu has real history; and it is a history no less splendid and important than the history of such great Islamic cities as Baghdad and Damascus.

The city was founded by the Tuaregs around the eleventh century. In his 1655 *Tarikh es-Sudan* (*History of Sudan*), the famous Sudanese historian, Abderrahman es Sadi (1594-1666), tells us how the city acquired its name. It is linked to the name of a slave to whom the Tuaregs gave the responsibility of guarding the encampment. He was called Buktu. 'Tim' means 'the place of'. The fusion of 'Tim' and 'Buktu' gives us 'Timbuktu': the place of Buktu. Others claim that Timbuktu means 'the well of Buktu', the well where the slave-watchman drew water. Timbuktu became a crossroads of civilisations, a meeting place between northern, Arab and sub-Saharan Africa. Historically, the city has been home to many different peoples. Two in particular shaped the history of Timbuktu: the Tuaregs and the Songhais – they are like rival brothers who have, despite themselves, been enriched by each other's contact. The city is marked indelibly by their respective influences.

The Songhais are the 'masters of water', people of the river living mainly from agriculture and fishing. They had their own language but used Arabic as the academic language. Abderrahman es Sadi was himself a Songhai and wrote in Arabic. The Tuareg are composed of Berbers from the north and the descendants of slaves taken from the populations of the south. The

Tuaregs speak Tamasheq, a Berber language, but their written language is Tifinagh. Contrary to the Songhais who were a sedentary people, the Tuaregs were livestock farmers, rearing goats, cattle and camels, who moved to find the best pasture for their animals. Historically each group excelled in complementary domains: the Songhais were like the Arabs, famous for their dexterity in commerce and the networks that they succeeded in developing, while the Tuaregs played an important role in trade security, since they offered their services to secure the caravan routes and the safe transportation of merchandise.

After being a great business centre due to its perfect location for trade, Timbuktu became an intellectual capital in the fourteenth century under the rule of the Mandingo Kings. The great traveller, Ibn Battuta, who visited the city in April 1353, reported that it was already well established as a commercial, intellectual and religious centre. By now Timbuktu was a mixed metropolis. A number of black African ethnicities came together in the city: Malinkes and Soninkes, later joined by the Peuls (Fulani). Gold became one of the main drivers of attraction.

Arab historians tell of the sumptuous pilgrimage to Mecca of Kankou Musa, King of Mali of the Mandinka dynasty, undertaken in 1325–6. He arrived at the head of a caravan of at least eight thousand men and hundreds of camels loaded with all the riches of Africa including two or three tonnes of pure gold. The glut in gold resulted in a catastrophic depression in the market for almost ten years.

In the fifteenth century, Timbuktu fell under the control of the Nomad Empire that grew out of the merging of trading and the Muslim faith. In 1469, the 'Great' Songhai King Sonni Ali Ber took possession of the city. It became the second capital of a vast empire that covered the whole Sudano-Sahelian region as well as part of the Sahara. Thousands of caravans from Marrakech, Fes, Tlemcen, Tunis, Tripoli or Cairo arrived, loaded with fabrics, silk, pearls from Venice, and that most precious of commodities – salt. New trades developed and again changed the face of the city.

The city experienced its golden age during the sixteenth century. It was due largely to King Askiaa al Hajj Muhammed, the great benefactor of intellectuals. The historical chronicles describe him as a pious and cultivated leader with an ardent love of books. Books became the key commodity of the city and intrinsic to its culture. Collectors came from all over the world to secure manuscripts for private and public libraries. Timbuktu became renowned for its books and learning; and attracted scholars from across the globe. Centres of learning and universities flourished, often linked to mosques where not only theology but also science, philosophy, poetry, grammar and logic were taught. The city experienced a new infusion of thought and knowledge, as well as architectural changes, after the arrival of Muslims and Jews who were driven out of al-Andalus after the fall of Granada. They brought manuscripts from Andalusia that they had saved from the fires of the Inquisition. The façades of houses became adorned with typically Muslim-Arab architectural elements, giving the streets an Andalusian ambiance.

This cultural radiance was interrupted by the Moroccan invasion, initiated by the Sa'did sultan of Morocco, Mawlay Ahmad al Mansour. The Sa'did Empire took advantage of the weakening of the Ottoman Empire to consolidate its power in the region. Timbuktu fell in 1591 ushering in a new era for the city: that of decline. The slave trade, transformed by the unquenchable Western demand for unfree labour in its colonies, modified the economic landscape and redirected the commercial activities towards the 'ebony' trade. It was accompanied by a 'necessary' repression of Muslim scholars and the descent of the country into anarchy, since the old trading rules based on sharia law were seen as getting in the way of the 'new' business. Thus, knowledge left Timbuktu to drain into the desert. The reputation and the wealth of Timbuktu became old memory. Sand entered Timbuktu the moment intellectuals and learning left the place.

France, which had been coveting Timbuktu's reputation for wealth and its strategic geographic position, took the city in 1894. It faced fierce resistance from the Tuaregs, which was eventually crushed – setting the scene for animosities that are now reasserting themselves. Since Mali obtained its independence in 1960, the country has gone through one turmoil after another. Mali's political experiences echo the mayhem repeated across ex-colonial Africa: socialist, authoritarian, then democratic, frequently punctuated by military coups.

Recent events have plunged Mali further into chaos. Several groups are jostling for power and political dominance: Tuaregs with their unilateral proclamation for the independence of 'Azawad'; armed 'jihadists' described by various labels and acronyms (AQMI, Ansar Eddine, MUJAO) and troops from the old colonial power, France. The French troops arrived in 2013 at the 'invitation' of the Malian government to eradicate the Islamic threat. This intervention, tainted by a self-interested paternalism, is more about serving strategic interests than driven by a purely humanitarian motivation.

Today, Timbuktu is a parable of a disease society. There is the disease of those whose roots, identity, culture and faith have been stolen from them by the plague of colonisation. There is the disease of corruption and political turmoil. There is the cancer of ever present jihadi violence. And a new pestilence that further accelerates the downfall of Timbuktu: the spread of neo-liberal globalisation, unhindered by any putative responsibility to state, economy or people. The citizens of Timbuktu are now forced to hide thousands upon thousands of ancient Islamic manuscripts, stored in their houses, or bricked up in walls and buried underground to save them from harm.

So, how does one tell the complex, multi-layered story of a city like Timbuktu?

Abderrahmane Sissako's *Timbuktu* achieves the task with symbolic gusto. It is an homage to the city's history and mythical power. At the heart of Sissako's *Timbuktu* is the original Timbuktu: fantastical, ancestral, Bedouin with tents and houses made of earth and straw. You feel as if you're experiencing a distortion of time and space. It is in part a tribute to a city that was once an intellectual centre, radiant in all of Africa, a smaller scale mix of 'Al Andalus' and an African 'El Dorado', where the Qur'anic command '*Iqra!*' ('Read') resounded like a mantra. But Sissako also presents it as disrupted, hurt, broken, suffocated – restrained by these messianic warriors of our times who want to use and destroy modernity simultaneously. How has Sissako managed to synthesise all this complexity? The history of the city and its inhabitants, its architecture, its evolution, what it is, and what it has been?

Timbuktu directed by Abderrahmane Sissako, produced by Sylvie Pialat, written by Abderrahmane Sissako and Kessan Tall, distributed by Cohen Media Group (Mauritania and France)
In Arabic, French, Tamasheq and Bambara, 2014

Given that the film's theme is religious extremism, you may be right to be nervous. There is always the temptation to pile clichés upon clichés to comfort (yet again) the binary black and white view of a world with the good, humanist, civilisation personified by the West on one side, and obscurantism and brutality, personified by violent jihadis, on the other. However, from the start of the film we realise that we are not going to be presented with a two-dimensional view of the world. We observe the world from three angles: from the point of view of a subject who is a human being, a woman and a Muslim. It proves to be impossible to disassociate the three as the opening scenes set in the seemingly pastoral idyll of a Bedouin family make abundantly clear. The scene is also Sissako's symbolic trademark. We follow a frightened gazelle fleeing before hunters in pick-up trucks and with automatic rifles. 'Don't kill her, tire her out!' one shouts. This is a reference to the mission of the jihadis occupying and seeking to control Timbuktu. Intimidation, harassment, hunting, enslavement... and fluttering over the trucks, a black flag with the message: 'There is no God but God and Mohammed is his messenger' – the 'logo' used by a movement to signify fear and cruelty. A message which has lost all its light and has become an instrument of messianic destruction. Other fleeting images catch our attention, such as the presence of a donkey, which is obviously not there by accident. He appears several times during the film, an allegorical representation of ignorance: ignorance of the sacred texts, of *jihad*, of the depth of faith.

We are elevated further by the presence of 'three wise men'. The first is Omar, the 'jihadist', who is teaching the local town leader (the now powerless) Abdelkerim how to drive a truck he has been given by the jihadists to buy him off. Omar is an empathetic, discerning young man who doesn't judge his ward – even though he knows Abdelkerim smokes which is forbidden under jihadi 'sharia'. The second is the imam of the mosque and shepherd of a flock threatened by wolves, who patiently but insistently pours words of truth upon his unwanted guests; counterbalancing their patent ignorance and literal reading of the sacred texts with enlightened counsel. The third wise man is also a shepherd but in a literal sense. Kidane, a husband and father, is a pastoral and almost biblical figure and symbol of the free and worthy people who built this city. However, he is flawed, and his wisdom is limited to the world of raising cattle and keeping his family. He tells his wife that one day the present situation will be over and normality will surely return. The one item of technology he has (apart from the ubiquitous mobile phone) is a revolver, which will be the instrument of his downfall.

It is within this context that Sissako sets the scene: a town under siege, the inhabitants held hostage. There are references to the antagonist origins of the city, the conflict between the masters of water and the desert people, represented through two characters who come face to face with each other in a fatal encounter: Kidane the Tuareg and Amadou the fisherman.

Sissako brilliantly tackled the destructive effects of globalisation in his film *Bamako* (2006) in which he knits two stories into one – one micro, one macro: a staged fiction showing the difficulties of a traditional Malian family, and then a mock trial of the World Bank and the IMF, led by real lawyers, staged in the yard of a house – quite a surreal setting. Here, globalisation is depicted not with the flow of money but with the circulation of people. *Timbuktu* is brimming with human diversity. The characters have multiple origins: Tuareg, Arab, Songhai. Their appearances are different and they speak different languages (Arabic, Tamasheq, French, English); an echo of the historical Timbuktu that was composed of varied ethnic groups and nationalities. The ontological aspects of character are exposed by giving them two faces: the light and at the same time the darkness that inhabits each of us. In some, the radiant part dominates; in others, the dark side comes to the fore, along with all the paradoxes that make men disoriented, lost beings.

There is another 'wise' person in the film – a 'crazy' woman, her hair uncovered, her torn robes dragging in the dirt, clutching her pet cockerel, with a suggestion of traditional African magical beliefs. This hirsute and imperious woman does what no one dares to do in Timbuktu. She walks down the deserted streets and insults the jihadis. Confused, they step aside to let her past. She denounces those that are 'cracked by life', empty, whose souls have fallen into a deep sleep, who have lost meaning and purpose in life. The jihadis are thus shown to be disconnected from the spirit of Islam, clinging to the form rather than the substance (ordering women to cover the hair, and men to pull up their trouser bottoms), without ever explaining or justifying anything. They forbid ball games; forcing young boys to inventively and subversively play a game of football – without a football (whilst we overhear a group of jihadis discussing the French football team and its stars). The turbans they wear serve as masks behind which hide disoriented, fractured beings full of contradictions, who don't hesitate to punish or execute their brothers in humanity in cold blood.

Abderahmane Sissako takes great care not to fall into the trap of dehumanisation – even of these 'cracked' men. His response lies in the beautiful scenes that anchor us to humanity. He shows us a man secretly performing a lyrical solo dance. This transcendental scene is beautiful and tragic at the same time: beautiful through the poetry it exudes, tragic because it is edited in parallel with a scene where a man and woman, buried up to their heads, are stoned to death. The movements take the man up to the sky, imitating a bird flying high and then down, grasping the earth with his hands. It reminds us of the battle of the soul that takes place in every being because of its two origins: an earthly origin, symbol of the temporal world, and a divine origin, the God-given footprint, the *fitra*, the innate nature of human beings, the spirit God has breathed into each of us.

It is this juxtaposition, so beautifully filmed and edited, that generates moments of pure poetry where the beautiful and the absurd merge: hatred and love, hope and despair, harmony and madness. Beyond the darkness, the film tells us about light, a light that emanates from the women. They radiate whether they are mothers, daughters, sisters, wives, or friends. They are dignified and resist, refusing to surrender, except to God. They rebel, they provoke, they challenge. They all are rays of the sun: the market woman who refuses the absurd order of wearing gloves while she sells fish; Satima, the Tuareg Kidane's wife, fair, beautiful, blessed with a 'great inner strength', and who weighs her every word; her daughter Toya, innocent and radiant; and finally the young woman with a celestial and pure voice (played by the superb Malian singer Fatoumata Diawara), who keeps singing, as a last act of resistance, while she is being publicly flogged.

There is one intriguing character left, half-dark, half-light: a character on a motorbike whose face is never shown. He comes and goes before the men, roaming the streets on his vehicle. We could see him as a messenger. He reminds us of a legendary character, El Faruk, a horse rider whose face is covered with a white scarf, haunting the streets and squares of the town on his horse at night. His task is to drive all malevolent spirits away from people. This protective genius is one of the symbols of the mystery of Timbuktu.

We return to the frame through which Sissako has us view his story – the oppressive scene during which the viewer holds his breath – the image of the gazelle running away from its hunters. Will it be caught and killed or will it escape? This graceful animal makes another appearance in the person of the girl Toya who, at the end of the film, finds herself in the same situation. She runs away from her pursuers, out of breath, but still alive – just like Timbuktu.

(translated from French by France Colle)

KASHMIR SPEAKS

Muddasir Ramzan

Kashmir has been a disputed territory ever since its erstwhile ruler Raja Hari Singh managed to botch up the issue of its accession to either India or Pakistan. Since its acquisition by India after Partition of 1947, the region has been enveloped in turmoil. Unrest in the Valley began in the late 1980s, when the eruption of violence and insurgency led to a military occupation of Kashmir and plunged the paradise of the East into the perpetual embers of fire. India exerts its control over Kashmir through its military occupation which it justifies by perpetuating the view that Kashmir is '*Atoot Ang*', meaning a fundamental, unassailable or 'integral part' of India. The Kashmiris have spent the last three decades in the perpetual shadow of unspeakable violence.

Shahnaz Bashir, *The Half Mother*, Hachette India, Delhi, 2014

Kashmiri writers have begun to explore the plight of their people only recently. Basharat Peer's memoir *Curfewed Night* (2009) was the first publication to break the long silence and retell the harrowing story of Kashmir. It was followed by Mirza Waheed's two novels, *The Collaborator* (2011*)* and *The Book of Gold Leaves* (2014), which encapsulated the bitter realities of the Kashmir conflict. These texts of resistance are filled with the tales of trauma and torture, wanton killings, arson, arrests, disappearances and terror that define post-1990 Kashmir. As a twenty-five-year-old Kashmiri, I have spent my entire life in the valley against the backdrop of the public struggles and private tragedies to which such writings bear witness. Both Basharat Peer and Mirza Waheed speak directly to me; and translate the tragedy of millions of innocent Kashmiris into a universal language. Now, there is a new, bold voice: Shahnaz Bashir. Born and brought up in Kashmir, Bashir intimately knows what he is writing about. 'People are born with certain responsibilities and writing is one of them,' he says. His debut novel *The Half Mother* is a powerful unflinching work that will leave readers shaken to the core.

We are transported to 1990s Kashmir, a period which saw the transition from calm to calamity. As the insurgency in the Valley intensifies, the government resigns, paving the way for Governor's rule. Tears, blood, death and war follow, as do curfews, encounters, raids, crackdowns, killings, army camps and bunkers, burning markets, schools and buildings. The novel tells the story of Haleema, who lives with her father Ghulam Rasool Joo, affectionately known as Ab Jaan. After a childhood of poverty and hardships, and the untimely death of her mother, she gets married to a medical assistant. Though her marriage proves a fiasco, it does bear fruit with the birth of her son, Imran. The narrative progresses smoothly, from Ab Jaan's struggle to find a job through to his retirement when he sets up a shop at the family residence in Natipora, and Imran's journey from childhood to his teenage years and his education. In his description of the minutiae of life of the Joo household, Shahnaz vividly exploits his powerful imagination and his entrancing art of storytelling. With masterful skills, including the majestic description of various physical and natural aspects of Natipora, he immortalises the place where he himself was born.

Imran emerges as a bold, courageous and sensitive boy. In one episode he asks his grandfather, Ab Jaan, a simple question: why are Kashmiris never taught their own history? When he asked this question in the class, the teacher tweaked his ear. How can one study Mesopotamia and the Indus Valley and Harrapa, this and that civilisation, but not learn anything about one's own community? Ab Jaan replies: 'because some people don't want it to be there. Not a bit of it. They don't want us to know ourselves. They don't want us to learn who we are'. The answer reveals how postcolonial India uses the same strategy of the much-hated colonisers to eradicate history and memory of a people. By snatching their existential identity from the Kashmiris, and preventing them from knowing their own culture and civilisation, and expunging their history from textbooks, India is denying the very existence of the Kahsmiri people. Such political injustices are not the only challenges faced by Imran. His mother Haleema's health deteriorates, putting extra responsibility on his young shoulders, forcing him to navigate the practical as well as ideological struggles of life in Indian-controlled Kashmir.

As the plot develops, Bashir paints a picture of the events following the unrest of 1989 when insurgents and soldiers from Pakistan-controlled Kashmir infiltrated Indian-controlled territory and triggered what became known as the Kargil War. Imran, emerging into adulthood, witnesses the conversion of his surroundings into army camps and other paramilitary bunkers. Soon insurgents attack an army party at Imran's locality and an army patrolling party begins to search houses, on the pretext of finding the attackers. Almost all the men in the neighbourhood receive their share of beatings in turns. The angry army soon reach Joo House. While Haleema assures them that they know nothing, her father Ab Jaan falls to merciless army bullets. Haleema frenetically slaps her own face and her chest and pulls her hair, while Imran is frozen with shock. The brutality of the Indian army is well illustrated: they behead those who protest against their tactics or question their actions, and they do so publicly so that nobody dares to repeat such resistance again.

After some days, another tragedy crushes Haleema when her house is raided again. Imran is whisked away, despite being innocent. All the tearful pleas and requests of Haleema are mercilessly rejected. Her life changes all at once. The fear and hysteria are picturesquely depicted, and bring verisimilitude to the novel. The heart-wrenching incident of Imran's arrest and his desperate mother's pleas before the troops for mercy is so poignantly described that it arouses emotions of awe and terror.

Much of the novel follows Haleema's epic journey to search for her son Imran, or rather to find out if he is dead or alive. Imran's arrest marks the beginning of the most agonising phase of Haleema's life, which affects her both physically and psychologically. Torn apart by her lonely existence, she battles for answers and seeks out army camps, torture centres, police stations, jails, wetlands and mortuaries. Social leaders, journalists, politicians, bureaucrats, NGOs and courts are approached. Clue after clue is traded but the truth remains lost in the fog of war. Though her health deteriorates rapidly, she continues to fight. She forms an 'Association of the Relatives of Disappeared Persons' so that they can strive for the cause together and support one another in this most desperate search.

The novel is divided into three parts. Book I comprises the first seven chapters, introducing the characters, main events and the context. Book II consists of ten chapters which are mainly concerned with the struggle. And Book III is a collection of random notes by a character called Izhar, a journalist, who plays a crucial role in helping Haleema in her quest to retrieve her son. It is through Izhar that we learn about the eventual fate of Haleema. For a non-Kashmiri reader the language may seem somewhat laboured; Bashir has translated his thought processes directly from his native language, Kashmiri, into English. The succinct inclusion of Kashmiri and Urdu words and phrases may also cause some problems for English readers. However, as a native reader, I find the Kashmiri and Urdu words and Kashmiri thought processes actually add to the impact of the story and position it firmly in its cultural context. Bashir's technique enables the reader to empathise not only with ill-fated Haleema but also with all those mothers whose sons have fallen prey to the atrocities of this conflict. As the Imam of Natipora says to Haleema, trying to console her: 'the greatest suffering bring the greatest hopes, the greatest miseries greatest patience, and the greatest uncertainties lead to the greatest quests'.

The Half-Mother is a trailblazing, brilliant novel. Its characters are delicately drawn, its descriptions of trauma, pain, separation, longing and undying hope in the middle of hopelessness are powerful. The apathy and high-handedness of the authorities are subtly rendered. There is also an illusion to the madness of despair in a dream-sequence in which Imran comes home and Haleema's joy knows no bounds. Haleema's portrait is crafted so captivatingly and in such detail that it is sometimes difficult for the reader to know whether they are reading a work of fact or fiction. The conclusion of the narrative will leave you speechless – indeed mindless for a while.

The Half-Mother is fiction as resistance – as you have never seen or read before.

OBSTINATE SOVEREIGNTY, AGAIN

S Parvez Manzoor

Despite the seductive appeal of its vision, Islamist politics is anti-politics, a search for a changeless world and a sinless humanity, a utopian longing that renders the pursuit of all politics and all dialogue with history superfluous. The misery of Islamist thought, however, is not due to the poverty of the historical tradition it is heir to, but it issues from its inability to comprehend the real nature of the modern Leviathan and its amoral ideology of sovereign power. This is the main verdict of Wael Hallaq's *The Impossible State*, a very incisive and merciless analysis of the logical incoherence and political imprudence of the Islamist project. But his book also leaves you in the dark about the ultimate target of Hallaq's censure - Islamic State or the Modern Leviathan?

Wael B. Hallaq, 'the Avalon Foundation Professor in the Humanities at Columbia University', has distinguished himself as a diligent and resourceful scholar of the history of Islamic law. His various works such as *Shari'a: Theory, Practice, Transformation* (2009); *Authority, Continuity and Change in Islamic Law (2001)*; *The Origin and Evolution of Islamic Law* (2005); *A History of Islamic Legal Theories: An Introduction to Sunni Usul al-fiqh* (1997); *Ibn Taymiyya Against the Greek Logicians* (1993), and others, amply testify to his erudition, intellectual acumen and moderating temper. Hallaq's present study reveals that this judicious interpreter of legal texts is also a philosophical inquisitor of no mean stature. His ability to conduct a sustained philosophical inquiry is as impressive here as was his facility earlier with the unravelling of a complicated legal argument. No wonder that the present volume reads like a prosecutorial indictment or a philosophical treatise. The legal and the philosophical are in perfect symbiosis; only the couple that cannot cohabit under the same political roof is made up of 'Islam' and 'State'. For, the 'Islamic state', so reads Hallaq's categorical judgement, 'is both an impossibility and a contradiction in terms'.

The ultimate challenge facing the Muslims, in Hallaq's highly schematised depiction, is the reconciliation of two facts: 'first, the ontological fact of the state and its undeniably powerful presence, and, second, the deontological fact of the necessity to bring about a form of Shariʻa governance'. The misery of Islamist thought stems from its inattention to history and its ensnarement by ontology: 'being' rather than 'time' was/is the truth of its metaphysics. The state thus conceived and propagated by it is the natural order of things and not a temporal entity. Having no inkling of its genealogy, metaphysical foundations and teleology, Muslim thinkers fell prey to the mystique of the state and took it for a timeless paradigm of political rule. It is this metaphysical confusion and philosophical naiveté that underlies some of the pathetic claims made by modernising Islamists who neither have a foot inside Islam's classical tradition nor know a thing about modernity. Hallaq exemplifies this by the following statement by the Muslim Brothers, who argue that the modern state 'does not stand in contradiction with the implementation of the Islamic Shariʻa, because Islam is the highest authority in Muslim lands, *or so it should be*. With its mechanisms, regulations, laws and systems, the modern state – if it contains no contradictions to the founding and indubitable principles of Islam – does not preclude the possibility of being *developed*... so that we can benefit from it in achieving for ourselves progress and development'.

To the Muslim Brothers' claim that 'there is no contradiction between the Nation-State and Islamic Shariʻa', Hallaq's firm rejoinder reads: 'But surely there is'. Indeed, the main argument of Hallaq's work is just that, that 'any conception of a modern Islamic state is *inherently self-contradictory*'. Significantly, however, by postulating this incompatibility between the Islamic and the modern forms of governance, Hallaq is neither lending his voice to the Islamophobic choir, whose tiresome refrain constantly reminds us of Islam's inherently undemocratic essence, nor is he championing the cause of secularism by suggesting that the only true Islam is a spiritual, apolitical one. No, his is not an apology for the modern regime, nor a reproach to traditional Islam. In fact, if anything, it is quite the reverse. For, he is bold enough to assert that 'the inherent self-contradictions entailed by a modern Islamic state are primarily grounded in modernity's moral predicament'. The significance of Hallaq's reflection, in other words, extends far beyond the limits of any debate on the 'crisis of modern Islam', beyond those inane assertions about Islam's singular ability to be self-referential, to create and sustain its own reality and to remain impervious to change. No, 'the inherent contradictions of a modern Muslim state', he insists, 'also implicate the moral dimensions of the modern project in our world from beginning to end'. Not inconsistently, he contends, his book 'is an essay in moral thought even more so than it is a commentary on politics or law'. One must also underline the fact that Hallaq does not subscribe to a conception of the moral which upholds 'the autonomy of the political'.

Wael B. Hallaq, *The Impossible State: Islam, State and Modernity's Moral Predicament*, Columbia University Press, New York, 2012.
Mehrzad Boroujerdi, Editor, *Mirror for the Muslim Prince: Islam and the Theory of Statecraft*, Syracuse University Press, New York, 2013.
Azfar Moin, *The Millennial Sovereign: Sacred Kingship and Sainthood in Islam*, Columbia University Press, New York, 2012.

Philosophically, Hallaq's volume may be conceived as an Alfarabian reflection for our times. It is a cautionary tale that alerts us to the dystopian reality of the Virtuous City of modernity, the modern secular state. That his project entails delineation of two paradigmatic, albeit morally incompatible, entities, 'Shari'a a governance' and 'modern state', is motivated by him in these words: 'it is legitimate to invoke any central domain of the moral, from past and present, that may provide us with a source of moral retrieval. While the past is materially and institutionally defunct, its moral principals are not. Thus, invoking the paradigm of Islamic governance is as plausible and legitimate a project as invoking Aristotle, Aquinas, or Kant'. The moral argument, which pervades throughout this reflection, owes a lot to the Catholic critics of modernity, notably Alasdair MacIntyre and Charles Taylor. Hallaq is convinced that Muslim revivalists who are equally repelled by a number of modernity's ills, 'not the least of which is the increasing collapse of organic social units, the rise of oppressive economic forms, and, most importantly, the havoc wrought against the natural habitat and the environment' display 'close parallels, even a virtual identity' with 'the internal western critiques within postmodernity'. Indeed, Hallaq's book ends with a plea for Muslims to make a common cause with these critics – morally and politically not a straightforward choice in our opinion.

The obdurate title of the book and the implacable temper of its righteous ideology need not, in our view, be taken at their face values: they distract us from fixing our gaze on the moral landscape of our time which Hallaq surveys with such keenness and intensity. Equally misleading would be to criticise him for presenting a circular argument, for confounding paraphrases of his ideological premises with logical conclusions, or to remind him that the putative incompatibility of Shari'a governance and nation-state is already built in the defining paradigms. Such, however, is the bane of all categorical thought: logical stringency in systematic thinking is achieved at the cost of ignoring all anomalies and paradoxes – the very stuff of human history and political existence. Indeed, it would be equally tempting to dismiss the upshot of his moral reasoning as a pious homily.

But this need not discomfort even the most demanding Muslim reader. For the earnestness and perspicacity alone, with which Hallaq expounds the two paradigms, Islamic governance and secular state, makes his work amply rewarding and gratifying. Hallaq's moral censure of modernity, just as his lyrical 'defence' of a paradigmatic Shari'a including the 'five pillars of Islam', is always conveyed with such moral pathos and philosophical sophistication that it is impossible to dismiss his labour as incarnating mere *ressentiment* or polemical fervour. Nevertheless, it is in the nature of his moral vision that his comparisons between Shari'a governance and the modern state be perceived unfair if not downright invidious. Or that he may be indicted for being exceedingly generous towards the former and inexcusably miserly towards the latter. Here is an example:

> In sum, the supremacy of the Shari'a meant a rule of law that stood superior to its modern counterpart, the present form of Western state that has come to be fused…with a claim to democratic legitimacy (or popular sovereignty) that "sits very awkwardly with its practical realities". For Muslims today to seek the adoption of the modern state system of separations of powers is to bargain for a deal inferior to the one they secured for themselves over the centuries of *their* history. The modern ideal represents the power and sovereignty of the state, which we have seen ….. to be working for its own perpetuation and interests. By contrast, the Shari'a did not – because it was not designed to – serve the

ruler or any form of political power. It served the people, the masses, the poor, the downtrodden, and the wayfarer without disadvantaging the merchant and others of his ilk. In this sense it was not only deeply democratic but humane in ways unrecognizable to the modern state and its laws. If the test is "what ought to constitute inalienable rights *beyond the reach of any government*," to borrow Robert Dahl's words, the Shari'a passed that test, privileging the rule of law over the state.

Only if we accept that Hallaq's ultimate focus is neither Shari'a nor statehood but morality, can we make sense of these schematic comparisons. The impossibility of an Islamic state is a theoretical exercise in which Islam functions as a metaphor. It is for the vindication of the belief, passionately held and cogently defended, namely that 'the state's *homo modernus* is, by definition, antithetical to the *homo moralis*' of Hallaq's vision, that the putative paradigm of Shari'a governance may be invoked. It has an instrumental value and an instructional role in this cautionary tale. The same may be said about the synthesis of the natural and the mystical that, according to Hallaq, was the outcome of al-Ghazali's intellectual labour:

> The Ghazalian project thus, represents not only an intellectual synthesis of morality, law, theology, mysticism, and philosophy, but also an "anthropological" foray into Muslim subjectivity – we can thus comfortably assert that Shari'a, in addition to its trenchant legal-moral character, represents at once a field of practical mysticism… If the Shari'a was *also* a psychological-mystical enterprise, and if it constituted the paradigmatic and undisputed "legislative" power of Islamic governance, *then this governance was not only about law, morality and their organic confluence; it was also and equally about a mystical perception of the world, a perception deeply anchored in a society – represented by a class of mystics-cum-jurists – that did not distinguish, in the practice of living, between the meanings of the legal, the moral, and the mystical.*

(The actual life-world of mystical Islam, as opposed to its metaphysical foundations, and the system of governance that is the fruit of 'the mystical perception of the world', is vividly described in Azfar's Moin's historical study, *The Millennial Sovereign,* to which I shall turn shortly.) In sum, while Hallaq's exposition of the traditional worldview of Islam is intellectually mature and refined, and will be music to many ears and a source of pride for the reactionary elite, it is better perceived as the bitter-sweet pill that one can neither swallow nor spit out.

If we transpose our vision from norm to history, if the historical Muslim rather than the ideal believer is allowed to present his/her testimony, we arrive at a less doctrinaire view of 'Islamic governance'. Or, rather, we are forced to concede that 'there is no unitary "Islamic" position on important issues of statecraft and governance'. It is with this in mind that Meherzad Boroujerdi's present volume seems to have been conceived. It offers a collection of some very insightful articles by the leading interpreters of the so-called Persian theory of statecraft and thus consciously positions itself at the opposite end of the juristic discourse. At the least, it shifts the perspective on 'Islamic politics' from being a quest for redemption, a utopian search for perfection and virtue to that of a more mundane 'art of the possible'. Paradoxically, it has been noticed by many scholars and critics that while both traditional ulema and modern 'Islamologues' are equally insistent upon positing the sacred and almost inviolable theory of Islamic political order, the historian is less inclined to espouse such a normative stance. Modern scholars, it appears, have accepted the authoritative claims of the *fiqhi* tradition as the following statement by A.K.S. Lambton, who, while discussing the three strands of political thought among the Muslims, categorically asserts: 'Of the three the most truly Islamic is the formulation of the jurist.' To this she adds almost as an afterthought, that the *fiqhi* model 'is in some measure expression of a religious ideal in opposition to practice'. Contemporary experts however conceive their task as that of demonstrating the unsuitability, indeed incompatibility, of the juristic paradigm with the modern ethos. (Hallaq, while striding both sides of the historical divide and lending traditional Islam a very cogent moral voice, is clearly no exception. His affinities with H.A.R. Gibb or W.C. Smith cannot be ignored.) The perplexity, indeed the anguish, of the protagonists of a non-dogmatic counter-discourse of Muslim politics is candidly revealed by Said Arjomand, who finds the community of interest between *fiqh* and modern scholarship academically unsound and Islamically insignificant (that is, 'Orientalist privileging of a narrow genre of "Islamic" juristic writing that was completely marginal to the *fiqh* corpus itself'.) His statement below thus faithfully captures the intellectual temper and moral élan of the whole volume:

The very short preface to Kwandmir's *Qanun-i-humayuni* is grounded in eight Qur'anic verses that are universally recognized by all Muslims as the word of God and the ultimate source of authority. What right do Gibb [H.A.R.] and Crone [Patricia] to consider it deranged and not "intrinsically Islamic"? Neither Crone nor I have any direct evidence for what "the Muslims" really thought, and we both must infer such evidence from a body of texts assumed to have been read by the literate. .... The evidence that I have presented on the care taken by the architects of Persio-Islamicate tradition of political ethic and statecraft to justify that tradition as Islamic by resting it on two scriptural sources of Islamic law suggests that the proponents of the thesis of the inescapably un-Islamic character of all Muslim governments are barking up the wrong tree. Rather than taking comfort in the Islamists' tendentious neglect of history, they should have the humility to let the Muslim historical subjects speak for themselves...

In the Introduction, the editor reminds the reader that recent uprisings in Arab lands have pitilessly demolished the credibility of 'the atavistic solutions offered by nativism', just as they have laid bare 'the pitfalls of unbridled cosmopolitanism'. The intellectuals now need 'to reanimate their communities', have an earnest dialogue with the past and produce a viable vision of the future. 'The (re)reading of the Islamic tradition' has thus become 'a part of the responsibility of intellectuals who wish to help future generations of Muslims contemplate a more humane style of statecraft'. The host of questions that arise in the wake of this challenge demand both a re-examination of the traditional debates and fresh intellectual creativity. Hence, the volume begins with the recapitulation of the 'pragmatic' reasoning, balancing *fact* and *text*, of the *fiqh* itself. Asma Afsaruddin looks at the juristic concept of *maslaha*, variously understood as 'public interest', 'utility', 'expediency' but which may equally be construed as 'equity' and 'politics of common good' and concludes that even though it was not termed as such, 'maslaha as a political concept' existed almost from the onset of Islam. (The tension between 'law' and 'politics', or more precisely between legal positivism and political prudence, it would appear, is also a congenital feature of the Islamic legal tradition.)

The first section of the book deals with the medieval 'Persian-Islamicate' works on political ethics and statecraft. Sa'di's *Treatise on Advice to the Kings*, along with the English translation of the Persian text, is lucidly expounded

by Boroujerdi and Shomali. While there is justified recognition of Sa'di's
political sagacity and universal humanism, the uncomfortable fact that his
moral realism turns quietist and at time borders on the cynical is not
commented upon. Said Amir Arjomand's probing of the relationship
between Persian political ethics and the sources of Islamic law is incisive
and suggestive. He is also critical of Orientalist scholarship's bid to
promote a normative view of Islamic politics and its indulging in polemics
by considering non-Arab rule as 'illegitimate'. As the historical focus on
Persia extends down to our times, it is not surprising that there's ample
room for critical perspective on today's Islamic Iran ('An Anomaly in the
History of Persian Thought' by Javad Tabatabi.). There is an additional
presentation of Atabeg Ahmad's work *Tufeh* ('Teaching Wisdom', by Louis
Marlow) which further testifies to the prevalence of 'Mirror for Princes'
(*Fürstenspiegel*) a form of political writing that was also common in Europe.
Muzaffar Alam extends this discussion to India and shows how the Mughals
relying on extra-fiqhi sources of legitimacy sought to create a more
inclusive polity and indeed largely succeeded in gaining the trust of their
non-Muslim subjects.

The other country in focus is Egypt, the intellectual heartland of the
Arab world. Three crisply written essays focus on Egyptian contribution to
the emergence of the current Islamist discourse. Peter Gran argues that
Al-Tahtawi's famous work *Takhlis* (1834) which is traditionally regarded as
a piece of travel writing, narrates as it does the author's trip to France, is
better understood as an example of the Mirror for Princes literature.
Bruce Rutherford's essay 'What do Egypt's Islamists Want?', in which he
scrutinises the significance of Yusuf al-Qaradawi, Kamal Abu al-Majid and
Tariq al-Bishri's thought for the ideology and politics of Muslim
Brotherhood, has unfortunately been overshadowed by the rapidity of
political change in Egypt and the uncertainty of her future. Charles
Butterworth's contribution is a very chaste, incisive and cogent
re-evaluation of Ali Abd al-Raziq's putative pleading for the separation of
religion and politics in Islam. Rather than dismissing him as a harbinger of
secularism, Butterworth asks, 'wouldn't it be more accurate to speak of
him as following in the steps of Marsilius of Padua .... by trying to show
that it is better for religion to be limited with spiritual concerns and for
politics not to intrude on the sphere of religion?'. Indeed, Butterworth

insists that 'far from seeking to distinguish himself from religion, Ali Abd al-Raziq aims in his work [i.e. *al-Islam wa usul al-hukm*] to show clearly how much religion has to gain by distancing itself from politics and how politics will gain in justice and wisdom as it distances itself from religion'. It is worth recalling that Machiavelli, another 'misunderstood' thinker whose discovery of the autonomy of politics provides the ultimate legitimacy of our world-order, also entertained similar thoughts. The meddling of religion in the affairs of the state, he opined, can only lead to two consequences: either the triumph of religion and ruination of the state, or the supremacy of the state and corruption of religion! Obviously, the strategy of 'separation' can only be applied when we have a clearer conception of the two protean entities, religion and politics, or where the institutional framework for the definition of state and church exists, Nevertheless, for all our uncertainties, the dialectics of state and religion does not admit of simplistic answers, whether from secularist or Islamists.

Unfortunately, the remaining three articles by Serif Mardin, Roxanne Luben and Aziz al-Azmeh are far too specialised and academic to be discussed here. There's no doubt however that specialists and other academics will give them the attention they merit. Despite the variety of subject-matter, perspectives and styles, *Mirror for the Muslim Prince* makes a welcome contribution not only to the academic scene, but also to the political debate. It provides a much needed counterpoise to *fiqh*-centred discourses, whether perpetuated by Islamists or by opinionated academics, those champions of the 'clash of civilisation' ideology who are equally adamant on dismissing, all historic evidence to the contrary, those manifestations of Muslim rule that do not conform to their essentialist paradigm, as 'un-Islamic'.

While political theorists, academics or activists, may continually debate about the nature of political order in Islam (Islamic, Islamicate, Secular, un-Islamic), or about the prudence of not defining it, history has its own say in this debate. Azfar Moin's seminal work on Mughal and Safavid history, *The Millennial Sovereign*, a superb feat of synthesis that, without laying any claim to being a work of political theory, nevertheless reveals the dialectic of state and religion, the nexus of saintliness and sovereignty, in a radically new, and one might add startling, fashion. It alerts us to the fact that the Sufi paradigm of Messianic kingship is not merely an anomaly. Along with the two established models of 'Islamic sovereignty', the Righteous Caliph and the Just King, the political languages of Islam have been suffused with 'the scriptural notions of the messiah (*mahdi*) and the renewer (*mujaddid*), the mystical concepts of the pole or *axis mundi* (*qutb*) and the perfect individual (*insan-i-kamil*) and the kingly notions of divine effulgence (*farri-izadi*) and Lord of Conjunction (*Sahib Qiran*)'. (The Timurid title, Lord of the Conjunction, which has no basis in the Islamic scriptural traditions, was 'in its most energetic form a millennial title which signified change in religiopolitical order on a global scale and, potentially, the end of the world'.) The political consciousness of Sufism thus reveals a thoroughly enchanted world in which 'the messianic myth' is made meaningful through an array of divinatory knowledge forms 'such as scriptural interpretation, apocalyptic lore, dream vision, and numerological and astrological predictions'. In this world, 'theology and astrology were sister disciplines' and 'theology was as "political" a science as history'.

The dismal state of affairs after the Mongol conquest, which destroyed the political order and flattened social structures across the Eastern Islamic world, provided a space for a number of religious movements that expressed themselves in the messianic idiom. The emergence of the divine matrix of kingship, however, owes to a number of factors and was facilitated 'by the influence of preeminent Sufism, Mongol universalism, millenarian technologies and dreams and Persian tradition'. The style of monarchy that developed in Safavid and Mughal times was premised on the unity of religion and politics: the claims of political power were inseparable from the claims of saintly status. That Muslim kingship became intertwined with the symbols and narratives of 'a shrine-centred Sufism organised around the hereditary cult of the saint', and as the fusion of saintly sacrality and sovereign power became more common, Moin argues, 'it led to a new synthesis of practical politics and spiritual practice'. The foundational monarchs of these two lineages modelled their courts on the pattern of Sufi orders and fashioned themselves as the promised messiahs, with the result that in their classical phases both the Mughals and the Safavids embraced a style of sovereignty that was "saintly" and "messianic", which rested on the belief that the monarch was in some sense the embodiment of the divine. Accordingly, remarkable rituals were developed, and forms of knowledge were created 'to make the body of the kind sacred and cast it in the mould of a prophesied saviour'.

In Moin's judgement it would be wrong to suggest that these Muslim sovereigns assumed the trappings of saintly piety and renounced the world and its sinful ways. More accurately, they adopted the trappings of saintly power and embraced the world as 'heaven-sent saviours'. It was not the case of the Monarch donning the woollen attire, as it were, but the mystic seizing the throne. Indeed, this is what actually happened, as Shah Isma'il, hereditary leader of the Sufi tariqa became the founder of the dynasty that carries its name. Though it is the Indian emperor Akbar who is generally associated with the foundation of a divine cult around his person (*din-i-ilahi*), it was indeed the Safavi Shah Isma'il, who deserves this honour. In the opinion of the author, however, 'the rise of Shah Isma'il was a cataclysm of a magnitude not felt in the region since the conquest of Timur'. India, by contrast, 'suffered much less "Islam" under the Mughals, who did not impose it upon the local population, than Iran did under the Safavids, who, over the long term, enacted a policy of forced conversion to Twelver Shi'ism'.

In sum, *The Millennial Sovereign*, whose historical perspective stretches from Timur to the end of the early modern dynasties of India and Iran, recovers the cultural world of this time by paying attention to the categories, symbols, and narratives that shaped its public discourse. Indeed, it broadens the scope of this inquiry by probing well beyond the Persian and Arabic chronicle tradition to incorporate genres such as miniature painting, illustrated epics and histories and Sufi hagiographies. The result is a very revealing and fascinating world with insinuations of ritual cannibalism (!), desecration of graves, full prostrations (*sajda*) before kings and saints, etc. We are certainly on a different planet than the one inhabited by the jurists of Islam! Little wonder that both in India and Iran, the two orthodoxies of Islam, Sunnism and Shi'ism, revolted against the extremes of 'millennial sovereignty' and sought to bring the political order more in line with the jurists' model – a process that is still unfinished and whose mechanics and strategies remain undefined. Moin's book convinces the Muslim reader that not to have a normative judgement at all on history is not a moral option, just as it makes plain for the academic scholar that, for all its inadequacy as an analytical tool, the notion of 'legitimacy' cannot be entirely dispensed with. History and politics acquire meaning only when these can be judged by norms that are external to them.

Since our focus is on the intractability of sovereignty for political thought, we'd like to bring the focus back to history and the problem of power. That Muslim empires crumbled before the onslaught of miniature western states and that it was the secular worldview of modernity that was responsible for the creation of the new world-order introduces an altogether new dimension in the intra-Muslim discussion. It is here that the following reflection is in order. Of the three pre-modern Muslim empires, the Ottomans, the Safavids and the Mughals, all of them Turkic dynasties, the Ottomans displayed the greatest willingness to stay close to the juristic model of governance. Some of this fidelity to the Shari'a had unintended consequences: it may have cost them their empire. This, at any rate, is how a prominent historian, William McNeill in his monumental reflection, *The Rise of the West: A History of the Human Community*, pursues this line of thought:

> In attempting to convert a freebooters' frontier principality into a great Moslem empire, the Ottoman sultans also called upon the *ulema* for help. This had two curious effects. On the one hand, by enhancing the place of the Sacred Law in Ottoman life, the *ulema* widened the breach between Moslem and Christian ways of life — a breach which had been minimal in the beginning phases of Ottoman expansion. Second, the Sacred Law itself inculcated tolerance for the People of the Book and forbade forcible interference with Christian or Jewish religion, thus checking the *ghazi* habit of headlong attack upon any and all infidels. Hence, as the rude frontiersmen of early Ottoman history gave ground before the slave family on the one hand, and before the orthodox *ulema* of Sunni Islam, on the other, conversion of Christian subjects almost ceased, save through the limited channel of the slave family itself. Only in remote and mountainous regions like Bosnia, where the prevalence of Bogomilism probably facilitated the reception of Islam, or in Albania, where continuous local warfare fostered a spirit resembling that of the old *ghazi*, did mass conversion from Christianity to Islam occur after the fourteenth century.

The dialects of power and morality that this reflection mercilessly exposes cannot be resolved by the theoretical claims of the incompatibility of Shari'a governance and the modern state. To the certainty of theory, history, which is made by human actors and their political will, responds by its own unfathomable logic. In politics, the possible and the impossible are reduced to historical contingencies, and human will overrides all theoretical constraints. When the political will is animated by a faith in the transcendent ends of man, totally unforeseeable futures open up. If a Jewish state can be resurrected after two millennia of suffering and diaspora, why must the Muslims be denied the *possibility* of a political order they can claim as their own? Why must 'Shari'a governance', in short, be defined in terms of such moral perfection that it cannot sustain itself in our sinful world? Islamist thought, must, in short, end its impasse and renew its dialogue with history.

ET CETERA

ON FATIMA MERNISSI

Stuart Schaar

I first met Fatima Mernissi, who died at the end of 2015 aged 75, in the 1960s when I was doing research for my doctorate in Morocco. Whenever I came to Rabat or lived there I made it my business to ring her up and visit her in her Agdal apartment. A parade of people made the pilgrimage to see her and since she had become so renown she had to ration her time and be very selective about who she let into the sanctuary where she lived and held court with several female servants. I was one of the privileged few who saw her at home on the average of two times a week.

She was a wonderful friend, and every time I saw her she plotted with me to work out plans to make me famous, not knowing that I really liked my anonymity, something she refused to understand.

When you visited her apartment you would be led into her living room by one or another of the women who looked after her, prepared her meals, and kept her home clean. While waiting for her to appear, behind the banquet where visitors sat were a pile of art books and other special editions written by her friends and offered to her as presents, which lined the wall. Invariably I would pick out one or another book to read while I awaited her appearance. Then in walked Fatima loaded down with reading material that she would share with me. These included articles from the press which she had just discovered, a new book about cutting edge technology, and something that she had just written in English which needed editing. Could I do it for her while I waited for tea? She shared everything she found curious, old and new, and did it with such gusto that you were swept up into her vortex of discovery just like a small child who had found a new toy.

Her style of writing was all her own. She would begin by recounting 'Khalid's' reaction to what she had just written. Was he real? Or just a foil to present a new argument? At any rate, it was her trademark and it worked, by drawing the reader into her vortex. Khalid told her this or that about her writing and in that way she would introduce a new subject to her readers. She wrote English as a native, but made small errors, which I promptly corrected.

She was a world renowned sociologist and writer; and a sought after celebrity at home. In a series of books – most notably *Beyond the Veil* (1975), *The Veil and the Male Elite* (1991), and *Women and Islam* (1991) – she painstakingly debunked the dominant traditional discourse that suppresses, degrades and relegates Muslim women to inferior position. She tackled a whole range of subjects, from polygamy to the harem, modernity to democracy, with fearless zest.

Fatima was born in Fez in 1940. Her family was affluent; and she grew up between two extended families, surrounded by a host of female kin and servants. But she found the harem into which she was confined suffocating. Despite the fact that her grandmother and mother were both illiterate, she was encouraged to attend school. Later, she went on to study sociology at Mohammad V University in Rabat. After a stint for graduate studies at the Sorbonne, she obtained her PhD from Brandeis University in the US. She returned to Morocco to teach at Mohammad V University; and began work on social and political reform – a passion that she maintained for most of her life.

Fatima was her own person. By the time she died she no longer worked on women's issues. Rather, she spent her time examining how technology was transforming Morocco and the wider Arab world. She read profusely magazines from around the world including the *Economist*, *Al-Ahram*, and all the many women's magazines in Arabic for clues as to how the society was changing rapidly. She always asked me to buy her books about new trends in the West and she knew which titles she wanted.

Over tea and cookies she would take out of her see-through plastic folder article after article that she had just found, which she wanted to share with me. She would make me read the articles right then and there so that we could discuss their contents. Her curiosity had no limits and she questioned what I thought of a given piece or if I could add anything to what I had read. I always felt as if I was back in graduate school on these occasions, being grilled by Fatima about what I had just perused.

We used to go out often in her chauffeured car to interview people to find out what they thought. She would run into cyber cafes in the slums around Rabat to see what literature clients were reading; then she would stop people and ask them a million questions and the wondrous thing was that they would always answer her. She also loved nature and she would race to see the sun set, with its bright colours lighting up the sky. She even had a false wrought iron window on her beach front summer home, which the state granted her during her lifetime, and we would sit on the veranda watching the sun set in a rainbow of colours. When it rained, she could not work. The only productive times for her were days of blue sky and bright sunshine. Otherwise she was morose. Happily, there were many sunny days in Rabat, so she produced in mad torrents – always original stuff.

She also took under her wings young people, especially young women, and started writer's workshops with them, to help them learn to write and get published. She told me once that she decided long ago to devote a third of her time to unpaid mentoring, whether for writers, or weavers of rugs, whose product she helped sell by organising caravans that roamed the country finding ready buyers. On one occasion, she decided that she wanted to see what women in the Rabat area were weaving in their houses. So, we jumped into her car and headed to the countryside where she stopped people along the road and asked them which women were weaving at home. Lo and behold, she found them, and we knocked at their doors, and they let us in, and we saw some magnificent specimens of rugs and tapestries being woven right next to the women's beds. It was an eye opener and an aesthetic delight. She asked questions of people that no one else would dare pose. As an interviewer, I have never witnessed anything akin to what I heard and saw when riding around with her on her mini field trips.

On a particular visit to a slum, she discovered that one of the most popular booklets poor people read was one written by a Saudi *shaykh* giving advice to the love stricken. On another tour of the outskirts of Rabat we came upon a series of high walls hiding abodes of some very rich people. She had her driver stop her car and beckoned two young men in the vicinity. 'Who lives behind these high walls,' she asked. Without hesitation, she was told that the high walled compounds in the vicinity belonged to the Qatari royal family. We discovered Moroccan royalty kept other royal households happy and content in their Moroccan vacation palaces. If I had wandered alone and asked such questions of strangers I probably would have been arrested by the police. No one dared stop or arrest Fatima who went about her business without fear of being confronted by agents of the law.

One day, Fatima decided that she wanted to see how people lived who had been forcibly moved from their jerry-built homes in the *bidonvilles*, the tin can shanty towns that surround most Moroccan cities. They are moved into new concrete dwellings specially constructed by the state, which consider them unsanitary and a blight on the nation. We found a half-finished site which already contained people displaced from their homes by bulldozers. Having nowhere else to go, they had moved into unfinished concrete shells.

It was winter and evenings were chilly and families sat around charcoal braziers shivering while trying to keep warm. Fatima found a young girl in one family who she cosied up to and began a conversation. We discovered that she wanted to become a doctor and was determined to succeed. First, Fatimah and I looked at each other in astonishment. Then we concluded that with that spirit and fortitude, the young girl would achieve all her ambitions!

Towards the end of her life, Fatima began designing her own clothes in bright red colours to match her hair. She had a local tailor make them up, including bright turbans, which were her hallmark. She loved popular culture and whenever a Moroccan artist had an opening at a gallery or a public space Fatima would pop in to pay homage. Immediately, she would be surrounded by dozens of people. Invariably she would whisper to me to join her later on for dinner at her place – her sanctuary from celebrity.

I would show up at around eight o'clock. I would sit with her around her round table with a rotating lazy susan on top, starting with delicious Moroccan appetizers, then some fish and Moroccan brouettes that the women surrounding her had made for us. We would proceed to discuss in some detail the art opening we had just attended, going over the paintings or photographs that we loved most. Nothing escaped her interest or attention. The artists knew well that her presence at the opening of their show would confirm their artistic worth.

She received a constant stream of invitations to speak or to use her name for a cause. We would go over the list of invitations; and she would now and then ask me to research a particular group and let her know my opinion about whether or not she should say yes. Sometimes invitations came from far-right groups and I would let her know their political colour, allowing her to decline the invitation quickly and definitively. Sometimes a magazine would write a notice announcing that Fatima will appear at an opening – when she had made no such commitment. She would immediately call an editor at the magazine and let them know that she never agreed to attend such an event and demanded that they write that in the next edition of their publication. No one could refuse.

She was a superstar. Her books were best sellers, translated into many foreign languages. A generation of young people have grown up reading her work. Many were transformed by her writing which affirmed a positive view of the Islamic corpus. Fatima loved her culture and tried to find the best in its past that might be used to forge a brighter future. She believed firmly that the past had to be mined in order to help young people transform themselves into whole and healthy human beings. Many people – women and men – related to her work and appreciated her optimistic reading of their past, which might be applied to the present.

Her generosity knew no bounds. Her door was always open to a constant parade of young researchers who made their way to Agdal to visit with her and get guidance in their work. I sometimes wondered how she managed her schedule, since so many people wanted to meet her and pick her brain. She managed to see many people each day, giving them an hour or two as the queue mounted. Those who were fortunate enough to know her well appreciated her honesty and friendship. An icon and a dear friend has passed away and she will be sorely missed.

Fatima Mernissi, writer, sociologist, feminist, born 1940; died 30 November 2015

TEN CITIES TO VISIT
BEFORE YOU DIE

You have to go on a package tour (as there is no other way) to Mecca at least once in your life. But we recommend that you take the once in a life-time recommendation literally. God knows how many Muslims take everything else about their religion literally. There is not much to see in the Holy City except the Kaaba, which on first sight ought to send a spiritual tremor through your very being. But there is no history, no cultural property, no culture, no museums, no galleries, as you would expect in any great city. Absolutely nothing but plenty of shopping, luxury hotels and ugliness that has to be seen to be believed. Ditto Medina, which you should visit as part of your hajj or *umra* package. We can thank 'the Custodians of the Two Holy Mosques' for this plight that leaves the eyes only to weep with.

But don't be a tourist, a slave to packaged tours. Tourists go on holidays. Travellers go to explore, discover, relate to others as human beings (instead of taking pictures), and soak themselves in their history, culture, cuisine and worldview. Tourists are after a quick fix; travellers take their time. Tourists return unchanged (as many do from a quick *ziyarat* from Mecca and Medina). Travellers come back enriched, more knowledgeable, more experienced, more spiritually elated – and hence, more aware, more tolerant, more open-minded and more enlightened. This is why the Qur'an asks the believers to 'travel throughout the earth' (29:20) and see why God has given His Bounty more to some than to others (17:21), how many lofty towns He has 'destroyed and left in ruins' (22:45), and learn the histories and stories of other people which contain 'lessons for those who understand' (12:111).

Incidentally, the Qur'an also tells us why Mecca and Medina are the way they are now: 'have these people (of Mecca) not travelled through the land with hearts to understand and ears to hear? It is not the people's eyes that are blind, but their hearts within their breasts' (22:46).

So open your hearts, sharpen your vision, refine your hearing and travel to these cities before your return to the bosom of the earth.

1. Fez

There is only one city that can be on the top of your travel list: Fez. After the destruction of Aleppo, it is the only Islamic city that not only retains its original character and cultural properties but still functions as a viable, living, thriving city. Established in 789 by Idris 1, Fez was built on a river bank with brilliant insight into the use and abuse of water. The carrying capacity of the city was determined by the amount of water available; the water supply for the city was taken from upstream, and used water was then flushed downstream. A wall around the city was built to ensure that the carrying capacity of the city was not exceeded. If you look closely at the size of the pipes taking water into the dwellings you can guess how big is the inside of the house and how many people live there! The houses are modelled on Dr Who's Tardis: they look small and unimportant from the outside, but step inside and the huge interior transports you to another place. Every house is a true marvel of beauty. There are other fabulous architectural monuments, including the oldest functioning madrasa in the world: al-Qarawiyyin, built in 859. And, by the way, the old leather, carpet, ceramic and tile industries are still there – be ready for an obligatory tour, good natter, endless cups of mint tea, and make sure you have a stuffed wallet.

2. Granada and Cordoba

Two cities with a single tale: the rise and fall of Muslims in al-Andalus. When the Umayyad were crushed by the Abbasids in Baghdad, they escaped to Hispania and established one of the most intellectually exciting and pluralistic cultures in world history. Granada is, of course, the site of Alhambra, an architectural wonder that mesmerises you the moment you walk in. In Cordoba you can walk in the footsteps of ibn Arabi, ibn Tufayl and ibn Rushd, whose statue stands in one of the squares of the city. And admire the Great Mosque (though you will not be allowed to pray in it). You need to spend several months in each city to truly appreciate their histories and cultures.

3. Bukhara

It is the city of Ibn Sina, Imam Bukhari, Al-Beruni, Al-Khwarizmi—and of course a place that was home to thousands of Jews for centuries as it had been for Zoroastrians, Hindus, Buddhists and others for such a long time. Bukhara's Ark (Fort) once prized itself with a huge library that Ibn Sina and Al-Beruni claimed to have absorbed in their early years. The city was once the Oxbridge of the Muslim world and visiting those madrassas even today takes one into 'a lost horizon'. Even after spending weeks in the old city next to its three ancient bazaars and surrounded by older buildings, mosques and seminaries, your quest will remain unquenched. Next to the Imam Bukhari Museum and not too far from the ancient city walls, and facing the Ark, is Chashma-i-Ayyub, the spring of Prophet Job reminding visitors that the city was once called Bukhara Sharif – the sacred. Our favourite building in Old Bukhara is the Kalan Minar (Kalan Tower) which is the only monument spared by Ghengis Khan when he destroyed Bukhara in 1212 during his stampede across Central Asia. At the height of 46 metres, this brick-built circular tower overlooks the charming Madras-i-Mir Arab and Kalan Mosque.

Further down right in the heart of old Bukhara there is another architectural gem – Chahar Minar – that reminds one of Taj Mahal and similar monuments in South Asia. Do remember to spend some time at the shrine of Bahauddin Naqshband, the founder of the Sufi Order of the Naqshbandis. Sit by the old *hauz* and watch the warmth, simplicity and devotion of Uzbek men and women rushing to offer their prayers.

4. Samarkand

Like Granada and Cordoba, Samarkand and Bukhara are essentially twins. One of the oldest cities in Central Asia, Samarkand was the first Islamic city to manufacture paper, which it supplied to the rest of the Muslim world, and from where it found its way to Europe. Its prosperity was based on its location on the Silk Road, and even Genghis Khan could not dent its reputation as a world-renowned centre for scholarship. Whatever Genghis and his Mongol herds destroyed was lovingly restored by Timurlane, and his mausoleum, Gur-Amir, is one of the main architectural sights of the city. But the city is most famous for the Ulugh Beg Observatory, built by the astronomer Ulugh Beg in 1420, where astronomers of such distinction as al-Kashi, Ali Qushji, and Ulugh Beg himself came close to discovering that the sun and not the earth was the centre of the solar system. To discover what the madrassas really looked like in Islamic history, visit the Ulugh Beg Madrasa, the Sher-Dor Madrasa and the Tilya Kori Madrasa – given their architectural splendour and beauty, one can only imagine the quality of education these madrassas provided. Dream about listening to one of Ulugh Beg's lectures and then reflect on what the madrassas are doing to our young today.

5. Timbuktu

Not much may remain of Timbuktu once the psychotic Jihadis are finished with the city. Of course, there are other hurdles to reaching the fabled city – desert, disease, killer bees, an odd charging hippo, lack of roads and not least any direct route from Bamako, the capital of Mali.

Maybe you will be better off travelling by water on the Niger River. But true travellers should not give up for this may be your last chance to stand in front of the Sankore Mosque and Madrasah, a true wonder of Islamic history. It is built of mud, with the courtyard that has the exact dimensions of the Kaaba in Mecca, and was financed by (alas unknown) a wealthy lady of the city. Then there is Ahmed Baba, the sixteenth/seventeenth century Songhai scholar who was appalled by how the Arabs justified slavery and denounced many classical jurists – some we worship – for using fabricated, manufactured hadith to defend the most brutal exploitation by humans with a superiority complex of other less fortunate humans. The Ahmed Baba Institute is home to countless invaluable manuscripts and a testimony to the scholarly heritage of Timbuktu. Go and rediscover Timbuktu and grasp the true meaning of learning.

6. Alexandria

Alexandria has to be on any discerning bibliophile's Bucket List. Perhaps after Beirut, Alexandria's old center has more bookshops per square inch than most comparable cities in the Arabic-speaking world. Arabic-speaking, however, is a misleading term because the world of Alexandria with its centuries-old hotels, squares, statues and its bookstores is a fading facsimile of Europe in the East. One of the oldest bookshops is Dar El Mostakbal, on Safya Zaghloul Street, opposite the old Metro Cinema. Here you'll find a small selection of new and used books, all with some connection to Egypt and the Arab world. A larger selection of newer books can be found in Egypt's book chain, Diwan, on the campus of the magnificent Bibliotheca Alexandrina, built adjacent to the site of the original library and in the city's old Hellenic quarter, Chatby. The Bibliotheca, too, has a well-stocked selection, including the works of E. M. Forster and Lawrence Durrell, the two empire-era authors who made the city their home and propelled it far into the orientalist imagination. Sadly, beyond their words, the city has no memorial. In contrast, fans of the poet C.P. Cavafy can visit his apartment, now a museum, where he lived from 1898 until his death in 1933.

7. Saskatoon

The perceived difficulty of pronouncing 'Saskatchewan' – derived from the Cree for 'swift flowing river' – contributes to many non-Canadians' impression of the province's second city, Saskatoon, as a remote, tongue-twisting mirage, but learning how to rattle off 'SAS-ka-toon, Sas-KAT-chuh-won' will be only the first benefit of visiting this small prairie city. Named for the misâskwatômina, or saskatoon berries, that grow wild and sweet along the city's verdant river banks, Saskatoon, though not yet a postcolonial Mecca, offers rich encounters with First Nations history and culture. At Wanuskewin Heritage Park, a 'gathering place' for over six millennia, you can view the site of a bison jump, stand in the presence of a 1,500-year-old Medicine Wheel, and experience contemporary expressions of Aboriginal spirituality, art and cuisine. Saskatoon's many nicknames, including the Science City, Saskabush, Toontown, City of

Bridges (there are eight), and POW City (for potash, oil and wheat), also speak to its human dynamism and natural beauty. Our favourite, Paris of the Prairies, spans not only the aforementioned bridges, but the city's thriving arts scene. Long known for its theatres, galleries, bistros and live music scene (bands on cross-country tours prefer to stop here rather than the province's staid capital, Regina) Saskatoon now boasts over forty public art installations. You can take a tour online — but there is no substitute for travelling to the city and experiencing it personally.

8. Melaka

Malaysians know Melaka as the 'historic city'. As the capital of Melaka, the first Peninsula-based Malay-Muslim Sultanate founded in the early fifteenth century, it exemplifies the everyday cosmopolitanism of Southeast Asia. UNESCO designates it, along with George Town in Penang, as a World Heritage Site. The city's cuisine provides the liveliest testimony to this centuries-old cosmopolitanism. Feast on Portuguese-inspired curry devils, Nyonya (creolised Chinese) cakes, cendol, *sate celup* (dipped satay), chicken rice ball, oyster omelette and other mouth-watering delights. Melaka's architecture also embodies the multiculturalism that infused pre- and early colonial life in the Straits of Malacca. Government buildings, houses of worship, squares and forts are legacies of Portuguese, Dutch and British colonial rule. Melaka is also home to creolised Arab, Chinese and Indian communities which trace their origins to the glory days of the Sultanate. 'Harmony Street' is home to three houses of worship nestled beside each other — the Kampung Kling Mosque, the Sri Poyatha Moorthi Temple and the Cheng Hoon Teng Temple. The Mosque is especially charming — originally built by Indian traders in the mid-eighteenth century, its minaret resembles a pagoda. The hall contains English and Portuguese glazed tiles, Corinthian columns, a Victorian chandelier, a wooden pulpit with Hindu and Chinese-style carvings, and Moorish cast iron lamp-posts in the *wudu* (pre-prayer ablutions) area. Melaka reminds us of the disconnect between politicised, aggressive expressions of Islam and everyday Islams that absorb, blend and play with a dazzling range of diversity.

9. Makhachkala

According to official chatter only the most fearless traveller would attempt the journey from Moscow to Makhachkala. Dagestan is not a recommended tourist destination with numerous military checkpoints seemingly illustrating the region's potential for volatility. More's the pity, for any visitor to this beautiful region's capital city will be handsomely rewarded in cultural wealth, culinary delights and an intoxicating collection of traditional textiles, jewellery and armoury. The city boasts some of the most celebrated wrestlers of the Soviet era, a prized sport in a society that is unapologetically machismo. Men gather on a Saturday night to watch cars racing along the main public highway, a natural progression from the Dzhigitovka, a traditional horse-riding technique to demonstrate bravery and valour practised during the Caucasian War before being adopted by Russian Cossacks. Over thirty ethnic groups, each with their own language, reside here, yet it is not without consequence that, nestled on the south-western shores of the Caspian Sea, Makhachkala was built as a fortress city, isolated by its breath-taking mountains and valleys punctuated by wistful waterfalls. The idyll belies the reality of a Muslim population standing at the cusp of modernity as competing forces of national government, imported Wahabbi influences and capitalism vie to replace the ebbing post-Soviet socialist experience.

10. Ciudad del Este

Crossing the bridge from Brazil over the River Parana into Paraguay you would think you had wandered into a Wild West frontier town occupied by a distinctly Asian population. The second largest city in Paraguay boasts a thriving community of Indians and Arabs, as well as some Japanese and Koreans, who haggle and sell everything from electronic equipment to Iranian rugs in shops imaginatively called Shopping Mina India, Beirut Market and Korea Mall. You are more likely to be greeted by a 'salaam' than an 'hola' in this hive of commerce. Ciudad del Este is famed for its 'enterprise zone' located on the outskirts, attracting Brazilians from across the border who venture over to buy a dizzying array of exotic as well as everyday tax-free items. On their return journey to Brazil the practice is to throw their newly acquired 'contraband', wrapped tightly in bin bags and cardboard, over the side of the bridge. Fifty feet below, multitudes of young men, scurrying like worker ants, carry their booty up the hill. Walking around this part of the city, visitors will encounter bustling mosques, Bollywood music blaring from shops and the waft of Arab and Indian food aromas. Paraguayans wander in and out of stores buying products that would cost double the price in the centre of town. If you want to visit South America, continue walking for a further ten minutes. This part of town is truly Asia.

(Thanks to Iftikhar Malik, Naomi Foyle, Burhan Khan, Samia Rahman, Ehsan Masood and Shanon Shah for their contributions to this list.)

CITATIONS

Introduction: Detroit Do Mind Dying
by Hassan Mahamdallie

Robert Lacy's *Ford: The Men And The Machine* (Heinemann, London, 1986) is an excellent history of the city, and can be found cheaply on online bookstores. *The Last Days of Detroit* by Mark Binelli (Vintage, London, 2014) is an entertaining up-to-date account of city's woes. *Detroit: I Do Mind Dying: A Study in Urban Revolution* by Dan Georgakas and Marvin Surkin (Haymarket, London, 2012) is a classic account of the 1960s-70s battle in the car-plants between radical black autoworkers, the trade unions and the bosses. It has lots of detail about the city's social, cultural and political life during this period, told through first-hand accounts. David Harvey's *Rebel Cities: From The Right To The City To The Urban Revolution* (Verso, 2013) is a brilliant little treatise that will make you think about what cities could and should be.

For accounts of Detroit's bankruptcy, corruption scandals and foreclosures go to the Detroit Free Press www.freep.com. Chris and Amany's LaunchGood can be found at www.launchgood.com. John Collin's Underground Resistance is at www.undergroundresistance.com. Find out about Lela's campaign and others at: http://detroitevictiondefense.org.

Istanbul: Capital of the World by Peter Clark

For background on Istanbul, see Andrew Dalby, *Tastes of Byzantium* (I B Tauris, London and New York, 2010); Erik J Zürcher, *The Young Turk Legacy and Nation Building* (I B Tauris, London and New York, 2010); Jonathan Harris, editor, *Byzantine History* (Palgrave Macmillan, London, 2005), and my own book *Istanbul: A Cultural History* (Signal Books, Oxford, 2010).

Medieval Basra: City of the Mind by Robert Irwin

The opening quotation from Sinbad's voyages is from *The Arabian Nights: Tales of 1001 Nights* tr. Malcolm Lyons (London, Penguin, 2008), vol.2, p.456. Louis Massignon's important essay on the topography of medieval Basra 'Explication du plan du Basra' can be found in Massignon, *Opera Minora*, 3 vols. (Beirut, Dar al-Maaref, 1963) vol.2, pp.61-87. The passage on the Marsh Arabs is from Michael Asher's *Thesiger*, (Viking, London 1994), pp.398-9. There is a short article on the literary importance of Basra by G.J.H. Van Gelder, in *Encyclopedia of Arabic Literature*, 2 vols. eds. Julie Scott Meisami and Paul Starkey, (London, Routledge, 1998), vol.1, pp.140-1. There are articles on Basra and the Mirbad in the second edition of the *Encyclopaedia of Islam*. On the Mirbad see also Odette Scendura 'Le role du Mirbad de Bassora dans le conservatisme poetique jusq'au début du 11e siècle', *Ibla* (1957) pp.369-79. The leading literary figures are discussed and excerpted in Robert Irwin ed. *The Penguin Anthology of Classical Arabic Literature* (London, Penguin, 1999). For Jahiz see especially Charles Pellat, *Le milieu basrien et la formation de Gahiz* (Paris, Adrien-Maisonneuve, 1953) and Pellat ed. and tr. *The Life and Works of Jahiz* (Berkeley and Los Angeles, University of California Press, 1969). There are excellent accounts of science, occult sciences and medicine by Sonya Brentjes, Robert G. Morrison and S. Nomanul Haq in *The New Cambridge History of Islam*, vol.4, *Islamic Cultures and Societies to the End of the Eighteenth Century*, ed. Robert Irwin (Cambridge, Cambridge University Press, 2010). On people arriving without any luggage and other lexical curiosities, see M.G. Carter, 'Arabic Lexicography' in *The Cambridge History of Arabic Literature: Religion, Learning and Science in the 'Abbasid Period*, (Cambridge, Cambridge University Press, 1990). On the polymath al-Kindi, see Fritz Zimmerman in the same volume. On the Persian embrace of Greek culture as their own, see Dmitri Gutas, *Greek Thought, Arabic Culture*, (London, Routledge, 1998).

The New Citadels of Culture by Boyd Tonkin

The official version of the development of Saadiyat Island can be found at www.saadiyat.ae. More detailed accounts of the museum projects, with impressive modelling of the buildings once completed, are collected at www.saadiyatculturaldistrict.ae. Hamed al Hamed's Ph.D thesis 'Establishing a Cultural Quarter in Abu Dhabi, UAE' (University of Portsmouth, 2014) uses quantitative analysis to explore the gap between elite ambitions and local perceptions, and argues that 'without properly cultivating native cultural entrepreneurship, efforts towards the establishment of a cultural quarter would be short-lived'.

In *After the Sheikhs: The Coming Collapse of the Gulf Monarchies* (Hurst, 2012), Christopher M Davidson offers a thorough critical overview of the recent history, present challenges and future prospects of states in the region. He is also the author of *Abu Dhabi: Oil and Beyond* (OUP, 2009). Amnesty International's report into human rights, 'There is No Freedom Here: silencing dissent in the United Arab Emirates' (2014) can be consulted at www.amnesty.org.uk. The investigations by the Gulf Labor group into workers' conditions on Saadiyat have now been published, along with interventions by artists in support of the campaign, as *The Gulf: High Culture / Hard Labor*, edited by Andrew Ross (OR Books, 2015). Molly Crabapple's reportage from Saadiyat appeared in *Vice* magazine in 2014 as 'Slaves of Happiness Island' (www.vice.com).

Abu Dhabi also hosts the annual International Prize for Arabic Fiction, which has an independent panel of judges drawn from across the Arab world and beyond. The winning and shortlisted novels, which sometimes present a critical or satirical picture of local societies sharply at odds with the official line, bear out the complex and unpredictable nature of sponsored culture in the Gulf. Recent winners include Abdo Khal's novel of corrupt development and autocratic modernisation in Saudi Arabia, *Throwing Sparks* (translated by Maia Tabet and Michael K Scott; Bloomsbury, 2013); and Saud Alsanousi's story inspired by the fate of children in Kuwait born to local fathers and migrant-worker mothers, *The Bamboo Stalk* (translated by Jonathan Wright; Bloomsbury, 2015).

Tashkent Odyssey by Eric Walberg

For the astonishingly brilliant Islamic history of Tashkent, see S Frederick Starr, *Lost Enlightenment: Central Asia's Golden Age from the Arab Conquest to Tamerlane* (Princeton University Press, reprint edition, 2015). For the Russian history of the city, see Jeff Sahadeo, *Russian Colonial Society in Tashkent,*

1865-1923 (Indiana University Press, 2010). And for how Tashkent was transformed into a Soviet city, see Paul Stronski, *Tashkent: Forging a Soviet City, 1930-1966* (University of Pittsburgh Press, 2010) and Philipp Meuser, *Seismic Modernism: Architecture and Housing in Soviet Tashkent* (DOM Publishers, Berlin, 2016). See also: Peter Hopkirk, *The Great Game: On Secret Service in High Asia* (John Murray, reprint edition, 2006), Wilfred Blunt, *Golden Road to Samarkand* (Hamish Hamilton, London, 1973), and Colin Thubron, *Shadow of the Silk Road* (Vintage, London, 2007).

Utopia in Tehran by Javaad Alipoor

For a critical description of how Utopian politics and analysis functions, the best starting point is Krishna Kumar *Utopianism* (University of Minnesota Press, 1991). Gregory Busquet's *Political Space in the Work of Henri Lefebvre: Ideology and Utopia* is a good practical account of the relationship between cities, space and utopian politics as critique (http://www.jssj. org/wp-content/uploads/2013/09/JSSJ5-3.en_1.pdf). For a discussion of the mystical significance of Nasir Khusraw's travel writings see S.H. Nasr's Introduction to the Nasir-i Khusraw section in *Ismaili Thought in the Classical Age* (I.B.Tauris & Co. 2008) or Peter Lamborn Wilson's *Sacred Drift: Essays on the Margins of Islam* (City Light Books 1993). Wilson's *Scandal: Essays in Islamic Heresy* (Autonomedia 1988) also lays out an introduction to the style of 'Orientalismo', that I have tried to develop in the essay, and in some recent plays. I have discussed it further on articles collected at www.attheinlandsea.wordpress.com and www.mybrotherscountry. wordpress.com. For an introduction to al-Farabi's philosophical and, broadly, 'political' writings see Majid Fakhry's *Farabi: Founder of Islamic Neo-Platonism* (Oneworld 2002). I re-read sections of Marcus Dod's critical translation of *The City of God* (Hendrickson 2014) for this essay.

Asset Bayat's *Street Politics: Poor People's Movements in Iran* (Columbia University Press 1998) is a great introduction to the reality of life for the urban poor in twentieth century Iran, and the form that politics of resistance have taken. Ervand Abrahamian's *Khomeinism* (Univeristy of California 1993) and Adib-Moghadam's *A Critical Introduction to Khomeini* (Cambridge University Press 2014) are brilliant guides to Khomeini's ever shifting politics and theology, and Abrahamian's book is the source of the discussion on May Day in the Islamic Republic. A good translation of Khomeini's *Guardianship of the Jurisprudence* is available online (http://www.iranchamber.com/history/rkhomeini/books/velayat_faqeeh.pdf).

Ali Shariati's *ReligionVersus Religion* (Kazi 1998) lays out some of the central issues of his political views, but there is yet to appear a decent critical summation of his thought in English. Hamid Dabashi's *Islamic Liberation Theology* provides some analysis of how Shariati's work sits in the context of similar anti colonial religious thought (Routledge 2008). The phrase about '99% of what we do' not being from Islam, is a phrase used by Rafsanjani in a speech delivered in 1992, quoted in Abrahamian's *Khomeinism*.

For an introduction to Iranian prison literature, as well as the writing of Bozorg Alavi, see *The Prison Papers of Bozorg Alavi* translated by Raffat (Syracus University Press 1985). *The Iranian Mojahedin* (Yale University Press 2009), by Abrahamian provides both a detailed account of the split in the guerrilla movement, and the original text of the letter that I have fictionalised. There isn't a huge amount in English on Ayatollah Taleghani, the left wing Ayatollah, but *Zendeginame-yeh Siasiy-eh AyatollahTaleghani* (The Political Biography of AyatollahTaleghani) (Tavani Nashr-e Ney 2013) is available. I also mention the seminal *Westoxification* by Aal-e Ahmad, which is available in English, translated by John Green (Mazda 1997).

The full text of Suhravardi's *Avaz-e Rak-e Par-e Jibra'il* (translated rather clunkily) as *The Sound of Gabriel'sWings*, is available at:https://www.scribd.com/doc/32993488/The-Sound-of-Gabriel-s-Wing-s-by-Suhrawardi. The description of torture at Gohar Dasht is taken from *Crime and Impunity*, a book about women's experiences of prisons in the Islamic Republic, available   online:http://www.wluml.org/sites/wluml.org/files/CrimeImpunity.pdf.

Ranking Cities by Jeremy Henzell-Thomas

Ranking websites include http://www.photius.com/rankings/ and https://rankingamerica.wordpress.com/

On the Muslim Population of Cities in the EU, see http://www.themuslimtimes.org/2013/10/europe-and-australia/europe/list-of-cities-in-the-

european-union-by-muslim-population. See also http://www.
pewresearch.org/fact-tank/2015/01/15/5-facts-about-the-muslim-pop
ulation-in-europe/.

On far right Islamophobic reactions to growing Muslim populations in
cities in the EU, see http://www.frontpagemag.com/point/214086/
french-city-40-muslim-population-most-dangerous-daniel-greenfield.

On the question of 'Liveability', see IMCL (International Making Cities
Liveable) at http://www.livablecities.org/; http://pages.eiu.com/rs/
eiu2/images/Liveability_rankings_2014.pdf; http://www.economist.
com/blogs/graphicdetail/2015/08/daily-chart-5;http://ec.europa.eu/
regional_policy/sources/docgener/studies/pdf/urban/survey2013_
en.pdf.

On the idea of a 'Muslim Liveability Index', see http://muslimmatters.
org/2010/01/06/best-place-for-muslims-to-live-lets-find-out/.

On 'Loveable' cities, see http://monocle.com/film/affairs/5-loveable-
cities-2013/. On the Global Power Index for 2014, see http://www.
mori-m-foundation.or.jp/gpci/pdf/GPCI14_E_Web.pdf. See also
http://www.mori-m-foundation.or.jp/gpci/index_e.html, and http://
forum.skyscraperpage.com/showthread.php?t=174953.

On the *Condé Nast* 'Best Cities in the World' Readers' Choice Awards' for
2015, see http://www.cntraveler.com/galleries/2014-10-20/
top-25-cities-in-the-world-readers-choice-awards-2014.

For Trip Advisor's 'Top Ten destinations for 2015', see http://www.tripad-
visor.com/TravelersChoice-Destinations.

For the National Geographic's 'World's Best Cities', see http://shop.
nationalgeographic.com/ngs/product/books/travel-and-adventure/
travel-best-sellers/the-world-s-best-cities.

For rankings of the 'Happiest Cities' see http://travel.nationalgeographic. com/travel/photos-top-10-happiest-cities/?utm_ source=Facebook&utm_medium=Social&utm_content=link_ fbt20141226happiestcities&utm_campaign=Content&sf6429484=1#/ happiest-koh-samui_86320_600x450.jpg. See also *Sustainable Development Solutions Network* (a UN global initiative), 2010-2012.

See also: http://www.telegraph.co.uk/men/thinking-man/11936981/ Who-in-their-right-mind-would-want-to-visit-Dubai.html.

On the most highly ranked cities for food, see http://travel.nationalgeo-graphic.com/travel/top-10/food-cities/; http://www.ucityguides.com/ cities/top-10-best-food-cities.html, and http://www.citiesjournal.com/ top-15-best-food-cities-in-the-world/.

On the 'Best Cities for Arts and Culture' see http://www.cntraveler. com/galleries/2014-09-19/the-world-s-best-cities-for-arts-and-culture-lovers; http://www.travelandleisure.com/slideshows/worlds-best-cities-for-culture-and-arts, and http://www.timeout.com/travel/ features/362/the-worlds-greatest-cityr.

On the 'World's Smartest Cities', see http://www.iese.edu/en/about-iese/news-media/news/2014/april/tokyo-london-and-new-york-the-smartest-cities/ and http://www.fastcoexist.com/3029331/ the-10-smartest-cities-in-the-world.

On the 'World's Deadliest Cities', see http://www.theguardian.com/ news/datablog/2012/nov/30/new-york-crime-free-day-deadliest-cities-worldwide.

On the 'Noisiest Cities', see http://citiquiet.com/the-top-10-noisiest-cities-in-the-world-2/ 16/7/2014.

On the 'Most Polluted Cities', see http://www.ibtimes.co.uk/world-environment-day-10-most-polluted-cities-world-1504260. See also http://www.theguardian.com/environment/2015/jul/15/

nearly-9500-people-die-each-year-in-london-because-of-air-pollution-study.

On the 'Greenest Cities', see http://www.citiesjournal.com/top-12-greenest-cities-in-the-world,/ and http://ecowatch.com/2014/10/24/top-ten-greenest-cities-world/.

On the 'Most Expensive Cities In The World', see http://www.photius.com/rankings/most_expensive_cities_real_estate_2008.html., and http://www.telegraph.co.uk/finance/property/pictures/11450782/The-worlds-10-most-expensive-cities-2015.html?frame=3220490.

On ranking of Gender Equality, see the *Global Gender Gap Report* 2008 by the World Economic Forum in collaboration with Harvard University and the University of California, Berkeley at http://www.allcountries.org/ranks/gender_gap_gender_equality_country_rankings_2008.

On ranking of World Health Systems, see the WHO *World Health Report* (last produced in 2000) at http://www.photius.com/rankings/heal-thranks.html, accessed 13/10/15. For a critique of this report, see Glen Whitman, 'Who's Fooling Who? The World Health Organization's Problematic Ranking of Health Care Systems', CATO Institute Briefing Papers No. 10 at http://object.cato.org/sites/cato.org/files/pubs/pdf/bp101.pdf.

Inside the Vatican by Paul Vallely

This article is adapted from Paul Vallely's biography *Pope Francis: Untying the Knot, the Struggle for the Soul of Catholicism* (Bloomsbury-Continuum, 2015). See also: John Pollard, *Money and the Rise of the Modern Papacy: Financing the Vatican, 1850-1950* (Cambridge University Press, 2009); and his more recent book, *The Papacy in the Age of Totalitarianism, 1914-1958* (Oxford University Press, 2014).

Muslim Life in Sydney by Irfan Yusuf

For a background to Muslims in Australia, see Nadia Jamal, *The Glory Garage: Growing Up Lebanese Muslim in Australia* (Allen and Unwin, 2005), Nora Amath, *The Phenomenology of Community Activism: Muslim Civil Society Organisations in Australia* (Melbourne University Press, 2015), and Joshua M Roose, *Political Islam and Masculinity: Muslim Men in Australia* (AIAA, Sydney, 2015).

Tim Blair's column, entitled 'Last drinks in Lakemba: Tim Blair takes a look inside Sydney's Muslim Land' appeared in *Daily Telegraph* on 18 August 2014. Sheikh Taj Din Al-Hilali's comments can be found at: http://news.bbc.co.uk/1/hi/world/asia-pacific/6086374.stm

Ed Husic's speech at the Sydney Institute in October 2005 was published in *Sydney Papers* Vol.18 No.1 in 2006 (pages 89-101), and Jihad Dib's speech of May 2005 can be downloaded as a pdf file from: www.parliment.nsw.gov.au/

See also: Liza Hopkins, 'A Contested Identity: Resisting the Category of Muslim-Australian', *Immigrants & Minorities: Historical Studies in Ethnicity, Migration and Diaspora* 29:01, 110-131 (2011)

The Pearl of Morocco by Martin Rose

The Mercier quotations are all from *Rabat: Description Topographique* published in *Archives Marocaines*, VII, pp 296-349 (Ernest Leroux, Paris, 1906) by Louis Mercier, Vice-Consul of France at Rabat. I have translated the whole document from French myself and have used extracts from my translation. The quotations are from page 301 (for the Alou and the cemetery), 303 for the roughing up of Jews and Christians, and 312-13 for the Mellah.

For the history of Rabat see: Janet Abu-Lughod, *Rabat: Urban Apartheid in Morocco*, (Princeton University Press, Princeton, 1980); Beebe Bahrami, *The Persistence of the Andalusian Identity in Rabat* (University of Pennsylvania PhD thesis, 996 (unpublished); Francisco J Alcala-Garcia et al., *Rabat: géodiversité et patrimoine socioculturel* (Editions Maarif, Rabsat, 2013); Jacques Caillé, *La Petite Histoire de Rabat*, (Chérifienne d'éditions et de publicité, Rabat, n.d) and *La Ville de Rabat jusqu'au Protectorat Française*, three volumes (Vanoest, Paris, 1945, repr. Casablanca: Editions Frontispice 2006); ; and Robert Chastel, *Rabat-Salé: vingt siècles de l'oued Bouregreg*, (Editions La Porte, Rabat, 1997) and *Rabat: Le destin d'une ville et des caprices d'un fleuve* (Editions Chastel, Rabat, 2013).

See also: Nina Epton, *Saints and Sorcerers, A Moroccan Journey* (Cassel, London, 1958);L P Harvey, *Muslims in Spain 1500-1614* (University of Chicago Press, 2005); Robert Irwin, *The Alhambra*, (Harvard University Press, Cambridge, Mass, 2004); Leila Maziane, *Salé et ses corsairs (1666-1727): un port du course marocain au XVIIe siècle* (Pole Universitaire Normand, Universités de Rouen et du Havre, Presses universitaires de Caen, Rouen et Caen, 2007); Richard Parker, *Islamic Monuments in Morocco* (The Baraka Press, Charlottesville, 1981); Douglas Porch, *The Conquest of Morocco* (Knopf, New York, 1982); G H Selous, *Appointment to Fez* (The Richards Press, London, 1956); and Kenneth Brown, *People of Salé: Tradition and change in a Moroccan city 1830-1930* (Harvard University Press, Cambridge, Mass., 1976).

Obstinate Sovereignty, Again by S Parvez Manzoor

The quotation from A.K.S. Lambton is from *The Legacy of Islam*, (Oxford University Press, Oxford, 1974), p. 404; and from William. M. McNeill, *The Rise of the West: A History of the Human Community* (University of Chicago Press, Chicago, 1963) P. 499.

CONTRIBUTORS

Javaad Alipoor is a British Iranian playwright • **Syima Aslam** is the co-founder of Bradford Literary Festival • **Maria Chaudhuri** is a novelist and author of *Beloved Strangers* • **Peter Clark** is an internationally renowned writer of many books, including *Istanbul* and *Damascus Diaries: Life under the Assads* • **Jeremy Henzell-Thomas** is a Research Associate and former Visiting Fellow at the Centre of Islamic Studies, University of Cambridge • **Robert Irwin** is the author or editor of seventeen works of fiction and non-fiction, including his autobiography *Memoirs of a Dervish* • **Nimra Khan** is a Pakistani journalist • **VMK** is a photographer based in the United Arab Emirates • **Zohab Khan** is a multiple poetry slam champion, didgeridoo player, harmonica beatboxer and hip-hop artist based somewhere in Australia • **Hassan Mahamdallie**, co-director of the Muslim Institute, is an art critic and playwright • **Zina Mamouni**, who works as a teacher in a primary school, is a member of the Strasbourg (France) based group *Abyssinie* • **Irna Qureshi** is the co-founder of Bradford Literary Festival (no, they are not sisters, just joined congenitally) • **Muddasir Ramzan**, who lives in Pattan, Kashmir, is a budding writer • **Martin Rose**, a career British Council officer, has served in Rabat, along with many other places in the Middle East, and is currently a Consultant to the British Council • **Stuart Schaar**, professor emeritus on North African and Middle Eastern history at Brooklyn College, CUNY, is the author of *Eqbal Ahmad: Critical Outsider in Turbulent Times* • **Boyd Tonkin** writes for *The Independent* • **Paul Vallely**, journalist and writer, is the author of *Pope Francis: Untying the Knot, the Struggle for the Soul of Catholicism* • **Eric Walberg**, journalist and writer, is the author of *Postmodern Imperialism: Geopolitics and the Great Game* • **Irfan Yusuf** is pursuing his doctorate at Alfred Deakin Research Institute for Citizenship and Globalisation, Deakin University, Melbourne.